GERMANY'S DUAL CONSTITUTION

This book offers a compelling and persuasive framework for understanding the German constitutional system. It argues that it can only be fully understood as a dual structure combining two layers with little in common. The first layer is the basic administrative institutional structure, comprising federal and bureaucratic institutions. The second layer is that of parliamentary democracy. It is the interplay between the two, as mediated by the Chancellery, the major political parties and the Federal Constitutional Court, which lies at the heart of the German constitutional arrangement.

This innovative hybrid perspective allows for a better understanding of the current challenges of parliamentary government in Germany and its potential long-term development. An updated translation of its impactful German edition, this book provides one of the most brilliant introductions to the governmental system of a key state.

Volume 7 in the series Parliamentary Democracy in Europe

Parliamentary Democracy in Europe

The European Union is founded on the idea of 'representative democracy'. Its citizens are directly represented in the European Parliament, but Union democracy is equally based on indirect forms of representation especially through the European Council and the Council – two Union institutions whose members will be democratically accountable to their national parliaments. The good functioning of the Union democracy assumes, therefore, the good functioning of the democratic institutions of each Member State.

What is the role and relationship between the European and the national parliaments in the democratic functioning of the Union? Do they exercise distinct or complementary functions? Has the European Parliament adopted a structure similar to national parliaments; and how do national parliaments assume their 'European' functions? These questions have gained particular relevance in recent years. Not only has the Lisbon Treaty conferred new functions upon national parliaments, especially concerning the scrutiny on the compliance with the subsidiarity principle (the so called 'Early Warning System'), the coordination of fiscal and economic policies at the European level has led to significant restrictions of national parliamentary powers.

The new Hart Series on 'Parliamentary Democracy in Europe', encompassing both monographs and edited collections, aims to answer some of these questions. The series offers new insights into rules and conventions shaping parliaments and parliamentary democracy in Europe. Its aim is to provide a better understanding of the role parliaments are playing in European constitutional law and its idea of 'representative democracy'.

Series Editors

Nicola Lupo
Robert Schütze

Interparliamentary Cooperation in the Composite European Constitution
Edited by Nicola Lupo and Cristina Fasone

The Italian Parliament in the European Union
Edited by Nicola Lupo and Giovanni Piccirilli

The Principle of Subsidiarity and its Enforcement in the EU Legal Order: The Role of National Parliaments in the Early Warning System
Katarzyna Granat

Parliamentary Oversight of the Executives: Tools and Procedure in Europe
Elena Griglio

The Internationalisation of Constitutional Law: A View from the Venice Commission
Sergio Bartole

Executive-legislative (Im)balance in the European Union: (Im)balance in the European Union
Edited by Diane Fromage and Anna Herranz-Surrallés

Germany's Dual Constitution: Parliamentary Democracy in the Federal Republic
Florian Meinel

Germany's Dual Constitution

Parliamentary Democracy in the Federal Republic

Florian Meinel

•HART•

OXFORD • LONDON • NEW YORK • NEW DELHI • SYDNEY

HART PUBLISHING

Bloomsbury Publishing Plc

Kemp House, Chawley Park, Cumnor Hill, Oxford, OX2 9PH, UK

1385 Broadway, New York, NY 10018, USA

29 Earlsfort Terrace, Dublin 2, Ireland

HART PUBLISHING, the Hart/Stag logo, BLOOMSBURY and the Diana logo are trademarks of Bloomsbury Publishing Plc

First published in Great Britain 2021

A catalogue record for this book is available from the British Library.

Library of Congress Cataloging-in-Publication data

Names: Meinel, Florian, author.

Title: Germany's dual constitution : parliamentary democracy in the Federal Republic / Florian Meinel.

Description: Oxford, UK ; New York, NY : Hart Publishing, an imprint of Bloomsbury Publishing, 2021. | Series: Parliamentary democracy in Europe ; volume 7 | Includes bibliographical references and index.

Identifiers: LCCN 2021004210 (print) | LCCN 2021004211 (ebook) | ISBN 9781509943395 (hardback) | ISBN 9781509943432 (paperback) | ISBN 9781509943418 (pdf) | ISBN 9781509943401 (Epub)

Subjects: LCSH: Constitutional law—Germany.

Classification: LCC KK4450 .M43913 2021 (print) | LCC KK4450 (ebook) | DDC 342.43/04—dc23

LC record available at https://lccn.loc.gov/2021004210

LC ebook record available at https://lccn.loc.gov/2021004211

ISBN: HB: 978-1-50994-339-5
ePDF: 978-1-50994-341-8
ePub: 978-1-50994-340-1

Typeset by Compuscript Ltd, Shannon

ACKNOWLEDGEMENTS

While thinking about the transformation of parliamentary democracy I have enjoyed the company of truly inspiring and intellectually generous friends who helped me to structure my observations and concepts, read my drafts, and discussed them with me. I am deeply indebted to Philip Manow, Christoph Möllers, Christian Neumeier and Matthias Roßbach. My warm thanks also to Martin Loughlin, Tom Wickham, Michael Koß and Benjamin Vauteck for exceptionally helpful correspondence. Some of the most outstanding and experienced protagonists of parliamentary government in Germany have shared insights and observations with me and helped answer my questions. Among them, I would like to mention Wolfgang Schäuble, Norbert Lammert, Peter Altmaier, and Horst Risse. Joe Paul Kroll's translation of the original German text laid the groundwork for this book. Lina Gebhardt, Xenia Heckmann, Darius Ruf and Samuel Nelkenstock have provided excellent research assistance.

Like the German edition (*Vertrauensfrage*, C.H. Beck, 2019), this revised, partly rewritten book is dedicated to the loving memory of my grandparents, Werner and Edeltraut Meinel. One year before the Berlin Wall was built, they left behind their home in Dresden for the Federal Republic to give their children and grandchildren the chance of a life in political freedom.

CONTENTS

NOTE ON THE CITATION OF CASE LAW

Rulings of the German Federal Constitutional Court are cited from the official publication in *Entscheidungen des Bundesverfassungsgerichts* (*BVerfGE*), where 68 *BVerfGE* 1 reads as the first page of vol 68. Most of *BVerfGE* is accessible online at www.servat.unibe.ch/dfr/dfr_bvbd140.html. Where available, the European case law identifier (ECLI) citation is added. The court has provided an official English translation of its more recent signature rulings at www.bundesverfassungsgericht.de/SiteGlobals/Forms/Suche/EN/Entscheidungensuche_Formular.html?language_=en. An '(en)' following the citation indicates these cases.

1

Introduction: The Two Crises of Parliamentary Government

The establishment of a far-right opposition party in the German national parliament marks both a watershed and the end of the great transformation the German postwar constitution has undergone since the country's reunification. For more than six decades, as long as the shared memory of defeat and reconstruction was passed on from the founding generation to its children, the Bundestag had known only a loyal opposition. Meanwhile the political polarisation of German society has reached the centre of the political system. A vociferous opposition to the existing order is expressing itself in attempts to destroy the moral and political code of the Federal Republic, while the defenders of the status quo believe that the constitution can be defended by invoking its 'values'. Both sides hold fiercely opposing views on the true constitution. Friends of the constitution pitted against its enemies, democrats against anti-democrats, insiders against outsiders, elites against populists, the institutions against those who scorn them, the upholders of democracy against the rule of elites. And yet, amid this challenge to its constitutional beliefs, the country seems to remain true to its own self in one respect: each and every one is the enemy of the constitution in the eyes of the other.

From the outset, the Federal Republic did not attach its notion of 'constitutional patriotism' (*Verfassungspatriotismus*), this idea of a civic compensation for the lack of a republican identity, to its political institutions and the rules of the political process. Constitutional patriotism is a matter of ideals, high-level constitutional principles and basic rights understood as material truths.[1] As the constitutional lawyer Christoph Möllers has recently put it, high-ranking 'principles' in German constitutional law

> substitute for the lack of effective political traditions. Where the American constitutional debates, French republicanism or English parliamentarianism serve less as a consensual basis than as a foil against which disputes take place, the prehistory of the Basic Law cannot offer the same.[2]

The political inclination to the absolute, however, brings with it two opposing dangers. When every opponent is framed as an enemy of the constitution, there is great difficulty to put a name to the constitution's actual enemy and resolutely to combat him as such. Yet another danger lies in the strategy of all too readily disqualifying unwelcome opponents as 'enemies of the constitution' and thus evading the awkward task of confronting

[1] JW Müller, *Constitutional Patriotism* (Princeton, NJ, Princeton University Press, 2007) 16–20.

[2] C Möllers, 'Demokratie' in R Poscher et al (eds), *Handbuch des Verfassungsrechts* (Munich, CH Beck, 2021, forthcoming).

them politically. As a result, the realm of political possibility keeps on shrinking, narrowing down to a simple alternative of loyalty or disloyalty. Any willingness to political and institutional change is lost, and the well-meaning defenders of policies with supposedly 'no alternative' themselves act as protagonists of what the ancient historian Christian Meier has called 'a crisis without an alternative',[3] accelerating the crisis much against their will.

Over the last decade the diagnosis of a crisis of liberal democracy has become an unquestioned commonplace of political and constitutional theory, while at the same time the concept of democracy serves as a somewhat vague and unspecific device of polemic. In public debates, not only in Germany, 'democracy' often figures as something that could once be taken for granted and was associated with high turnouts, moderate and broadly based parties, an efficient welfare state, measured statecraft, the West, journalistic objectivity in the mass media, and the absence of Facebook and Twitter. Yet to recall a sense of political stability that has come to seem unfathomable, though it belongs to times only just past, is no substitute for political analysis. As the Greek word 'crisis' signifies the turning point in a disease, it seems fitting to examine the patient's *state*, his *constitution*, rather than to lament too much about the way of life that brought about the depression. The crisis of democracy without a reasonable alternative is a global phenomenon, but its manifestations, driving forces and development logics differ in each particular polity. What are the constitutional peculiarities of democracy in Germany? To what extent does the German model of parliamentary democracy differ from other comparable models? In what direction is it developing? What are its political strengths and weaknesses, and where do its vulnerabilities lie?

Democracy first and foremost is a set of political institutions that guarantee political freedom by submitting the exercise of political power to authorisation and control of the people. Its core therefore comprises the rules that spell out the meaning of representation by defining and intertwining parliaments, parties, government and the administration. Traditionally preoccupied with basic rights and judicial review, German constitutional law and theory has too often taken most of that for granted. To glance today at a standard textbook of German constitutional law is to behold the image of a coherent, self-contained constitutional framework: reasonable gradations of democratic legitimacy embodied by the Bundestag and Bundesregierung, federalism based on the principle of subsidiarity, embeddedness in the supranational federation of the European Union, comprehensive and sophisticated protection of basic rights, the rule of law; the institutional safeguard provided by the Federal Constitutional Court as the 'guardian of the constitution'. No mention is made of the internal contradictions of the constitutional system, of the unpredictably rapid changes to which it might be subject, of returning ghosts of times past, of niggling doubts whether the constitution suits a society so different from the one of the old Federal Republic – no mention, in brief, of the forces slowly eating away at the institutional foundations of parliamentary democracy in Germany. Yet these forces are what this book is about. It asks how Germany is governed today and how it can expect to be governed in the future.

[3] C Meier, *Res Publica Amissa: Eine Studie zur Verfassung und Geschichte der späten Römischen Republik* [1966] (Stuttgart, Steiner, 2017) 201.

I. Brexit and the Europeanisation of Westminster Parliamentarianism

Parliamentary politics in the What makes the German case special in the world of parliamentary democracies? Federal Republic is operating under constant critical scrutiny by a constitutional court and shows strong features of bureaucratic autonomy in a complex federal system. This makes its current transformation interesting for anyone interested in the contemporary crisis of representative democracy. But the German case is also interesting because in many respects it represents a radically different type of parliamentary democracy compared to the United Kingdom, where it has been undergoing a profound transformation during the last decades, too. Political science and constitutional thought have long treated continental and Westminster-style parliamentarism as two different institutional models connected only by their name. Perhaps that was wrong. Perhaps critical developments of parliamentary government in Britain and on the continent are more closely connected than they appear at first glance. Perhaps one aspect of the crisis of the British constitution is that it is taking on continental features. This is a remarkable development in every respect.

The English role-model of parliamentary government contributed much to the political ideals of German liberals throughout the nineteenth and twentieth centuries. From the early admirers of Edmund Burke's defence of the Westminster institutions to Max Weber's outline of Germany's interwar constitution and constitutional theorists of the Federal Republic such as Wilhelm Hennis: responsible government, a two-party system and the respective set of constitutional conventions represented the desired opposite of both the German tradition of bureaucratic autonomy and the dangers of revolutionary mass democracy. It was not by chance that the first systematic analysis of British parliamentary procedure was written by an Austro-German liberal lawyer.[4] But the adoption of this model failed or remained patchwork. German parliamentary democracy has always been and still is different.

Like Montesquieu, who famously misinterpreted eighteenth-century British parliamentary government to model his theory of a mixed constitution, German fascination with British parliamentary democracy has not always been free of prejudices or clichés. The most recent example is the German public's imagination of the Brexit process as a foolish rebellion of irrationality. This view of the British struggle for EU withdrawal was formed by the Leave campaign and the result of the referendum, but even more by the agony of the House of Commons under Theresa May's government after the UK Supreme Court's judgment in *R (Miller) v Secretary of State for Exiting the European Union*[5] and the events surrounding Boris Johnson's prorogation of Parliament and *R (Miller) v The Prime Minister*.[6] How could this admired institution of British statecraft fail to present a workable solution? German debates on the British constitutional crisis were touchingly idealistic. Not a word about the fact that withdrawal was an option provided for in the Lisbon Treaty –something that German constitutional theory, too, at the time of the drafting had strongly advocated for reasons of democratic legitimacy. German observers also tended to ignore that the Tories

[4] J Redlich, *The Procedure of the House of Commons: A Study of its History and Present Form* [German edition 1905], 3 vols (London, Constable, 1908).

[5] *R (Miller) v Secretary of State for Exiting the EU* [2017] UKSC 5; see M Gordon, *Parliamentary Sovereignty in the UK Constitution. Process, Politics and Democracy* (Oxford, Hart, 2015) viii–x.

[6] *R (Miller) v The Prime Minister; Cherry v Advocate General for Scotland* [2019] UKSC 41.

had won a parliamentary majority in 2017 with their promise 'no deal is better than a bad deal'. It was Johnson who at least publicly took the stand on this election promise, while Theresa May, who was bid farewell on the continent with a heavy heart after her resignation, had herself pushed the rift between her and her party when she took this option off the table after the election. Most of all, German commentators did not want to understand why Brexit wasn't stopped by a non-partisan coalition of the reasonable and why the courts couldn't stop the madness. Why could there not have been better integration of Scottish and Irish regional interests? When the UK Supreme Court eventually declared the prorogation unconstitutional, it was unanimously celebrated by German and European constitutional scholars as a victory of parliamentarianism. But was it? The intervention of a constitutional court may have been cheered also because it met European expectations. In short, anyone following the German debate had to reach the conclusion that everything could have turned out for the better if Britain were to become more like the Federal Republic: with a multi-party system, parliamentary election of the head of government, the option of grand coalitions for exceptional challenges, federalism and powerful constitutional review.

The continental democracies may have been overlooking that the Brexit drama highlighted the accelerating assimilation of Westminster parliamentary democracy to its continental type. The admired institutions of liberal statecraft were in fact becoming more like their counterparts in countries such as Italy, the Netherlands or Germany. The British constitutional crisis of 2017–19 may not have been solely about Brexit. It was also a conflict between the traditions of the English constitution and the standard type of constitutionalism established worldwide, defined by the separation of powers, fundamental rights and constitutional review. In its breakaway from the European Union, the British constitution ironically seemed to be becoming more European.

The modern notion of parliamentary government in the United Kingdom was based not on the separation of powers, but on a prime ministerial government accountable to parliament and its constant public control by the opposition. Political authority was concentrated in the prime minister as head of government, party and parliamentary leadership in one. Walter Bagehot had famously situated political authority under the British constitution in a 'fusion of legislative and executive power'.[7] The institutional separation between legislative and executive power does exist as a distinction between parliament and government, but it is overshadowed by the political antagonism between government and opposition, which has never existed in such sharpness in continental parliamentarism.

The assimilation of British parliamentary government dates back to the 1990s, when the Labour government introduced certain elements of European constitutionalism. In 1998, the Human Rights Act created binding basic rights that also restrict parliamentary sovereignty.[8] The devolution of Scotland, Northern Ireland and Wales later introduced a kind of asymmetric federalism, the Constitutional Reform Act of 2005 established a Constitutional Court, the UK Supreme Court, which is no longer part of Parliament. It is certainly no coincidence that these institutions have played a major role in the Brexit crisis. In 2017, the Supreme Court bound the government to parliamentary approval of its Brexit policy, thus separating the government's basis of confidence in the House from the

[7] W Bagehot, *The English Constitution* (London, Chapman & Hall, 1867) 12, 36.

[8] Gordon (n 5) 120–26; JD Goldsworthy, *Parliamentary Sovereignty: Contemporary Debates* (Cambridge, Cambridge University Press, 2010); JL Hiebert, 'Parliament and the Human Rights Act: Can the JCHR Help Facilitate a Culture of Rights?' (2006) 4 *ICON* 1.

House's approval of certain major issues. The Scottish National Party, too, was a force of resistance against Brexit, not least because devolution greatly accelerated the crisis of the British party system and majority representation. Since British quasi-federalism makes it less hazardous to send representatives of regional parties to Westminster, a considerable number of seats are no longer allocated to the two major parties, which makes one-party governments structurally less likely. After the Second World War, only the elections of 2010 and 2017 resulted in a hung parliament (with the minor exception of 1974, when a hung parliament only lasted half a year). If there were only negative majorities in the House of Commons from referendum day to the general election of December 2019, this was ostensibly related to the political question as such, but at the same time to a deep-seated dysfunction in the formation of majorities in parliament. The plebiscitary representation of the referendum only made this dysfunction particularly visible: A huge majority of Labour constituencies notoriously voted 'Leave'.

A second element of continental constitutionalism changed the British constitution in 2011, not coincidentally pushed for by David Cameron's coalition government with the Liberal Democrats. The Fixed-term Parliaments Act (FTPA) addressed the very centre of parliamentary government. It was only the Brexit crisis that fully revealed its institutional consequences. Ever since the modern type of prime ministerial government emerged when the party leader successfully reclaimed the right to the premiership at the turn of the nineteenth and twentieth centuries, the basis of prime ministerial power was control over his parliamentary party. His most important instrument to keep together centripetal factions within the party was the right to dissolve Parliament and call new elections at any time. This gave the head of government the power to ensure that the major policies pursued by his government and the majority in Parliament are consistent with the electorate. Albert Venn Dicey in his classical analysis of parliamentary government under modern mass democracy, conceived the free dissolvability of Parliament as the flipside of its outstanding constitutional position. Since Parliament is the legal place of sovereignty, there must be a guarantee for the 'sympathy between the action of the legislature and the will of the people': '[A]nd this security is given by the right of dissolution, which enables the Crown or the Ministry to appeal from the legislature to the nation.'[9]

The FTPA abolished this power. Ever since, the only way to call new elections has been through a successful no-confidence motion by the opposition, an Act of Parliament or a two-thirds majority. In consequence, the prime minister has since then needed other means to control his own party. The drifting apart of government and parliamentary majority, of government and Parliament is the almost inevitable consequence, which occurred soon after the FTPA and long before Brexit: when David Cameron in 2013 had to turn round his Syria policy, he was the first prime minister since the end of the eighteenth century to lose a parliamentary vote on a military issue without being forced to resign. Boris Johnson's attempt to force the approval of snap elections through a combination of parliamentary prorogation, a motion under the FTPA and a series of government defeats in the Commons failed, but it did not cost him office either.

In this situation, the referendum of 2016 acted as an amplifier in the process of dissolving the complex fabric of the British constitutional system. It was yet another alien

[9] AV Dicey, *Introduction to the Study of the Law of the Constitution*, 8th edn (London, Macmillan, 1923) 429, 433.

element in that system; however, no one was allowed to say so openly. After all, who could officially ignore the will of the people? It was so diffuse that all sides could appeal to it. A grotesque situation that paralysed the political system until December 2019: although there was a simple majority of 51.9 per cent from the referendum and different majorities for and against different propositions in Parliament, there was no institutional way of resolving this contradiction and bringing about a conclusion.

The strictly majoritarian logic of the House of Commons, the logic of confidence and control, has thus been doubly weakened by the referendum and by the hidden supermajority of the FTPA. How far the government's control over the agenda of the House of Commons was affected by this process is demonstrated by the rise of a hitherto politically largely insignificant office at the centre of the constitution: who beyond the shores of Britain knows even one Speaker of the Commons by name between the legendary Arthur Onslow (1691–1768) and John Bercow? Bercow's spectacular discharge of his office, which made him a political popstar worldwide, shows the tragedy of institutions formerly integrated into parliamentary government becoming 'more independent': he was no longer able to play the mediating role between government and opposition the office is based upon. But he was ill-prepared for the mediating role between government and the majority party, between government and the situational majorities, and hence often seemed biased.

This process points at an apparent dilemma of parliamentary government in Britain today. Its present structure emerged in the eighteenth century, when the power to control the parliamentary agenda was monopolised by government.[10] Ever since, the standing order requires that 'government business shall have precedence at every sitting'. It was that agenda power that gave rise to what Walter Bagehot called the 'fusion of executive and legislative power'.[11]

If control over the parliamentary agenda is therefore not a formality, but the centre of parliamentary democracy,[12] then it was not an ordinary procedure or a necessary protection of minorities in a perilous situation but a constitutional amendment when Bercow broke the monopoly on the agenda in late March 2019 in favour of the Letwin amendment in order to wrest sole control over voting from the May government. The direct consequences were far-reaching, the indirect consequences for the institutional fabric are hardly foreseeable: since Bercow himself did not hesitate to rewrite the rules, his rebellion against Boris Johnson's threatened disregard for the Benn Act (which sought to outlaw leaving the European Union without an agreement), which would never have existed without Bercow's own intervention, could not be fully convincing.

As a way out of the stalemate of the House of Commons over Brexit in 2019, international commentators often recommended two things which amount to the same: a written constitution and bipartisan if not non-partisan majorities.[13] It is the way the German political system has almost always taken on particularly important issues. It is one of the

[10] GW Cox, *The Efficient Secret: The Cabinet and the Development of Political Parties in Victorian England* (Cambridge, Cambridge University Press, 1987); S Patrick, 'A History of Standing Orders' in P Evans (ed), *Essays on the History of Parliamentary Procedure* (Oxford, Hart, 2017) 189, 195–201.

[11] Bagehot (n 7) 12, 36.

[12] M Koß, *Parliaments in Time. The Evolution of Legislative Democracy in Western Europe, 1866–2015* (Oxford, Oxford University Press, 2018).

[13] B Ackerman, 'Why Britain Needs a Written Constitution – And Can't Wait for Parliament to Write One' (2018) 89 *Political Quarterly* 584.

difficult-to-understand characteristics of German political culture that majorities tend to be looking for even larger majorities that also involve the opposition. But this is precisely what the British institutions are worst equipped for. Majority voting offers little incentive for the formation of stable coalitions, and Parliament lacks the bargaining systems of the legislative committees in which coalition positions are formed. It is therefore unjust to blame the House of Commons for the course of the Brexit drama. Certainly, it has not managed to form a positive majority for anything in months and has thus to some extent worked towards its own disempowerment. Yet, it was neither Parliament nor government but the Supreme Court who transferred a key principle of German constitutional law into British constitutional law in the first *Miller* case, according to which certain key government decisions require a preceding act of Parliament. The Court thereby confronted Parliament with a task for which it was institutionally unprepared. This left the Prime Minister, any prime minister, only one way out, which is aggravating the underlying crisis: he needs to use the media and other means of executive power in a targeted anti-parliamentary way and to demand from his party, through plebiscitary mobilisation, the willingness to follow suit, which the instruments and institutions of parliamentary government no longer guarantee.

In the meantime, Britain's withdrawal from the European Union has been decided. What is not decided is whether the assimilation of the British constitution to the continental and US type of constitution alism will continue after Brexit, or whether, on the contrary, Britain's reclaimed 'sovereignty' will be followed by a glorious revolution of the old British constitution. A first step in this direction may be the elimination of the FTPA, which the Johnson government has announced in the December 2019 Queen's Speech and which is the objective of a private bill introduced in February 2020.[14] Not quite a revolution yet, since the bill's section 7 provides that a committee shall carry out a review of the operation of the FTPA and, if appropriate in consequence of its findings, make recommendations for its repeal or amendment by late 2020. But other steps might follow.

II. Master Narratives of the German Democracy – and Recent Doubts

The crisis of the German parliamentary system, as enshrined in the German Basic Law (Grundgesetz),[15] has different origins – and a different historical narrative. Parliamentary democracy has been historically vindicated by the stable democracy of the Bonn republic – the prosperity, pluralism and peace experienced seemed to provide for prosperity, pluralism and peace. According to this conventional master narrative, the fathers and mothers of the Basic Law did not repeat the mistake of the 1919 Weimar constitution, which placed alongside the parliamentary system a president as a dictator-in-waiting equipped with extraordinary powers. Instead, the founders in 1949 held the political parties

[14] Fixed-term Parliaments Act 2011 (Repeal) Bill [HL] 2019–21.

[15] Following the German practice, the abbreviation 'GG' is used when reference is made to a particular provision (eg Art 4(1) GG).

responsible for forming majority governments. But who dares to judge how great a contribution a constitution or a constitutional court ultimately makes to stabilising a political order? Might a state in the social, economic and above all international situation of the Federal Republic before 1989 not have done equally well under the Weimar or indeed any other constitution? In the postwar years, there was little resistance to the banning of disloyal parties such as the national-socialist SRP in 1952 and the communist KPD in 1958, whereas the confrontation with their latter-day successors has only just begun. Also, the powers of the presidency in Weimar became a problem only when voters chose to bestow these upon the charismatic war hero General Paul von Hindenburg who had made an astonishing career for himself under two regimes while making no secret of his disdain for parliaments, parties and civilian politics.[16]

The largely tactical attitude to the rules of parliamentary life today is represented by the right-wing party Alternative für Deutschland (AfD, Alternative for Germany), which was born in 2013 out of agitation against Angela Merkel's economic policy concerning the eurozone crisis and has grown to its present strength during the European migrant crisis, when it adopted an increasingly extremist approach. The party confronts the Federal Republic with a question striking at the heart of its constitution: how much of its stability does the German state owe to a singular historical constellation, and to what extent does it still live on that political capital? Historical studies of parliamentarism broadly agree that a cultural background and an environment shared by the political actors increase the likelihood of a parliament forming stable governments, for constant contact and familiarity are conducive to compromise.[17] Such a sense of belonging was far likelier to arise naturally in Bonn, so often mocked for its provincial character – the 'small town in Germany' of John Le Carré's eponymous novel – than in sprawling Berlin.[18] However unlike London it was in other respects, the spatial compactness of the functions of parliament and government in Bonn resembled the British arrangement between Westminster, Whitehall and Downing Street. The social world surrounding career politicians was likewise narrower, as were the opportunities for amusement, and it was common knowledge who took advantage of them and how. Chancellor Helmut Kohl was a master of informal power not least on account of his legendary knowledge of the personal lives of those who enjoyed his confidence and those who lost it.[19] How little those directly involved were aware of those sociocultural determinants of their own parliamentary system of government is evident in one of the most curious decisions of constitutional politics during the reunification years: in the Bonn–Berlin Act of 1991, in large parts still in force today, the Bundestag undertook to form and control, from Berlin, a government of which large parts were to remain in Bonn.[20]

[16] A von der Goltz, *Hindenburg: Power, Myth, and the Rise of the Nazis* (Oxford, Oxford University Press, 2009); W Pyta, *Hindenburg: Herrschaft zwischen Hohenzollern und Hitler* (Munich, Deutsche Verlags-Anstalt, 2009).

[17] T Mergel, *Parlamentarische Kultur in der Weimarer Republik: Politische Kommunikation, symbolische Politik und Öffentlichkeit im Reichstag*, 3rd edn (Düsseldorf, Droste, 2012); T Raithel, *Das schwierige Spiel des Parlamentarismus: Deutscher Reichstag und französische Chambre des Députés in den Inflationskrisen der 1920er Jahre* (Munich, Oldenbourg, 2005).

[18] See also the excellent essay by L Haffert, 'Metropole des Populismus – Berlin als Totem der Elitenkritik' (2018) 825 *Merkur* 71.

[19] The best analysis of Kohl's strategies of informal power is P Bahners, *Helmut Kohl: Der Charakter der Macht* (Munich, CH Beck, 2017).

[20] V Gransow and KH Jarausch (eds), *Uniting Germany: Documents and Debates, 1944–1993* (Providence, Berghahn Books, 1994) 233 (doc 3).

Even some of its political opponents hoped that the success of a party to the right of the Christian Democrats might give a new lease of life to parliamentary procedures and debates; after all, the AfD had entered the scene with a claim to represent a 'silent majority' that supposedly have become politically homeless. And the AfD's accession to the Bundestag has indeed enlivened its debates, if only superficially. The media gratefully seize upon any of the stage-managed provocations that have become the party's strategic mainstay since its far-right wing (led by Björn Höcke) trounced the slightly less far-right wing in the summer of 2017. Such high jinks had already been well-rehearsed in the parliaments of several *Länder*, in which the AfD takes full advantage of parliamentary sessions to stage headline-grabbing interventions. Meanwhile, however, its representatives seem rather less eager to engage in their oversight and control function and in committee work, leaving aside occasional questions in the house that are limited largely to the fields of migration and law and order.[21] Conservative policymakers may still dream of isolating the AfD's radical wing and incorporating the remaining moderates into a mainstream centre-right coalition. Yet all previous experience of the trajectories of right-wing protest parties from Front National and Lega Nord to UKIP suggests that the Christian Democrats would be the first victims of such a strategy. Any enlivenment that extremist parties such as the AfD might bring to the institutions of democracy and parliament in particular is thus set to be either short-lived or fatal.

Fatal, in the present context, would mean a return to the predicament of the Weimar Republic, with the parties at the centre moving ever closer together while the fringes grow stronger. The divide between government and opposition would be increasingly supplanted by that between the defenders of the constitution and its enemies. With the parties of the centre closing ranks, following the defensive imperative of holding firm, any impetus to political and institutional change is likely to be lost. In the worst-case scenario, only the Constitutional Court would remain as the bearer of some vague hope for rescue, though no one today can say with any certainty how justified such hope might be. The Federal Constitutional Court's ruling of January 2017 on the neo-Nazi National Democratic Party (Nationaldemokratische Partei Deutschlands, NPD) shows why: although its principles were clearly inimical to the constitution, the party did not yet pose a sufficiently concrete danger in the eyes of the court and thus did not need to be banned. The solution represents the court's attempt to claim the moral authority of the 'guardian of the constitution' while reserving the right to exercise it only in situations of genuine peril.[22]

Short-lived, on the other hand, would mean those forces scorned as 'the old parties' pulling together to enact constitutional reforms that by their nature would also have to entail a reform of parliamentary democracy. The specific measures to be taken, however, are far from obvious, though lists of grievances and desiderata seem remarkably consistent across decades.[23] Ever since the Adenauer years, public intellectuals in continental democracies have been at hand to call for a 'livelier' parliamentary politics, at least when there was nothing worse to complain about. The remedies proposed at regular intervals

[21] W Schröder, B Weßels and A Berzel, 'Die AfD in den Landtagen' (2018) 49 *Zeitschrift für Parlamentsfragen* 91.

[22] *Party ban procedure NPD*, Second Senate, 144 *BVerfGE* 20 (2017), ECLI:DE:BVerfG:2017:bs20170117.2bvb000113 (en).

[23] See P Cancik and H Pünder, 'Wahlrecht und Parlamentsrecht als Gelingensbedingungen repräsentativer Demokratie' (2013) 72 *Veröffentlichungen der Vereinigung der Deutschen Staatsrechtslehrer* 191.

to emulate the British model tend always to be the same: relaxed party discipline, shorter but better speeches, abolition of the speaker's rostrum that marks the most obvious visual difference between Westminster and continental parliamentary traditions, more head-to-head confrontation between government and opposition, fewer chat shows, and, most of all, more public participation. In June 2020, the Bundestag launched a 'citizens' council' (Bürgerrat), which is supposed to represent a social cross-section of the German population. The 160 members, assembled by lot rather than by vote, are expected to draw up, in dialogue with experts, a report on no less a topic than 'Germany's role in the world', supposed to be debated in parliament later. Seldom has a parliament made itself so small with so little effort; a parliament that, on the other hand, is generally considered to be far too large. Since the complicated electoral law leads to additional mandates when the share of votes of the major parties declines, the Bundestag now has 709 members instead of its regular 598. No doubt a parliament of 700 members presents a less congenial arena for political talents than one of, say, 400. This problem is exacerbated by the huge debating chamber of the Reichstag building in Berlin, whose very expanse seems to preclude any intense personal confrontation. (The architectural dimensions of the plenary hall only became an advantage during the 2020 pandemic, as they are almost ideal for social distancing.) In short, the reform proposals have been on the surface of the political phenomena for too long. It is time to think bigger and at a more fundamental level, asking questions about the electoral law, the organisation of government and the bicameral system.

III. Realities of Mass and Social Media

Few things have so thoroughly transformed the functioning of democratic institutions as television and radio. Totalitarianism was not least a media event. In his famous essay on 'The Work of Art in the Age of Mechanical Reproduction' (1937), Walter Benjamin gave the following diagnosis:

> Parliaments, as much as theatres, are deserted. Radio and film not only affect the function of the professional actor but likewise the function of those who also exhibit themselves before this mechanical equipment, those who govern. Though their tasks may be different, the change affects equally the actor and the ruler. The trend is toward establishing controllable and transferrable skills under certain social conditions. This results in a new selection, a selection before the equipment from which the star and the dictator emerge victorious.[24]

Benjamin knew that old-style parliamentarianism had few means of competing with the plebiscitary uses to which radio and film were put in the interwar period, for technology enabled the executive to be ubiquitous in a manner that shattered the aggregation of power and its exercise within a closed, representative assembly.

Yet after World War II, the once-deserted parliaments reinvented themselves and successfully recast their rules of procedure, their agenda, their seating arrangements and their very

[24] W Benjamin, 'The Work of Art in the Age of Mechanical Reproduction' in *Illuminations* (New York, Schocken, 1968) 247.

language in accordance with the logic of television. They adapted to the rules of what the German sociologist Niklas Luhmann called the 'reality of mass media'.[25] It may even be that a decisive role in the renaissance of parliamentary government after 1945 falls to the establishment of televised debates, of a perspective centred on the television viewer, a perspective that today's so-called 'social media' seek to abolish. We may thus have not so much as the first inkling of the extent to which the decentralisation and de-hierarchisation of political speech will change all parliamentary institutions. Digital swarms, too, will 'result in a new selection', and since November 2016 the world knows what its beneficiaries may look like.

It is almost certain that one day the Covid-19 pandemic will also be seen as a turning point in the history of parliaments. Parliament, the grand assembly, became an impossible place almost overnight due to the great physical proximity of people who are disproportionately at risk. And yet parliaments did not give up in the crisis. Many of them around the world have modified and adapted their rules of procedure with a remarkable amount of innovative spirit to allow remote working and remote voting by videoconference and speeches to be broadcast to members, ministers to be questioned in semi-virtual set-ups or to scrutinise the government outside the select committee framework.[26] It is not yet possible to say whether these are signs of progress or decline. After all, the physical presence of the government, the physical exposure of the decision-makers to the representatives, is one of the key elements of parliamentary government, deeply inscribed in the architecture and seating arrangements of parliaments.[27] It will certainly need more than just technology to transfer these arrangements into the virtual sphere.

Democratic institutions are once again faced with the need to reinvent themselves, although nobody yet knows how such an institutional renewal might succeed. What is certain, on the other hand, is that the future of parliamentary democracy hinges less on loyal attitudes and rhetorical confessions to the importance of democracy than on a reasonable structure of its constitutional institutions. It is to that debate that this book is intended to contribute by trying to understand the constitutional and legal peculiarities of this system of government, its political strengths and weaknesses, and the direction it seems to be heading in.

IV. Outline

In this book I start off with the question of what the term 'parliamentary democracy' means for the constitutional structure of the Federal Republic. A schematic distinction is commonly made between democracies of the parliamentary and the presidential type.[28] Yet

[25] N Luhmann, *The Reality of Mass Media* [1995] (Cambridge, Polity Press, 2000).

[26] A survey on the measures taken by parliaments to cope with the corona crisis has been conducted by the Interparliamentary Union: www.ipu.org/country-compilation-parliamentary-responses-pandemic (updated 18 September 2020). A fairly optimistic view on virtualising parliamentary procedure is expressed by F-A van Lier, 'Towards Virtual Parliaments?' *Open Democracy* (blog), www.opendemocracy.net/en/can-europe-make-it/towards-virtual-parliaments/ (12 May 2020).

[27] P Manow, *In the King's Shadow: The Political Anatomy of Democratic Representation* (New York, Polity, 2010).

[28] H Fix-Fierro and P Salazar-Ugarte, 'Presidentialism' and AW Bradley and C Pinelli, 'Parliamentarism' in M Rosenfeld and A Sajó (eds), *The Oxford Handbook of Comparative Constitutional Law* (Oxford, Oxford University Press, 2012) 628, 650.

as far as the Federal Republic of Germany is concerned, that is far from being the whole truth. Its constitution follows neither type. In Chapter 2 I show that the German peculiarity rather resides in a dualism specific to the country's entire constitutional structure, of which the parliamentary system is, as it were, but one layer, one institutional system. A second layer is formed by an intricate arrangement – part constitutional-legal, part political – of administrative and federal institutions: state executives, the second chamber or Federal Council (Bundesrat) and informal bodies coordinating policies among the various federal states. This second layer of the constitution, moreover, is older and subject to quite different rules of political functioning. In Chapter 3, I discuss the historical reasons why Germany nonetheless warrants the title of a parliamentary democracy: the Federal Republic's three distinctive institutions – the broadly based main or 'popular' parties (*Volksparteien*), the Federal Chancellery and the Federal Constitutional Court – have proved able to mediate between and indeed to tie together the two layers of the constitution. Since, however, the evolution of the Federal Republic towards a parliamentary system of government thus took place outside the purview of the constitution's formal institutions, the basic normative question of this form of government, the principle of representation embodied in the German Bundestag, has remained remarkably unclear, which is due not least to the peculiarities of the voting system (Chapter 4). Yet all three of these mediating institutions have for some time now been caught up in a process of change. The role of the major parties as pillars of the constitutional order is eroding in plain sight, whereas the Constitutional Court and the Chancellery are becoming increasingly unbounded. This state of affairs represents a fundamental challenge to the parliamentary system of government, for it means that the mediating institutions are less and less able to fulfil their function (Chapter 5). This is of particular relevance with regard to the capacity and functioning of parliamentary oversight over the executive, a function already under severe strain from shifting paradigms of government action (Chapter 6). As a result, technical questions relating to the organisation of political life rapidly turn into fundamental questions concerning the Federal Republic's constitutional and legal identity. But no diagnosis of this malaise can shy away from first seeking to understand German democracy in its day-to-day workings.

2

The Two Worlds of German Constitutionalism

I. What is Parliamentary Government?

Germany is usually and rightly referred to as a parliamentary democracy. In constitutional terms this means something far more definite than the commonplace blanket term 'parliamentarianism' suggests. The parliamentary system of government is a profoundly specific thing. It denotes a type of constitution in which the highest power among political institutions is located, as it were, between the parliamentary majority and its government. Yet this description, too, leaves many questions unanswered. Whereas the English model of parliamentary government rests on the notion of sovereignty being vested in Parliament itself, continental thought does not recognise parliamentary sovereignty but holds parliament and government to be 'constituted' institutions – institutions derived, that is, from the sovereignty of the people.

What distinguishes parliamentary from presidential constitutions is the constitutional relationship between parliament and the executive. Parliamentary government does not emerge from direct elections, but through the election of parliament. This does not necessarily, not even regularly entail the government being elected by parliament. Investiture rules differ considerably across different parliamentary constitutions:[1] in Germany, the chancellor needs an absolute majority in the Bundestag to assume office (Article 63(1)–(3) Basic Law). In the United Kingdom, for instance, the prime minister continues to be formally appointed by the monarch. The president of Italy's Council of Ministers is appointed by the president of the Republic (Article 92(2) of the Italian Constitution of 1947). In every case, however, the formation of a government depends on a parliamentary majority. The government comes into office with the support of a parliamentary majority, and no government can remain in office against the will of a majority in parliament. This bears the consequence that the legislature and the executive cannot be viewed as separated, independent powers or branches of government, each legitimised in its own right. Rather, they are held together by the closest of political and constitutional ties. This is why a parliamentary government is responsible to parliament for the discharge of its duties.

[1] BE Rasch and S Martin (eds), *Parliaments and Government Formation. Unpacking Investiture Rules* (Oxford, Oxford University Press, 2015).

A. The Monism of Powers

Walter Bagehot, author of the classic account of *The English Constitution* first published in 1867, was thus right to distinguish the parliamentary government from the doctrine of the separation of powers by calling it a 'fusion' rather than a separation of powers.[2] In translating this idea into the concept of the 'monism of powers' (*Gewaltenmonismus*), Richard Thoma, an eminent scholar of Germany's first democratic constitution after World War I, was accurate enough.[3] Yet he left himself open to misunderstanding by using a term that seemed to imply the illegitimate concentration of powers. What is more, the term 'monism' is far more appropriate to the British system of government, in which the very appearance of the cabinet as the front bench even creates a spatial unity with the majority party in the House of Commons. In Germany, on the other hand, as in all continental states, parliamentary government emerged from an altogether different historical constellation. The decisive factor here was the separation between absolutist states and their bureaucracies on the one hand, and parliaments on the other, that had to be bridged by the principle of ministerial responsibility.

What parliamentary governments of all types have in common is the political front line between government and opposition that cuts across the institutional link knitting together parliament and government. Governments and their parliamentary majorities cooperate and pursue shared political goals. Moreover, the party leadership typically rests with that of the government, which means that governing parties, in particular, do not form counterweights to governments. Meanwhile, the parliamentary opposition is directed not only against the government of the day, but also against the agenda pursued by the government's majority in parliament. This affects all key functions of parliaments beyond government formation, namely legislation, control and representation. The role of the parliament in a parliamentary system is not simply or even principally that of a legislature. Control over the legislative process is usually shared by government and the parliamentary majority. Nor does parliamentary control serve as some kind of external democratic watchdog over government policy, as a mere representative of the popular interest vis-a-vis the government. It is rather the bearer and embodiment in its own right of political power, which it exercises jointly with the government. This form of parliamentary democracy is thus the explicit rule of a democratically elected assembly, from which a government emerges and draws its support – until such time as it is withdrawn.

B. Reservations about Parliamentary Rule

The German public and political theory remain subject to the most astonishing misapprehensions regarding the political purpose and the institutional logic of parliamentary democracy. The simple fact that parliament is a form of democratic rule continues to be viewed with particular suspicion. Carl Schmitt and Jürgen Habermas, each of whose accounts of parliamentarianism foregrounds the element of rational public discussion,

[2] W Bagehot, *The English Constitution* (London, Chapman & Hall, 1867) 12, 36.

[3] R Thoma, 'Sinn und Gestaltung des deutschen Parlamentarismus' in H Dreier (ed), *Rechtsstaat – Demokratie – Grundrechte* (Tübingen, Mohr Siebeck, 2008) 233.

are only the most prominent exponents of an attitude that quietly doubts or openly challenges the idea that parliament's actual task should be to bring about democratic decisions.[4] It is still common in Germany to hear the parliament referred to as the *Volksvertretung*, an untranslatable term that alludes to the people as a metaphysical entirety, avoids the notion of political representation and power, and keeps alive an idea of parliamentarianism dating back to the nineteenth century, when German parliaments could not yet hold governments responsible. German constitutions since 1871 have held that deputies 'shall be representatives of the whole people, not bound by orders or instructions and responsible only to their conscience' (Article 38 GG).[5] It is all too easily forgotten how fundamentally the meaning of that phrase changes when parliament does not merely *limit* the rule of a monarchical bureaucracy by safeguarding certain rights and reservations of the people, but actually *rules* itself.

Democratic rule is a complex and laborious process, in which open debate in the chamber – which the mere fact of etymology would lead one to believe was the most important aspect of a *parliament* – is the exception rather than the rule. Nonetheless, images of a Bundestag chamber that is often quite empty and lacks the regular spectacle of PMQs still serve as clichés for a critique of parliamentarianism in which backroom deals, lobbying and party discipline serve as ciphers lamenting the decline of what it was purportedly all about in the first place, namely the representation of the people. The AfD's parliamentary style hypocritically lives up to this idea. Its deputies seem to enjoy the sound of their own voices in the chamber, while leaving committee work to others, not to mention the work of governing. 'Have people forgotten', the politician and political scientist Hans Maier asked the German public as long as fifty years ago, 'that parliaments are packed only in dictatorships and that attendance in the chamber tends to decline rather than rise in line with a parliament's increasing power – to the degree, that is, that parliaments function as something other than an ornamental assembly of yes-men?'[6]

C. Confidence, Power and Control

At the centre of the idea and form of parliamentary government stands an informal principle that in the constitutional tradition goes by the name of 'confidence'. What in British parliamentary procedure is the function of confidence motions by which the opposition can test the 'confidence of the House in Her Majesty's government',[7] in Germany is the way of electing a chancellor. Every chancellor must successfully claim the confidence of a majority of the Bundestag's members – the so-called 'chancellor's majority' – to be elected

[4] C Schmitt, *The Crisis of Parliamentary Democracy*, trans E Kennedy (Cambridge, MA, MIT Press, 1988); J Habermas, *The Structural Transformation of the Public Sphere: An Inquiry into a Category of Bourgeois Society*, trans T Burger (Cambridge, MA, MIT Press, 1991); E Kennedy, 'Carl Schmitt and the Frankfurt School', 37 *Telos* 20 (1987).

[5] Art 29 of the 1871 constitution of the German Empire: 'The members of the Reichstag are representatives of the entire people [*Vertreter des ganzen Volkes*] and are not bound by orders and instructions.' Art 21 of the Weimar Constitution: 'The deputies shall be representatives of the entire people. They are subject only to their conscience [*Gewissen*] and are not bound by instructions.'

[6] H Maier, 'Parlamentsreform – aber wie?' (1969) 254 *Merkur* 516.

[7] *cf Erskine May*, 25th edn (2019), part 3 ¶ 18.44, https://erskinemay.parliament.uk.

to office (Article 63(1) GG). He can seek an affirmation of this confidence by calling for a 'vote of confidence' (Article 68(1) GG).[8] A new parliamentary majority can withdraw its confidence from a government by electing another chancellor by means of a so-called 'constructive vote of no confidence' (Article 67(1) GG).[9] A government formed by such means is every bit as legitimate as another, as history proves. The political leadership of the GDR tried to help overthrow Willy Brandt's government when it famously bribed opposition MPs before the confidence vote in April 1972. Helmut Kohl, too, used a constructive vote of no confidence against Helmut Schmidt to launch his sixteen-year chancellorship in 1982.

Yet unlike the related concept of 'trust', 'confidence' is to be understood here as neither a moral nor a legal, but as a political category. Gertrude Lübbe-Wolff, a justice on the Federal Constitutional Court, has prominently made this point in her dissenting opinion on Gerhard Schröder's dissolution of the Bundestag in 2005: the question asked in a vote of no confidence

> is, much like the question posed at the marriage altar, not a question of knowledge, which anybody might answer as well as or indeed better than the one to whom it is addressed. By posing the question of confidence, the chancellor is not enquiring into a point of knowledge, but into the will of parliament and its members, to whom the question is to be addressed according to art 68 of the Basic Law: The question, that is, concerning their willingness to support him and his political programme by means of their voting behaviour.[10]

Among their crucial institutional provisions, the parliamentary rules of procedure contain a striking contradiction: whereas the chancellor is elected by secret ballot, the vote of confidence is held in the open, with deputies voting by name. Only this latter procedure is truly consistent. After all, the most politically significant procedure for which this system of government provides has nothing to do with safeguarding individual deputies' feelings about the head of government. Instead, what is at stake is the public demonstration of a deputy's willingness to support a particular government or not.

Within the remit of the Constitution can thus be found the borderline cases of confidence: its manifestations, its revival in situations of peril and its withdrawal. How political confidence is created and sustained is not a matter of legal definition. How parliamentary support for government policy can be secured within the parliamentary groups of the governing parties and how, conversely, cabinet members can be made to support policies likely to gain parliamentary approval are questions of political instinct and statecraft. 'Experience suggests that this can best be achieved by leading a group into parliamentary battles requiring thorough preparation and in which leadership material is likely to come to the fore', as Hans-Peter Schwarz, a political scientist, brilliant biographer of Helmut Kohl,

[8] The clause reads: 'If a motion of the federal chancellor for a vote of confidence is not supported by the majority of the members of the Bundestag, the federal president, upon the proposal of the federal chancellor, may dissolve the Bundestag within twenty-one days. The right of dissolution shall lapse as soon as the Bundestag elects another federal chancellor by the vote of a majority of its members.'

[9] 'The Bundestag may express its lack of confidence in the federal chancellor only by electing a successor by the vote of a majority of its members and requesting the federal president to dismiss the federal chancellor. The federal president must comply with the request and appoint the person elected.'

[10] *Dissolution of the Bundestag*, dissenting opinion LübbeWolff, 114 *BVerfGE* 121, 182 (2004) ECLI:DE:BVerfG:2005:es20050825.2bve000405 (en).

and himself intimately acquainted with the political system of the Bonn Republic, once remarked.[11] It is recognised for every government in the history of the Federal Republic that fading support in the chancellor's own parliamentary party significantly contributed to the loss of power.

D. The Asymmetric Juridification of the System of Government

This political logic of parliamentary government poses a challenge to constitutional doctrine. The interrelation of parliament and government in a parliamentary democracy rests on what might be called its asymmetric juridification. Interactions between opposition and governing majority must be governed by minority rights and thus be heavily juridified, be it in the form of the right to submit motions, obligations to inform and consult, or rules governing the funding of parliamentary parties or the distribution of committee seats and chairs. The same applies, for the same reason, for the laws concerning political parties and elections. By contrast, there are hardly any constitutional rules governing the relationship between the government's parliamentary majority and the cabinet, aside from those surrounding the election of the chancellor. This is neither an omission nor an accident. After all, this system of government is all about the institutional and political link between the governing majority and the cabinet. The rule that members of parliament can at the same time hold a cabinet post is, in the terms of the parliamentary system, not a worrying infringement of some 'separation of powers', but rather one of that system's vital preconditions.[12]

If, then, the formal relationship of support between the parliamentary majority and the government lies at the very core of this form of parliamentarianism, it would be a mistake to imagine the relevant constitutional laws as particularly static. This relationship is founded not on fixed institutions with clearly demarcated powers, but rather on a kind of open institutional synthesis. As Wilhelm Hennis, one of the greatest admirers of the British constitution and its most forceful advocate in the Federal Republic, once put it, parliamentary government hence is 'the most demanding and vulnerable' of all forms of government.

> Like no other, it is dependent on external circumstances and conditions, its character changing with every new constellation of parties and coalitions. … Parliamentary government is thus the form of government which is the least rigid. It is always possible to expect different things from it and invariably, it leaves some questions unanswered.[13]

Of course, the informal systems of regulation developed by the parliamentary system are decisively shaped by the constitutional framework within which actors operate.[14] Within these boundaries, however, there is a great deal of space for the development of political

[11] H-P Schwarz, 'Die CDU/CSUFraktion in der Ära Adenauer' in H-P Schwarz (ed), *Die Fraktion als Machtfaktor* (Munich, Pantheon Verlag, 2009) 13.

[12] *cf* AW Bradley, KD Ewing and CJS Knight, *Constitutional & Administrative Law*, 16th edn (Harlow, Pearson, 2015) 269.

[13] W Hennis, 'Die Rolle des Parlaments und die Parteiendemokratie' (1974) in *Regieren im modernen Staat* (Tübingen, Mohr Siebeck, 1999) 227.

[14] The classic analysis is G Lehmbruch, *Parteienwettbewerb im Bundesstaat: Regelsysteme und Spannungslagen im politischen System der Bundesrepublik Deutschland*, 3rd edn (Wiesbaden, VS Verlag, 2000) 17.

rules that can ultimately solidify into reliable conventions and be brought to bear on the understanding of constitutional institutions. This is particularly true in the Federal Republic of Germany.

II. The Dual Structure of the German Constitution

Germany's particular difficulties with the proper understanding of parliamentary democracy and parliamentary government arise from the constitution itself. One cannot understand the structure of the German constitutional system if one interprets it as a parliamentary democracy as a whole in its institutional workings. Whereas in Great Britain most political institutions can be understood in terms of a sovereign parliament on the one side and a government responsible to it on the other, this has never been the case in the Federal Republic. The principles of parliamentary democracy explain only one dimension, one set of possibilities, one political component of the German constitution – a constitution that is dualistic at its core, a variable disposition of two layers which embody a peculiarly German version of the 'division of powers': the politics/bureaucracy divide.

The specific institutional elements of the parliamentary mode of government – the distinction between government and opposition, the link between parliament and government, and finally the responsibility of ministers – are hallmarks of one layer of the constitution, the more recent. As remains to be shown, it is a creation of the Basic Law only in some of its rudiments, being in most respects rather a product of the Federal Republic's constitutional history.[15] Against this more recent layer is set the constitution of the federal and administrative state, the elementary structures of which date back to Bismarck's constitution and the creation of the German nation-state after the Franco-Prussian War of 1870–71. Although this older layer of the constitution has been significantly altered since the late nineteenth century, it has never been fundamentally challenged.[16] The federal order is deeply inscribed in the Basic Law through its history: under Allied supervision, the constitution was drafted in 1948 and 1949 by envoys from the *Länder*.

It is only a slight overstatement to say that federalism, in the context of the German constitution, is a camouflage name for bureaucratic autonomy. What are its building blocks? At the federal level, the individual ministries continue to enjoy a high degree of autonomy from parliamentary control, as do large parts of the administrative apparatus, for instance the large administrative bodies of the welfare state. That autonomy of the federal bureaucracy is based on a mediating role between the government and the administrative bodies in the several *Länder*. Their governments and their bureaucracies on the other hand can wield considerable political influence on national policy via the federal second chamber (Bundesrat). The institutional control they exercise over public broadcasting places another vast resource of power in state hands. State power is further amplified by informal bodies that coordinate between the states and the federal level, for instance the influential standing conferences of ministers of the interior or of education.

[15] See ch 3 below.

[16] The best historical account of German federalism is S Oeter, *Integration und Subsidiarität im deutschen Bundesstaatsrecht: Untersuchungen zur Bundesstaatstheorie unter dem Grundgesetz* (Tübingen, Mohr Siebeck, 1998).

A. The Administration's Uncoupling from the Political System

From the very outset, there was an anti-parliamentary thrust to the German model of the administrative state and so-called administrative federalism.[17] Its most important constitutional principle, devised by the cunning political genius Otto von Bismack, consists in systematic detachment of political responsibility for the administrative implementation of law on the one hand and the government's responsibility towards parliament on the other. This detachment is based on a principle of decentralised responsibility similar to EU law: whereas most legislation is the responsibility of the federal level (Articles 73 and 74 GG), its implementation – and thus the considerable powers that come with administrative discretion and local autonomy – is in most cases left to the *Länder* (Article 83 GG).[18] Administrative institutions on the federal level can only be created if explicitly allowed for a certain matter by the constitution; federal oversight of the decentralised administrations is in most cases limited to special cases of unlawful administrative action. In most cases, the governments of the *Länder* are responsible for how federal law is implemented. It is the regional legislatures rather than the Bundestag that pass rules on administrative procedure and the organisation of administrative authorities. And it is the *Länder* governments rather than federal government that shape administrative discretion, flesh out implementation policies and are ultimately responsible for decisions taken in individual cases. The key problem with this responsibility is its addressee. It is not to the parliament that has passed the law implemented. The regional parliaments (*Landtage*) can enforce responsibility but they have little incentive to put much energy into it, as they cannot change the substantive law in question so that any policy reaction can only take place on the federal level anyway.

To illustrate the problem with an example: migration and asylum is entirely within federal law-making powers. Yet the enforcement of deportation orders in cases where asylum was refused is largely left to the local authorities. If therefore, for political reasons, a *Land* is generally opposed to deporting any rejected asylum seekers or if on the contrary it takes a particularly harsh stance, the federal government usually has little choice but to comply. It is thus a fairly blatant violation of the principles of federalism if an amendment of the German Residence Act enacted during the migration crisis gives the federal minister of the interior the right to assume responsibility for enforcement in the case of individuals considered a security threat and in which the federal government can claim a particular interest in their deportation.[19]

For this reason, the Covid-19 crisis, too, was a phase of intensive intra-federal coordination on an administrative level, bypassing the *Länder* parliaments to an alarming extent. It is true that the most important legal basis for all administrative measures of containment is a federal law (Infection Protection Act), which was amended in a rapid legislative

[17] R Miller, 'Executive Extremes: German Lessons for our Authoritarian Era' (2021) 68 *Jahrbuch des öffentlichen Rechts der Gegenwart*, forthcoming.

[18] Art 83 reads: 'The *Länder* shall execute federal laws in their own right insofar as this Basic Law does not otherwise provide or permit.'

[19] § 58 a s 2 of the German Act on the Residence, Economic Activity and Integration of Foreigners in the Federal Territory (as of March 2020) www.gesetze-im-internet.de/englisch_aufenthg/englisch_aufenthg.pdf.

process at the beginning of the crisis. However, its implementation is the sole responsibility of the *Länder*. Although the federal chancellor tried to play a leading role in the Minister-Presidents' Conference that she moderated, the *Länder* governments have more than once refused to follow her lead.[20]

The democratic principle of parliamentary responsibility is dangerously enfeebled by the deliberate sundering of legislation and implementation. Nor is there much scope for the effective control by state parliaments over policies pursued by their governments on the federal level, where they exercise considerable powers of bargaining through the veto powers of the second chamber. Overstated or not, parts of what is often decried as the European Union's 'democratic deficit' have long been a familiar feature of the constitutional order in Germany, albeit one level further down. The Federal Republic continues to be faced with the fundamental problem of reconciling a parliamentary system of government structured around the dualism of government and opposition with the federal structure of both the country and its party system.

The institutional preconditions of parliamentary government could hardly be more ambivalent, particularly in comparison with Britain, which has no written constitution to trump legislation and no constitutional court, but does have a centralised system of government and a first-past-the-post electoral system still organised around two main parties. Against this model, the parliamentary system of government must appear as an altogether unlikely constitutional order for a country of Germany's political, social and federalist structure. How it nonetheless managed to consolidate itself in the Federal Republic hence must appear as the great unanswered question of its constitutional history.

Many postwar liberals such as Wilhelm Hennis had long clung to the hope that the Federal Republic's political elites might succeed in shedding the ballast of the Bismarckian legacy and organise the second German democracy along English lines. Like many liberals, he expected the first grand coalition of the late 1960s under chancellor Kurt-Georg Kiesinger to introduce majority representation with a first-past-the-post system, thereby eliminating the centrist Free Democratic Party and placing a two-party system with an alternating divide between government and opposition on a permanent footing.[21] Later, he persuaded Helmut Kohl, after the latter had triumphed in the popular vote of the 1976 Bundestag election and yet had to leave the chancellorship to Helmut Schmidt, to give up his office as prime minister or 'minister president' (*Ministerpräsident*) of Rhineland-Palatinate and to move to Bonn. There, he was to act as leader of the opposition and build a shadow cabinet – a term previously unfamiliar in Germany. It was a tremendously symbolic act in a constitutional system in which the *Länder* are often a more powerful place of opposition than the national parliament.[22] Yet few of this had a lasting impact. Hennis underestimated the intransigence of the dualistic constitution, which he, with mounting bitterness, ultimately dismissed as a pathology.[23] He increasingly came to view the informal dualism of parliamentarianism and federalism as an aspect of the institutional impossibility of

[20] A slightly too euphemistic account of the role of parliaments in the 2020 crisis is given by J Kersten and S Rixen, *Der Verfassungsstaat in der Corona-Krise* (Munich, CH Beck, 2020).

[21] Hennis's key studies are collected in the volume *Regieren im modernen Staat: Politikwissenschaftliche Abhandlungen I* (Tübingen, Mohr Siebeck, 1999).

[22] S Schlak, *Wilhelm Hennis: Szenen einer Ideengeschichte der Bundesrepublik* (Munich, CH Beck, 2008) 174.

[23] W Hennis, *Auf dem Weg in den Parteienstaat: Aufsätze aus vier Jahrzehnten* (Stuttgart, Reclam, 1998).

majoritarian politics. His theory of a crisis of 'governability' (*Regierbarkeitskrise*) became the moderate German echo of what Western conservatives in the 1980s described as a structural lack of political leadership in advanced welfare states.[24]

B. Continuity as Principle

Why have the full institutional consequences of parliamentary democracy never been drawn in more than seven decades of the Federal Republic? There are good reasons why a pure form of parliamentary government would hardly be its appropriate constitutional structure. Like it or not, German political culture is deeply distrustful of the majority principle in its undiluted form and displays a marked preference for negotiated solutions, a fact that is often put down to centuries of dealing with religious divisions in the fragile institutional fabric of the empire before 1806. Indeed, this dualistic structure is also one of the great strengths of the German system of government, which has never displayed the kind of fickleness that is sometimes held against the Westminster model. A standard American objection to the British constitution argues that a new governing majority tends to meet with little resistance in toppling even fundamental political settlements. A radical rupture of the kind visited by Margaret Thatcher on postwar British corporatism would be hard to imagine in the Federal Republic. In fact, no new federal government has ever truly questioned, let alone rescinded, fundamental decisions made by its predecessor. The coalition of social democrats and liberals, which came to power in 1969, continued Adenauer's policy of firmly embedding Germany in the Western alliance. And though that coalition's successor, the conservative government led by Helmut Kohl, had famously proclaimed the need for a 'spiritual and moral renewal' (*geistig-moralische Erneuerung*), the call went unheeded in the pluralist consumer society of the 1980s and 1990s. Not only that, but Kohl also left completely untouched the social and welfare legislation enacted by the social democratic governments of Willy Brandt and Helmut Schmidt. It its turn, the social democrat–green coalition led by Gerhard Schröder upheld Kohl's policy both on the domestic and European front. And even though Angela Merkel's chancellorship began with the radical free-market rhetoric announced at a legendary party conference of her Christian Democrats in Leipzig, she eventually reversed none of the signature achievements of the red–green coalition. Even in nuclear policy, her government, after a brief turnaround of six months, quickly fell back in line with the nuclear phaseout that the Greens had rung in. None of this was in any way legally or constitutionally mandated, but was perhaps rather an expression of the supposed German love of continuity, to a certain extent no more than a cliché, accurate though it often is. A more helpful explanation may be found in one political effect of the dualistic constitution: all principal parliamentary decisions are always already the product of negotiations with the other actors in the federal system, whose position gives them veto rights to insist on any compromise achieved, even if the parliamentary arithmetic has since changed. This mode of decision-making reconciles a political culture deeply sceptical of the majority principle with an institutional form of parliamentarism.

[24] G Chamayou, *La société ingouvernable. Une généalogie du libéralisme autoritaire* (Paris, Fabrique, 2019).

C. The Constitution as an Achievement

This book argues that, to this day, there is no stringent legal link between the parliamentary and the federal-administrative sides of the constitution. Nor is there even so much as a constitutional model that might provide an intellectual framework for their integration. On the contrary: the only theory of parliamentary democracy that is viable from a constitutional-legal perspective, and to which the Constitutional Court has so far subscribed, emphasises only the parliamentary aspect of the constitution, leaving the other virtually invisible. The foundations of this conception are the work of Ernst-Wolfgang Böckenförde, internationally known for a constitutional theory that combined Carl Schmitt's notion of popular sovereignty with liberal elements.[25] According to Böckenförde's account, parliamentary democracy is a layered, ultimately self-referential institutionalisation of popular sovereignty. Hence, any public body, office or institution is the bearer of democratic legitimacy to the extent that it can show that it does what it does as a result of parliamentary decisions and thus expressions of the sovereign will: parliament supports the government and makes laws that bind it, the government controls the ministries, which in turn control their subordinate authorities, in a chain of democratic legitimation that ultimately, in the shape of binding decisions, connects back to the citizenry from which it is originally derived.

The Constitutional Court recently gave a pithy reaffirmation of this principle at the heart of its jurisdiction:

> Art 20 sec 2 sentence 2 GG sets out the principle of sovereignty of the people. It determines that all state power is derived from the people, who exercise it through elections and other votes, as well as through specific legislative, executive and judicial organs. This requires that the people have an effective influence on the exercise of state power through these organs. Any actions of these organs must be attributable to the people's will and be justified before it. … In addition to being ensured by parliamentary elections, laws adopted by Parliament as a standard for the executive, and the fact that the administration is generally bound by instructions of the government, this bond of answerability between the people and power of the state also operates through Parliament's influence on the government's policies. The fact that 'all state authority is derived from the people' must be noticeable for the people as well as the state organs and take effect in practice. An adequate substance of democratic legitimacy – a certain legitimacy standard – must be achieved. … Only a Parliament elected by the people can transfer democratic legitimacy to the organs and functionaries of the administration at all levels. In case functionaries and organs are not legitimated by way of direct elections, the democratic legitimation for the exercise of state power requires as a rule that the appointment of functionaries is attributable to the sovereign people and that their acts undergo sufficient factual and substantive legitimation. In personal terms, a sovereign decision is democratically legitimised if the appointment of the respective person can be traced back to the sovereign people in an uninterrupted chain of legitimation. Factual and substantive legitimation is conveyed through the binding nature of statutes and of government mandates and instructions. The latter has a legitimising effect due to the government's responsibilities vis-à-vis the Parliament. … Keeping secrets from Parliament limits parliamentary oversight and may thereby impair or disrupt the necessary democratic legitimation.[26]

[25] EW Böckenförde, *Constitutional and Political Theory: Selected Writings*, ed M Künkler and T Stein (Oxford, Oxford University Press, 2019).

[26] *Arms export permissions*, 137 *BVerfGE* 185, 232 (2014) ECLI:DE:BVerfG:2014:es20141021.2bve000511 (en).

Which is to say, the more directly the exercise of legal power is tied to a democratic election, the greater its legitimation is; conversely, the further it recedes into the murk of the administrative organisation, the weaker its legitimation is. And finally, the further-reaching a particular decision-making power and its exercise are, the closer they must be tied to the fount of legitimacy. What this reading in the spirit of Böckenförde has in common with that of Hennis is that it quite blithely assumes the development of the Federal Republic in the direction of a full parliamentary democracy. And as with Hennis, this is a problem – because it is at odds with reality. In this standard model of parliamentary democracy constitutional doctrine operates upon, the key institutional features of the constitution – namely the lack of control of both the legislature and the federal government over the administrative level – simply have no place.

The institutional fabric of the Basic Law has failed to ease the tension between executive federalism and parliamentary government. To have succeeded in yoking the two layers of the constitution together is rather the shared historic achievement of the three genuinely new institutions of the Federal Republic that were unknown to its Weimar predecessor: the two grand mainstream parties, the office of the federal chancellery and the constitutional court. *This yoking together of parliament and government, of which they are the guarantors, forms the institutional core of the Federal Republic.* A constitutional opinion on the current state of parliamentary government can be ventured only if the mechanisms by which the party system, the chancellery and the constitutional court have hitherto mediated between the parliamentary and the federal-bureaucratic layer of the constitution are well understood. It will then soon become apparent that the troubling history of parliamentarianism under the monarchy and in the Weimar Republic has retained a latent presence in the institutions of the Federal Republic. This is revealed when the yoke weakens and the mediating institutions fall into crisis, as has recently been the case under the grand coalition.[27] Whenever that happens, the system of government seems to adapt at the surface while its constitutional structure relapses into an earlier state and functions according to its other potential logic.

III. The Outsider's Republic: Parliamentary Government and the Political Culture of the Merkel Era

The Federal Republic's chancellors were usually insiders, who had power bases both within their parties and at the level of their respective *Land*. The writer and historian Patrick Bahners recently described Helmut Kohl as the consummate political insider, whose power was founded not on charisma, but on a stunning familiarity with the inner workings of politics, both within the party and at state and federal levels, acquired from an early age. But Gerhard Schröder, Helmut Schmidt and Willy Brandt were likewise insiders, compared to whom Angela Merkel entered the chancellery as an outsider and without a strong and reliable power base in her own party. Under the governments she has led, the constitutional situation of the Federal Republic changed to an extent comparable only with that of the SPD/FDP-dominated era of the 1970s. 'Merkel not only administered

[27] I shall discuss this in more detail in ch 5.

the republic; she rather performed a controlled detonation of the rules of the old Federal Republic', as the political scientist Philip Manow put it in a valediction marking the inauspicious beginning of her fourth term in office.[28]

A. Technocracy or Morality?

Complaints about Angela Merkel's supposedly 'undemocratic' style of government have been legion, long before a movement of conspiracy theorists, radical ecologists and libertarians attacked her matter-of-fact handling of the corona crisis and even before her political stance in the refugee crisis polarised the German political landscape. What critics mean by 'undemocratic' remains strangely vague. Leaving aside obscure claims such as the 'great replacement' narrative, two main lines of interpretation can be distinguished. The first locates the democratic problem of this administration primarily in an ideology of factual constraints and hence of an apolitical technocracy.[29] Recently, the original sin of the Merkel era has been found in the chancellor's language, an amalgam of 'toxic phrases' invoking a purported lack of alternatives (TINA, 'there is no alternative') and frustrating any kind of democratic decision-making.[30] This criticism adds up to an image of the chancellor as the chief administrator of an affluent society with a declining need for political orientation: live your life, she seems to say, and I'll take care of the rest. Yet what truth there is in this indictment applies neither to the chancellor nor to her politics specifically, but rather to an entire era. In the 2000s, the soothing jargon of technocracy was used equally by management consultants, political scientists and self-help gurus. Gerhard Schröder's aggressive interpretation of his political leadership, on which he began to double down in the spring of 2003, seemed untimely at any rate. But who would hold it against politics that it should speak to a society that has come to disdain power in a language that casts a veil over power and puts management in its place? That fatigue with this language has set in, although it continues occasionally to be rewarded in elections, is hardly the fault of politics. During the corona crisis in 2020, once again, her political rhetoric of 'there is no alternative' has met the need of the hour.

Others consider undemocratic the very opposite of 'TINA'-politics, namely highly contingent and disruptive about-turns of policy. The poorly debated abolition of conscription in 2011, the phasing out of nuclear power contrary to previous election manifestos, the refugee crisis and gay marriage all stand for an approach to politics founded on the deliberate railroading of both the chancellor's own party and parliament as a whole. In the time of chancellors Kohl and Schröder, there had always been conservative criticism of the inability of German politics to reform and to make quick decisions. Conservative commentators since the postwar era had criticised the Federal Republic for the lack of a constitutional executive emergency ordinance, as the Reich president famously had after Article 48 of the Weimar Constitution.[31] To say the same about the Merkel era would obviously be mistaken.

[28] P Manow, 'Das Ende der Situationsvernunft' *Die Zeit*, 14 July 2018.

[29] See, for instance, D Kurbjuweit, *Alternativlos: Merkel, die Deutschen und das Ende der Politik* (Munich, Hanser, 2014).

[30] A Séville, *Der Sound der Macht: Eine Kritik der dissonanten Herrschaft* (Munich, CH Beck, 2018).

[31] *cf* D Dyzenhaus, 'State of Emergency' in M Rosenfeld and A Sajó (eds), *The Oxford Handbook of Comparative Constitutional Law* (Oxford, Oxford University Press, 2012) 442–62, 449–50.

The fundamental political decisions since 2005 were mostly reached not by technocratic means, but for quite explicitly moral reasons, always backed up by the judicious use of opinion polls. The constitutional lawyer Christoph Möllers recently drew attention to this:

> In many of the European Union's member states, the combination of austerity with regard to Greece and openness towards non-European refugees is considered somewhat erratic. … In both cases, the decisions made seemed to express virtues – self-reliance and thrift in the former case, helpfulness in the latter – that were considered national virtues.[32]

B. The Weakness of Parliamentary Instruments of Power

What unites these mutually exclusive interpretations, however, is the dissatisfaction they express with regard to the structural weakness of the tandem pairing of parliament and government. Both the technocratic obliviousness of parliament and its disruptive bulldozing appear merely as variants of an increasing disjuncture between the formation and articulation of political will in parliament on the one hand, and the actions of government on the other, while making no claim as to the causes. One thing this certainly would mean is that a whole set of explanations currently in public circulation, which seek to explain the chancellor's supposedly conflict-averse personality in terms not least of abstruse, gendered clichés ('mummy', 'Mother Teresa'), must be wide of the mark. It is certainly remarkable that no political use is currently made of certain constitutional options for acting within the framework of the parliamentary system. Although it would be absurd to pretend that the politics of the past had not been disruptive, such disruption was usually channelled through parliament. Although it had not of course itself been previously discussed, Helmut Kohl introduced his historical ten points for German reunification in the Bundestag's budgetary debate in November 1989. Gerhard Schröder announced his far-reaching programme of welfare state and labour market reforms (known in Germany as 'Agenda 2010'), which often is given as one of the reasons for Germany's comparatively good performance after the 2008 economic crisis, in his policy statement to the house in March 2003. Indeed, Schröder tied both his major political about-turns – the decision to send troops to Afghanistan to take part in the coalition war after the attacks of September 11 and then the Agenda – either tacitly or explicitly to a vote of confidence according to Article 68 of the Basic Law and hence to the disciplining instrument constitutionally available to the chancellor. In doing so, Schröder made explicit his claim to leadership over the parliamentary groups of the governing parties.

Angela Merkel, on the other hand, introduced her government's new energy policy in the form of a nuclear moratorium, which in turn was announced in a press statement from the chancellery some days before being proclaimed in the Bundestag as part of her policy address. Her U-turn on gay marriage was made during an interview on stage at Berlin's Maxim Gorki Theatre. The event in question was subsequently described by the theatre's blog as having taken place

> at the invitation of a rather mumsy women's magazine, one that is usually preoccupied with telling its readers how to produce the perfect cheesecake and how to find the perfect trousers with

[32] C Möllers, 'Wir, die Bürger(lichen)' (2017) 71 *Merkur* 12.

> the perfect fit. A glossy mag, in other words, whose stock-in-trade is the outright avoidance of anything political.[33]

And according to the rules of parliamentary government, the chancellor might rather have been expected to enforce the consent of the coalition parties to her decision to leave the borders open to refugees by laying the authority of her office on the line – not least to avoid so much as the suspicion of a political sleight of hand premeditated to bypass parliament. As leader of a coalition with the liberal Free Democratic Party, Angela Merkel had always been careful to secure a parliamentary majority of her own for her policies related to the Greek bailout. Although the Social Democrats supported the substance of her policies in the eurozone crisis, she was loath to rely on opposition votes.

C. The Drama of the Social Democrats

But it would be exaggerated, indeed, almost wrong, to blame the chancellor's style and personality for the declining esteem in which the instruments of parliamentary government are held. This is evident from the vacillation on the part of the Social Democrats, when Martin Schulz, the former president of the European Parliament, ran against Merkel in the 2017 general election. For the first time since Schröder, the SPD was able to present a candidate who was able to inspire enthusiasm because he appeared to be a fresh face, untainted by the infighting within the grand coalition. But when he announced his ambition and was elected leader of the party at a special conference held roughly six months before the election – nothing happened. His party did not think for a second to call the shots, terminate the coalition government and elect Schulz chancellor with the majority of Social Democrats, Greens and Left Party in the eighteenth term of the Bundestag (2013–17). This would have been Schulz's only coalition option after the election anyway. Forming a new government by parliamentary means would have given the SPD the incumbency advantage in the election. The SPD might not have needed to make more than minor concessions to the Left before the election, at which point the deck would have been reshuffled anyhow. Although Schulz would not have been a member of parliament before the next election, this situation had not stopped Kurt Georg Kiesinger from being elected chancellor by the Bundestag following Ludwig Erhard's resignation in 1966. Moreover, by depriving the ruling Christian Democrats of their politically most profitable assets, the chancellery and the chancellor, the SPD would have caused major problems for the losing party. After spending long years holding power, parties usually react to its loss with a phase of ideological struggles and turf battles.

The SPD did not seize that opportunity. The 2018 elections plunged the party into a crisis of a different order. Yet the structural aspects of these events continue to pose questions. Why did nobody at the time even raise the possibility of a change of power emanating from parliament? Would a government that owed its existence to a shift in coalitions with in a single parliamentary term even be thinkable today as it so clearly was in the old Federal Republic, before reunification? Could the Bundestag still muster the institutional authority

[33] M Kiyak, 'Angela Merkel sitzt im pinkfarbenen Sesselchen und modernisiert Deutschland', http://kolumne.gorki.de/kolumne-74/.

to bring about a change of government by means of a constructive vote of no confidence without the so-called mandate of the electorate? If not, the scope for democratic politics within a constitutional framework would indeed have shrunk substantially.

In any case, the Social Democrats seem to have learned nothing from the process. The interaction between party leadership, parliamentary group and ministers is becoming increasingly poor. The SPD could not even find it within itself to make its continuing support of the coalition in summer 2018 conditional on the sacking of Horst Seehofer, although the minister of the interior was in violation of all rules of cabinet discipline by scheming to discredit both his successor as prime minister of Bavaria and the chancellor herself. And ever since Schulz's successor, Andrea Nahles, was forced to retreat, the SPD has adopted a model of dual leadership with two chairpersons without any parliamentary experience (Norbert Walter-Borjans and Saskia Esken) and a *Spitzenkandidat* for the 2021 election (Olaf Scholz) who is a member neither of the larger party leadership nor of the parliamentary party.

IV. Merkel's Legacy and the Cautionary Tale of the Grand Coalition

A. The Supermajority as Working Principle

The constitutional present began in the autumn of 2005 with the first in a chain of grand coalitions. After the parliamentary election had failed to produce a majority for the Christian Democrats and Liberals, Angela Merkel finally came into office through an alliance with the Social Democrats, who were already having to contend with a split on the party's left, after the trade union wing had broken away in 2005 over Schröder's welfare reforms. The grand coalition has since become second nature to all its protagonists, and its interruption from 2009 to 2013 seems superficial in retrospect. As early as 2009, the SPD knew that it would get no closer to power in 2013 than as junior partner in a grand coalition. Even during the intervening period of the CDU/CSU–FDP coalition, the SPD parliamentary caucus stood at the ready to back up the chancellor whenever she could not quite rely on her own parliamentary majority, for instance in the matter of the eurozone crisis. In fact, Europe is a key issue here. Particularly under the system of government of the EU's largest and most influential Member State, the structure of European legislative procedure entails a certain disposition to decision-making by grand coalition. Not only is the German government confronted, in the Council of the European Union, with a legislature lacking clear party majorities and in which positions reached by a grand coalition are hence more likely to win approval, but in addition, a majority of CDU and SPD also maps onto a majority of their pan-European party organisations, the European People's Party (EPP) and the Party of European Socialists (PES), in the European Parliament, which may further increase the preference for decision-making by grand coalition.

It is a distinctive constitutional feature of the Merkel era that no major decision ever had to fear a narrow margin of victory in a parliamentary vote. The majority of at least a virtual grand coalition was a sure thing before an important matter even came before legislators. Philip Manow recently called attention to a stunning fact: in cases of dissent between the

Bundestag and Bundesrat over a bill, the constitution provides for a mediation procedure, which takes place in a special mediation committee (*Vermittlungsausschuss*), whose thirty-two members are selected half-and-half by each chamber.[34] The mediation committee and the mediation process were at the centre of the constitutional discussion during the first reform of the federal system (effective 2006), since both left and conservative oppositions had used the Bundesrat for obstruction tactics beyond *Länder* issues. During the Merkel years, the mediation process has become virtually irrelevant.[35] Whereas the committee was called upon more than a hundred times during the three years of the second red–green coalition (2002–05), it was summoned a mere three times during the eighteenth term of the Bundestag (2013–17).

B. The Democratic Costs of the Multi-Party System

These developments challenge the idea of parliamentary democracy, which rests on the continuous political confrontation between government and opposition in parliament, that is to say, *within* one institution. The norm of parliamentary government is thus competition within parliament for dominance within parliament – and for the right to form a government. Changes in voting behaviour and of the party system since the end of the red–green coalition have thus struck at the very heart of the parliamentary system of government. After the secession of its left wing, the SPD lost nearly 10 million votes compared to its 1998 victory. These votes were lost to all competitors, but disproportionately to the so-called 'minor' parties. This loss means that the SPD has de facto forfeited its claim to the office of chancellor, though it continues to put up candidates by ever more bewildering manoeuvres. The candidate for 2021 (Olaf Scholz), too, will have a hard time serving as Angela Merkel's loyal minister of finance and at the same time presenting himself as a convincing political alternative. Hence, for a decade and a half, the CDU has been the only party seriously and consistently able to make a claim to leadership at the federal level. The option of a change of power thus seems to have been taken off the table. There is no opposition capable of presenting itself to the public as a government in waiting.

The problem no longer seems to be the parties' lust for power, but rather their reluctance to assume power, which took on a stranger aspect following the 2017 elections to the

[34] Art 77 Basic Law:

> (2) Within three weeks after receiving an adopted bill, the Bundesrat may demand that a committee for joint consideration of bills, composed of Members of the Bundestag and of the Bundesrat, be convened. The composition and proceedings of this committee shall be regulated by rules of procedure adopted by the Bundestag and requiring the consent of the Bundesrat. The members of the Bundesrat on this committee shall not be bound by instructions. When the consent of the Bundesrat is required for a bill to become law, the Bundestag and the Federal Government may likewise demand that such a committee be convened. Should the committee propose any amendment to the adopted bill, the Bundestag shall vote on it a second time. …
>
> (3) Insofar as its consent is not required for a bill to become law, the Bundesrat, once proceedings under paragraph (2) of this Article are completed, may within two weeks object to a bill adopted by the Bundestag. The time for objection shall begin, in the case described in the last sentence of paragraph (2) of this Article, upon receipt of the bill as re-adopted by the Bundestag, and in all other cases upon receipt of a communication from the chairman of the committee provided for in paragraph (2) of this Article to the effect that the committee's proceedings have been concluded.

[35] Manow (n 28).

Bundestag than at any point since the 1920s. The period of nearly six months following the 2017 Bundestag election provided a vivid depiction of the political costs of forming a government that is the result, not so much of the voters' will, as of unpredictable negotiations. As long ago as 2013, the Greens shied away from entering into a coalition with the CDU, which at the time would have been possible even without the FDP. Four years later, weeks of negotiations between the three parties passed before being terminated for reasons that nobody remembers. It took a federal president, Frank-Walter Steinmeier, suddenly to reassume the role of his Weimar-era predecessors and browbeat the SPD into continuing the grand coalition, which the party had only just passed a solemn political resolution not to do.

This development poses a fundamental challenge to a great many things that until recently were taken for granted. After all, the modern system of parliamentary government built around a democracy of parties had only emerged when the power to decide on the leadership of the government passed from parliament to the voters by falling to the leader of the victorious party. In fact, it was only by the acceptance of this constitutional convention both in the United Kingdom and in the continental democracies that the old form of parliamentary government as the class rule of the bourgeoisie has become democratic in the twentieth century.[36]

C. The Future of the Constitution

Nonetheless, there is barely any discussion of fundamental constitutional reform of the kind that accompanied the first grand coalition in the late 1960s. Something approaching a constitutional question now only ever arises as a matter of expediency. An example is the debate, deliberately fuelled by the Federal Constitutional Court and taken up by senior politicians, over whether the increasingly vast bailouts in the eurozone crisis might not exceed the scope of the constitution and only be manageable under a new Basic Law, approved by popular vote.[37] The then minister of finance, Wolfgang Schäuble, only feigned indifference to the question when he publicly pondered a referendum according to Article 146 of the Basic Law. It is worth remembering, after all, that the last words of the constitution still provide, that 'this Basic Law, which, since the achievement of the unity and freedom of Germany, applies to the entire German people, shall cease to apply on the day on which a constitution freely adopted by the German people takes effect'. That particular debate did not outlast the consolidation of the markets.

This, too, may be a legacy of reunification. After the fall of the Wall, the German public debated intensively whether the country would rather simply extend the Basic Law to the GDR (which then Article 23 GG allowed for) or whether both parts of Germany should

[36] W Selinger, *Parliamentarism. From Burke to Weber* (Cambridge, Cambridge University Press, 2019) 194 et seq; K Kluxen, 'Britischer und deutscher Parlamentarismus im Zeitalter der industriellen Massengesellschaft' in *England in Europa* (Berlin, Duncker & Humblot, 2003) 216; H te Velde, 'The Domestication of the Machine. The Debate About Political Parties Around 1900' in H te Velde and M Janse (eds), *Organizing Democracy. Reflections on the Rise of Political Organizations in the Nineteenth Century* (Basingstoke, Palgrave Macmillan, 2017) 255.

[37] On the role of the FCC in the eurozone crisis, *cf* FC Mayer, 'Judicial Power and European Integration. The Case of Germany' in C Landfried (ed), *Judicial Power: How Constitutional Courts Affect Political Transformations* (Cambridge, Cambridge University Press, 2019) 183.

work out a new constitution together (the path actually intended for such a situation by the framers in Article 146 GG). More than a few West German constitutional law scholars tried to discredit the latter option through a virtual sanctification of the Basic Law.[38] The constitutional projects of the unification era largely failed, the chance to give a united Germany a new constitution was never taken, and nor did theoretical proposals for a new civic constitutional movement find any lasting resonance.[39] The project of a European constitution was scuppered by referenda in France and the Netherlands. Nor is there currently cause to expect any sudden leaps towards closer European integration, of the kind that might result from a new process for European parliamentary elections involving Europe-wide party lists. There is no point even asking such questions in today's Germany. 'Are we so afraid', asks Horst Dreier, 'of the idea of an open constitutional future? Or is the panicked debate over how to defend democracy obscuring the question of whether it is of sound constitution?'[40]

The suppressed questions nonetheless arise: is the parliamentary system of government still up to date? Is it still the appropriate constitutional form in light of the tasks faced by the Federal Republic today, both at home and abroad? With regard to the Bonn Republic, such questions have already been answered historically: it succeeded in integrating a post-totalitarian industrial society with weak social bonds as well as ideological opposition to the political system as it arose post-1968. Can the same be said, 30 years later, of the integration of the former German Democratic Republic? For the Berlin Republic, the answers must be political: the integration of an increasingly diverse immigration society is more than a question of administration and the allocation of resources; it is above all a constitutional question that cannot be indefinitely delegated to the courts through anti-discrimination legislation. The increasing difficulties of forming parliamentary majorities might soon confront the Federal Republic with stark alternatives: to muddle through with minority governments or to remove parliament from the process of forming governments? Might there be something to be said for a form of presidential government? Are hybrid forms thinkable? Germany's normative affiliation with Western constitutionalism was an unquestionable political imperative for survival only during the cold war and only for its Western part.

After the experience of Nazi rule, the choice for parliamentarianism was synonymous with the choice for a system of government that would keep a permanent check on the tendency of a monocratic executive to lapse into a plebiscitary autocracy. After all, a parliamentary head of government as a rule requires both the confidence of the voters to gain office as well as that of a majority of deputies to keep it – deputies, moreover, who maintain close scrutiny of the government's actions, on which they have staked their own political existence. No leader at the head of a mass movement is yet in sight in Germany, but the question of the continued relevance of such considerations also shows how timely it is to think about the future of the parliamentary system of government. Does the Federal Republic's

[38] *cf* H Dreier, *Gilt das Grundgesetz ewig? Fünf Kapitel zum modernen Verfassungsstaat* (Munich, Siemens-Stiftung, 2009) 100.

[39] UK Preuß, *Revolution, Fortschritt und Verfassung: Zu einem neuen Verfassungsverständnis* (Berlin, Wagenbach, 1990).

[40] H Dreier, 'Das Grundgesetz unter Ablösungsvorbehalt?' in *Idee und Gestalt des freiheitlichen Verfassungsstaates* (Tübingen, Mohr Siebeck, 2014) 455.

constitution, a largely consensual matter-of-fact political approach and its administrative culture make it less vulnerable to the scenario of an authoritarian uprising and populist politics?[41] The kind of historical and philosophical scepticism that might lead one to think the constitution's time had passed is a luxury we may ill be able to afford.

V. Parliamentarianism and Anti-Parliamentarianism

No constitutional institution has been given up for dead quite as often as parliamentarianism. 'In parliament', wrote Karl Marx in 1852, 'the nation made its general will the law, that is, it made the law of the ruling class its general will. Before the executive power it renounces all will of its own and submits to the superior command of an alien will, to authority. The executive power, in contrast to the legislative power, expresses the heteronomy of a nation, in contrast to its autonomy.'[42] Most of what is written and said today in the face of social media against the principle of representation is a mere repetition of old familiar positions. Even before the transition to a semi-parliamentary system of government after World War I, Georg Jellinek, the leading constitutional lawyer of the late Wilhelmine period, in turn became the first representative of the bourgeois class to declare parliamentarianism out of date: plebiscitary mass democracy now allowed 'the people to participate directly in the power of the state' and in doing so gradually rendered parliamentary institutions obsolete.[43] Lenin held their destruction to be the foremost task of the revolution.[44] Carl Schmitt, too, in a book published in 1923 and influential to this day, ranked parliamentarianism among the political forms of liberalism and thus in opposition to the mass democracy of the twentieth century.[45] After World War II, left-wing authors such as Johannes Agnoli and Peter Brücker revived Schmitt's critique of parliamentarianism from the opposite side.[46] In a welfare state, the premiums of the possession of power had grown to the point where parliament was nothing more than a front for authoritarian government and hence opposition was possible only outside of parliament.

Since the 1983 Bundestag elections, Germany's self-declared extra-parliamentary opposition movement (*Außerparlamentarische Opposition*) has itself, in the shape of the Green Party, become integrated into the parliamentary system and the theoretical anti-parliamentarianism of Marxist observance has largely disappeared. Yet the critique of parliamentarianism has not so much fallen silent as shifted to a largely functionalist perspective. In more debates over the interweaving politics with outside interests, and over the future of democracy at the level of the European Union's Member States, the

[41] See the account by J Kampfner, *Why the Germans Do it Better: Notes from a Grown-Up Country* (London, Atlantic Books, 2020).

[42] K Marx, 'The Eighteenth Brumaire of Louis Bonaparte' in K Marx and F Engels, *Collected Works*, vol 39 (New York and London, International Publishers, 1975) 185.

[43] G Jellinek, *Verfassungsänderung und Verfassungswandlung: Eine staatsrechtlich-politische Abhandlung* (Berlin, O Häring 1906) 76.

[44] VI Lenin, *The State and Revolution* [1918] (London, Penguin Books, 1992).

[45] C Schmitt, *The Crisis of Parliamentary Democracy* [1926] (Cambridge, MA, MIT Press, 1985); on Schmitt's theory of mass democracy, see BA Schupmann, *Carl Schmitt's State and Constitutional Theory. A Critical Analysis* (Oxford, Oxford University Press, 2017) 40–59.

[46] J Agnoli and P Brückner, *Die Transformation der Demokratie* (Berlin, Voltaire-Verlag, 1967).

question of the future prospects of parliamentarianism was always a more or less latent presence.

Anti-parliamentarianism is a chameleon that has recently assumed, more often than not, the colour of a utopian ideology of transparency. Information available online about conflicts of interest, voting behaviour, financial circumstances, additional income, biographies, offices or kinship relations of MPs make parliaments observable to a degree unimaginable until very recently. However valuable the existence of such information may be in certain respects, it inevitably contributes to a latent suspicion of normal parliamentary business and makes 'politics as a vocation' (as Max Weber put it) less attractive. Must committees really meet in camera? Why are only members of parliament but not the public kept abreast of the negotiations over the free trade deal? By its own excessive and increasing use of social media, the political bubble has helped create expectations that, in the long run, it cannot live up to. That citizens may permanently be 'in touch' with their representatives online, yet are unable to see through everything is a consequence not least of the fact that good policy-making requires good politicians. It is, in other words, a question of their professionalism. Naturally today's parliaments, highly bureaucratic and supported as they are by thousands of staffers in administrative, research and service departments of every imaginable kind, seem barely to resemble the assemblies that went by their name in the nineteenth century. Yet it is an inevitable fact of specialisation that it reduces transparency for outsiders. After all, nobody would expect a major research institution or a trade union to be transparent either. To demand that parliaments be both professional and transparent is self-contradictory. Unfortunately, however, complaints about the lack of transparency in politics tend to come from the very quarters that demand vigorous political action on all manner of issues.

Meanwhile, right-wing anti-parliamentarianism is enjoying something of a revival – not just on the streets, where parliamentarians are routinely branded 'traitors' and 'enemies of the people', but also in the academic landscape. Scholars such as Egon Flaig are thus able to appeal to today's 'enraged citizens' by rehashing the stale fare of anti-parliamentarian cliché and bemoaning 'unconstitutional party discipline', the 'suppression' of free opinion and the degeneration of committees into horse-trading.[47] Several years ago, Peter Sloterdijk took to the pages of the weekly news magazine *Der Spiegel* to reproach the political class for performing 'the monologue of a club of autists'.[48] Similar insinuations, albeit with different political aims, could be detected at the peak of the eurozone crisis, when none other than Jürgen Habermas lamented the transformation of the welfare state as civic democracy into a sham democracy deferring to market needs.[49] The term 'political class' has also seen a revival, though it is an almost grotesque misrepresentation of the social structure of German politics in particular.[50] For all that happened in the last century, the critique of parliamentarianism seems barely to have moved at all. As the next chapter will show, the opposite is true of its target, the parliamentary form of government.

[47] E Flaig, 'Wie entscheidungsfähig sind Demokratien?' in FW Graf and H Meier (eds), *Die Zukunft der Demokratie* (Munich, Siemens-Stiftung, 2018) 122.

[48] P Sloterdijk, 'Der verletzte Stolz', *Der Spiegel* 45/2010.

[49] J Habermas, P Bofinger and J NidaRümelin, 'Einspruch gegen die Fassadendemokratie', *Frankfurter Allgemeine Zeitung*, 3 August 2012.

[50] On the social geography of political representation, see M-L Recker, *Parlamentarismus in der Bundesrepublik: Der Deutsche Bundestag 1949–1969* (Düsseldorf, Droste Verlag, 2018) 153–77.

3

Transformations of Parliamentary Government in Germany Since World War I

I. The Written and the Real Constitution

German constitutional theory tends to overestimate the contribution a constitution makes to its own functioning. The very idea of the constitution prevailing in Germany imagines the relationship between the constitution and the political system as something static[1] – static in both time and structure. In spatial terms, the constitution is imagined as the solid and immutable framework, within which political business is conducted. Since the constitution makes provision for its amendment only by means of a formal revision of the text (Article 79(1) GG), its gradual change over time begins to take on the appearance of a pathology. Such a static conception of the constitution may possess a certain degree of plausibility for a highly traditional notion of the division of powers, one in which the competencies of the three powers of the state are precisely delineated and their mutual checks and balances conclusively defined. Yet even in US constitutional theory such a notion has by now revealed itself to be untenable.

As far as the parliamentary system is concerned, the idea of a static arrangement of institutions enshrined in constitutional law should in any case be consigned to the realm of legal fantasy. Constitutional history proves why. The parliamentary system of government was never to be taken for granted, least of all in Germany. Not even German liberals were unreservedly in favour of it. Nor has it simply taken its present shape through an act of constitution-making. At the centre of parliamentary government stands not the *separation*, but rather the *connection* between parliament and government. It is, therefore, a much more variable political form and is actually reorganising itself.

If nonetheless it is often thought of as a static institutional arrangement, this characterises the German constitution as a distinctly 'lawyerly' type whose management and interpretation has fallen to professional interpreters, with the Federal Constitutional Court (Bundesverfassungsgericht or BVerfG) at their head. Professional interpreters of the constitution have a professional interest that leads them to a knee-jerk rejection of the idea that, at the heart of the constitution, there might lie not a rigid arrangement of competencies, but rather an open institutional understanding between parliament and government. But that is precisely what distinguishes parliamentary government, and what is amply clear of its Westminster form, which was never enshrined in a written constitution. Yet in Germany, too, the parliamentary system of government is not exclusively – indeed, not even

[1] The classical critique is that of W Hennis, *Verfassung und Verfassungswirklichkeit: Ein deutsches Problem* (Tübingen, Mohr Siebeck, 1968).

principally – the creation of the 1919 and 1949 constitutions, but largely an achievement of the political system of the Federal Republic.

A. A Constitution without a Theory

One reason why this connection tends not to be clearly understood is that the German constitutional system to this day lacks a political theory of its own. Whereas theories with an interest in the constitution exist for American, British and French democracy, German lawyers persist in administering their lawyers' constitution. In so doing, they conceal their mounting inability to bring the constitution's normative foundations into some sort of systematic correlation with its organisational provisions. Political scientists, concerned as they are largely with the empirical workings of the political system, have a fairly easy time ignoring them. Of course, the very specific historical circumstances under which German parliamentarianism emerged have long been quite well examined.[2] There are, moreover, excellent studies of the functioning of the Federal Republic's parliamentary system of government, beginning with the pioneering works of Gerhard Loewenberg – an émigré still largely unknown in Germany – or the political scientist Gerhard Lehmbruch.[3] Yet the dominant image in the German theory of parliamentarianism is still of a parliament engaged primarily in Habermasian public deliberation. German intellectuals have largely remained suspicious of the reality of a parliamentary system of government. Since the days of Immanuel Kant, they have shown a marked preference for general legislation and rational law-making and hence have profound reservations about a form of parliamentarianism whose decisive political role is, in reality, anything but legislation. The same reservations can be found – without, of course, the corresponding affection for the law – in the intellectual current of anti-rationalism running from Romanticism to Carl Schmitt. As a result, scholars of public law, though tasked with interpreting the Basic Law, must do so without much of a workable theory of the German system of government. To fill this gap, they cope partly by borrowing from the classical theorists of the Weimar era, partly by appropriating American theories of democracy.

B. The Link between Parliament and Government

The German parliamentary system is a child of the revolution. It was introduced shortly before the end of the First World War, in a few sentences, by amendments made to the existing imperial constitution, meant to facilitate negotiations for a peace treaty.[4] It then became

[2] A summary of arguments can be found in C Schönberger, 'Der Deutsche Bundestag zwischen Konstitutionalismus und parlamentarischer Demokratie: Historische und vergleichende Variationen auf ein Thema Gerhard Loewenbergs' in H Schöne and J von Blumenthal (eds), *Parlamentarismusforschung in Deutschland* (Baden-Baden, Nomos, 2009).

[3] G Loewenberg, *Parlamentarismus im politischen System der Bundesrepublik Deutschland* (Tübingen, Wunderlich, 1969); G Lehmbruch, *Parteienwettbewerb im Bundesstaat: Regelsysteme und Spannungslagen im politischen System der Bundesrepublik Deutschland*, 3rd edn (Opladen, Westdeutscher Verlag, 2000).

[4] M Jones, *Founding Weimar. Violence and the German Revolution of 1918–19* (Cambridge, Cambridge University Press, 2016) 10–11; on the historical background, see M Hewitson, 'The Kaiserreich in Question: Constitutional Crisis in Germany before the First World War' (2001) 74 *Journal of Modern History* 725, 761–778;

a political reality just over one hundred years ago, in the form of the Weimar constitution of 11 August 1919.[5] Yet the moment of its introduction already contains the fundamental problem that has remained in place ever since: the difficulty of institutionally anchoring a fully formed and extraordinarily powerful bureaucratic government, accustomed to acting in a federal state, in a parliament that was unlike its nineteenth-century bourgeois ancestors. The political realities of the twentieth century had arrived, and with them came parties staffed by functionaries, plebiscitary techniques of propaganda, and universal suffrage. How, then, to forge a link in constitutional law between two institutions which for a long time were strictly separate and, in an age of mass democracy, were both subject to increasing centrifugal forces?

To proclaim, in constitutional law, the establishment of a government responsible to parliament alters nothing about the fact that the government must indeed be reliant upon constant interaction with parliament if the constitutional provision for parliamentary responsibility is to be of any practical, political consequence. The 'responsibility' of a government is exhausted in an abstract principle no more than that of the board of a publicly traded company; it instead depends on processes and sanctions in which that responsibility is embodied and enacted. Parliament's budgetary rights are an important means to this end, but by no means sufficient on their own. The US Congress has the right to approve expenditure, as did the Reichstag of Germany before 1918. Nor can parliamentary responsibility be ensured by making the passing of legislation its preserve, for the monopoly of legality does not give parliament control of matters going beyond legislation: those of implementation, organisation, planning, communication, foreign relations, crisis response, etc – in short, matters of government and administration.[6]

The processes by which parliamentary responsibility is brought to bear may differ significantly. At Westminster and in similar parliaments, the weekly 'Prime Minister's Questions' (officially and more accurately called 'Questions to the Prime Minister') are both a media event and a palpable expression of democratic accountability. Ministers, too, appear before parliament and its committees to answer questions far more often than they do in Germany. In nineteenth-century French parliamentarianism, formal interpellations followed by votes on the ministers' policies emerged as the means of holding the government to account.[7]

Such processual rules were, at first, more or less alien to German constitutional law. The right to summon ministers (Article 33(1) WRV; equivalent to today's Article 43(1) GG)[8] made exceptional demands for ministers' presence dependent on a majority vote. The rule tended to acquire significance only when the government lacked a parliamentary majority.

the most comprehensive German analysis is C Schönberger, 'Die überholte Parlamentarisierung. Einflußgewinne und fehlende Herrschaftsfähigkeit des Reichstags im sich demokratisierenden Kaiserreich' (2001) 272 *Historische Zeitschrift* 623.

[5] C Gusy, *100 Jahre Weimarer Verfassung: Eine gute Verfassung in schlechter Zeit* (Tübingen, Mohr Siebeck, 2018) 156; G Lübbe-Wolff, 'Das Demokratiekonzept der Weimarer Reichsverfassung' in H Dreier and C Waldhoff (eds), *Das Wagnis der Demokratie* (Munich, CH Beck, 2018) 116.

[6] A comparative model is developed in P Cane, *Controlling Administrative Power. An Historical Comparison* (Cambridge, Cambridge University Press, 2016) 2–5.

[7] On this period, see J Garrigues and E Anceau, 'Discussing the First Age of French Parliamentarism' in P Ihalainen, C Ilie, and K Palonen (eds), *Parliament and Parliamentarism. A Comparative History of a European Concept* (New York, Berghahn, 2016) 49.

[8] The clause reads: 'The Bundestag and its committees may require the presence of any member of the Federal Government.'

Today, too, the governing parties have far more effective means of influencing their own ministers – through informal channels – than by summoning them to appear before the house. The opposition parties in parliament have no such means, and the Bundestag lacks a culture of verbal response. The federal government responds to 'major' and 'minor' parliamentary enquiries (*große Anfrage/kleine Anfrage*) in writing. During question time, it exhibits the politically unfortunate habit of having questions answered by parliamentary state secretaries who are not of cabinet rank and hence are not responsible to parliament.

This fundamental problem of the German constitution has remained virulent ever since. Nor has the Basic Law 'solved' it, as it is fondly believed. That a parliamentary system of government was nonetheless able to take root in Germany is the historical achievement and the post-constitutional attainment of three genuinely new institutions of the German system of government for which, in their existing form, provision was not even made in constitutional law: the party system, the federal chancellery and the constitutional court. These three are the unsung heroes of parliamentary democracy in the Federal Republic. The federal chancellery is the institutional clearing-house for nearly everything that passes between parliament and government. The leadership of the government by the two major parties (or 'popular parties', *Volksparteien* as the German term calls them) ensures a close personal and political link between the cabinet and the parliamentary parties. And finally, the constitutional court, by the extensive use it made of its power to review federal legislation and the legislative process, helped parliament – and parliamentary opposition in particular – to consolidate its position.

The nature and peculiarities of the parliamentary system of government can therefore only be explained in historical terms.

II. 1919: Weimar – A Semi-Parliamentary Bureaucracy

A. The Very Different Example of England

When the Weimar constitution came into force, in August 1919, contradictory ideas were held concerning the functioning of a parliamentary government. The British system of government was often invoked as an example. This is still true today, even though the implosion of the House of Commons over Brexit has caused considerable damage. Yet the circumstances in which the Westminster parliament attained its dominant position have no counterpart in German history. The customary principle of the cabinet's responsibility to parliament emerged in England in the eighteenth century, when parliament forced the resignation of several governments. In this complicated process, parliament was aided no least by the political capital it had gained by its defeat of the monarchy in the civil war of the previous century.[9]

Eighteenth-century England was neither an absolutist state like the continental monarchies, nor was it a democracy as we would understand the term today. No universal suffrage was granted, no parliamentary public sphere existed, political parties in their modern

[9] C Roberts, *The Growth of Responsible Government in Stuart England* (Cambridge, Cambridge University Press, 1966).

form as groups professionally organised alongside ideologies and interests were unknown. What the term 'parliamentary government' denoted was a form of control of the government by a small, homogeneous ruling class, whose reciprocal loyalty was safeguarded by their shared social background. People, in a word, knew one another. Amidst all the power struggles, this prevented the kind of stark ideological polarisation that became typical of parliamentarianism from the late nineteenth century on. Political parties co-evolved with parliamentary government as vehicles for managing the emerging parliamentary system. Moreover, ministers responsible to parliament developed from a collegial body advising the Crown well before obtaining, by ruling over the administrative apparatus attached to their departments, the kind of autonomous political power characteristic of the modern office of the cabinet minister. What makes the case of the United Kingdom unique is that its parliamentary system of government emerged before democracy, before modern political parties and before bureaucracy.[10]

Elements of this historical context have persisted to this day. The principle of parliamentary sovereignty continues to rest on custom.[11] Parliament has no constitutionally enshrined powers, and nor is there a constitutional court, at least not in the German sense. Whether the Supreme Court will continue to take on the role it played in the two exceptional *Gina Miller* cases is a question that can only be answered after the consolidation of the British constitution after Brexit.[12] In other respects, too, the British system of government rests on altogether different premises: in the absence of federalism, there is no need to worry about state administrations that are not responsible to the federal parliament. A particularly important factor is the first-past-the-post electoral system, which can usually be expected to produce a parliamentary majority and hence a government without the need to form a coalition. Cabinets tend to be single-party bodies, in consequence of which parliamentary responsibility consists not of minsters' individual responsibility, but in the collective responsibility of the cabinet as a whole, under the leadership of the prime minister.

B. The German Problem

In both the circumstances of its emergence and in the path dependence of its subsequent development, the German system of government differs radically from the British. It developed in several highly distinctive phases, by which an already fully formed bureaucracy was brought under parliamentary control. Before the First World War, the Reich government (Reichsleitung) had been subject to the control of the imperial chancellor (Reichskanzler, nominated by the emperor) and the upper house or Bundesrat (dominated by the Prussian bureaucracy). The old lower house or Reichstag was able neither to drive out the government nor to control its actions effectively. The famous second sentence of Article 9 of

[10] Ernst Fraenkel in particular repeatedly underscored the significance of this 'asynchronicity in the development of bureaucracy and parliaments': 'Historische Vorbelastungen des deutschen Parlamentarismus' (1960) in *Deutschland und die westlichen Demokratien*, 9th edn (Baden-Baden, Nomos, 2011) 53.

[11] JD Goldsworthy, *Parliamentary Sovereignty. Contemporary Debates* (Cambridge, Cambridge University Press, 2010).

[12] The consequences of the introduction of constitutional review independent from Parliament are discussed in M Gordon, *Parliamentary Sovereignty in the UK Constitution. Process, Politics and Democracy* (Oxford, Hart, 2015) 126–27.

the 1871 constitution ensured that parliament and government remained carefully separated even at the organisational level: 'No one may at the same time be a member of the Federal Council and of the Reichstag.'

Although the electoral system was extremely progressive at the time (it excluded women, however), the Reichstag was unable to support a parliamentary government. It was thus left with the power of legislation, to which it was all the more devoted. That it tried, like all German parliaments since the early nineteenth century, to exert by public oratory and debate the influence which it was constitutionally denied[13] was of course to be expected of an institution endowed with such competencies, but it need not be understood as a sign of a strength. Far too late – in the last weeks of the First World War – the imperial government was made responsible to parliament. At the same time, Max Weber wrote a series of essays which were published while the constituent assembly was meeting at Weimar and which were published under the title 'Parliament and Government in Germany under a New Political Order'. Together with Weber's lecture on 'The Profession and Vocation of Politics', delivered in the summer of 1919, they form what to this day remains the only political theory of the parliamentary system of government in Germany. With remarkable clarity of vision, Weber recognised that the autonomy of a fully developed bureaucracy lay at the heart of the institutional problem faced by the parliamentary system of government in Germany. In the middle of the Second World War, an admirer of Weber's, the Austrian economist Joseph Schumpeter, described this problem as that of 'keep[ing] the leading group's hands on the bureaucratic engine'.[14]

To Weber's mind, it was not enough to introduce universal suffrage, the majority principle and the parliamentary accountability of the government. His concern was above all to ensure that the leading parliamentary politicians, who at the same were the leading lights of their respective political parties, had access to power – that is, to government offices in which they were able to take the political initiative. Weber, in other words, found the significance of the parliamentary system of government to reside in securing for politics, understood as the sphere of ethically responsible and future-oriented decision-making, a sphere of autonomous action vis-a-vis bureaucracy. This was to be accomplished by giving the large-scale political organisations operating in parliament a share of the responsibility of government. This, in turn, depended on nothing so much as on professional politicians who were not content to use oratory to call upon the government to change its policies and thereby merely to perpetuate, as Max Weber once put it, the 'negative politics' of 'philistine democracy in the old bourgeois mould'.[15] Weber saw a crucial part of the role of the professional parliamentary politician as residing in the active control of the government while himself striving to take over government responsibility. Yet Weber, who was well aware of the German penchant to an ethic of conviction as a reproach to professional politics, did not for a minute deceive himself as to the likelihood of such an attitude ever taking hold in Germany. That is why, in the constitutional deliberations of 1918 and 1919, he spoke in a favour of a system that was not to be purely

[13] A Burkhardt and K Pape (eds), *Sprache des deutschen Parlamentarismus. Studien zu 150 Jahren parlamentarischer Kommunikation* (Wiesbaden, VS Verlag, 2000).

[14] JA Schumpeter, *Capitalism, Socialism and Democracy* (London, Harper, 1943) 278.

[15] Letter from Weber to Ludo Moritz Hartmann, 3 January 1919, in *Max Weber Gesamtausgabe*, vol II/10,1, ed G Krumeich et al (Tübingen, Mohr Siebeck, 2012) 387.

parliamentary, but in which a president of the *Reich*, endowed with plebiscitary legitimacy, would act as a disciplining force upon parliament. The Weimar constitution, as we know, followed Weber's advice.

Another aspect of the problem, as revealed by Weber, was to prove no less consequential. The belated adaptation to parliamentarianism of a ready-formed national government meant that the model of bureaucracy and administration characteristic of the latter was constitutionally enshrined and carried over in the transition from monarchy to republic. The German administrative system basically still has the form it always had: many local and independent administrative bodies, different administrative cultures in the several *Länder* and a federal administration that is dominating in some sectors but less important in others. Rather than the structure of the administration being adapted to the parliamentary system of government, what took place was the reverse. Bureaucracy was accepted as a constitution-building force as it were; its functioning within the system of government has thus been able to go unquestioned and unchallenged to this day. That the structure of the administration might be altered is a thought so audacious that no constitutional reformer in Germany has ever dared utter it.

C. Organising Responsibility

Although the *Reich* constitution of August 1919 did not abolish the previous organisational division between parliament and government, it did at least allow for parliamentary mandate and government office to be united in the hands of one person. Article 54 summarised the parliamentary principle in the following terms: 'The Reich Chancellor and the Reich Ministers require for the exercise of their office the confidence of the Reichstag. Any one of them must resign if the Reichstag by formal resolution withdraws its confidence.' The consequences of this provision for the emergence of a specifically German constitutional model of parliamentary government have been legion. The crucial difference compared to the UK system in particular is the following: the German model envisages the collegial government of the chancellor and 'his' ministers not as a group united in collective responsibility under the leadership of the prime minister, but rather as a convocation of the heads of the federal government's departments, each of them *individually* responsible to the Reichstag.[16] It took decades to establish, against this constitutional model, the political leadership of a parliamentary head of government. From the outset, this marks a contrast in the organisation of government in the German constitutional model – not only to its supposed archetype, England, but also, for example, to Italy: 'The Ministers are collectively responsible for the acts of the Council of Ministers; they are individually responsible for the acts of their own ministries' (Article 95(2): 'I Ministri sono responsabili collegialmente degli atti del Consiglio dei Ministri, e individualmente degli atti dei loro dicasteri'). The second part of that sentence is echoed in the Weimar constitution and the Basic Law; the first is not. The political consequence of this purely individual responsibility established in 1919 is immediately apparent: each member of the government of

[16] I have discussed this in greater detail in *Selbstorganisation des parlamentarischen Regierungssystems: Vergleichende Untersuchungen zu einem Verfassungsproblem der Bundesrepublik Deutschland* (Tübingen, Mohr Siebeck, 2019) 350–60.

the *Reich* – particularly of a minority government – had to guard against the emergence of negative majorities in the Reichstag aimed at removing *him* from office. And hostile though the Communist and Nazi parties were, they were not above joining in a vote of no confidence in the Reichstag.

Scholars have often found this rule to have been a mistake, making it too easy for the Reichstag to remove unpopular or inconvenient politicians from office. A coherent and stable government policy was further impeded by special arrangements made by individual ministers to secure personal and changing parliamentary majorities for themselves for fear of being driven from office. From the perspective of the Basic Law, which abolished such individual sanctions, this assessment makes obvious sense. However, the individual responsibility of ministers was in accordance with the structure of the *Reich* executive to a degree that the national assembly at Weimar had very little choice in the matter: As heads of powerful national ministries, the ministers each wielded such enormous personal power that it could not simply be subsumed in the 'cabinet'. Before the era of the crisis cabinets appointed by the *Reich* president without parliamentary approval after 1930, the dominant political voices accordingly were often those of prominent ministers such as Matthias Erzberger, Gustav Stresemann or Otto Geßler – more so, in many cases, than those of their heads of governments. And since the Reichstag was elected by proportional representation, the likelihood of coalition governments had to be reckoned with from the outset. And what is 'collective responsibility' supposed to have meant, in the absence of strong ideological agreement, in the so-called 'Weimar coalition' of Social Democrats, the Catholic Centre and the moderate liberal German Democratic Party (DDP)? In a Reichstag vote held in November 1928 on the suspension of battleship construction, Chancellor Hermann Müller and the ministers Carl Severing, Rudolf Hilferding and Rudolf Wissel – all Social Democrats – voted against their own government's express policy not to pursue the matter.[17] Yet in the following vote of no confidence brought by the Communist Party, they supported Wilhelm Groener, a minister with no party affiliation, whose policies they had hitherto openly opposed.

Such occurrences are much rarer today. As late as 1955, Konrad Adenauer's old rival, Jakob Kaiser, who was brought into the fold as minister of intra-German relations, voted with FDP ministers against ratification of the Saar Treaty concerning the return of the Saar Protectorate to West Germany. By contrast, Sabine Leutheusser-Schnarrenberger – at the time minister of justice representing the same party – resigned when the cabinet, against her resistance, had agreed to go forward with measures allowing a hitherto unknown surveillance of communications by the police. Again in contrast to this latter example, it is remarkable that the current minister of the interior, Horst Seehofer, was able to keep his cabinet post in the summer of 2018 in spite of his public opposition to his government's migration policy. He thus openly challenged the constitutional convention, established over the course of decades, of discipline within both the cabinet *and* the parliamentary party.

Whereas ministers' individual parliamentary responsibility was quite consistent with their considerable powers as chiefs of department, the actual problem was rather the truncated parliamentary responsibility of the chancellor himself. Of course, he too relied on

[17] ER Huber, *Deutsche Verfassungsgeschichte seit 1789*, vol VII (Stuttgart, Kohlhammer, 1984) 647–48.

parliament's confidence. Yet he also had to assure himself of the support of the president, who was able to dismiss a chancellor at any time if he found a parliamentary majority to do so (Article 53 WRV) or to remove the chancellor's parliamentary support by dissolving the Reichstag (Article 25 WRV). Accordingly, torn as he had been between the two poles of the constitutional system, the president and the Reichstag, the chancellor was able truly to establish a leading political role for himself only once any kind of parliamentary responsibility had been nullified – that is, in the era of the presidential crisis cabinets. Herein lies the core from which arose the sombre analysis that Carl Schmitt published in 1932.[18] It also is a key reason why the Weimar-era Reichstag remained stuck in the defects inherited from the constitutional order of the monarchy.

D. Distorted Images in Parliamentary Theory: A Weimar Legacy

Carl Schmitt had already used the precarious nature of parliamentary government to make a systematic argument in his 1923 account of *The Crisis of Parliamentary Democracy*, a book that was to prove as fateful as influential. Free public deliberation, of which pre-democratic parliaments had made a principle to compensate for their exclusion from power, was proclaimed by Schmitt as representing the supposedly eternal ideal image of parliamentarianism. Having done that, it was easy to expose how far the parliamentary business of his age had strayed from that ideal: decisions made in the house had long before been settled on away from the public eye, in committees, while the deputies themselves, rather than being free citizens who followed their conscience and represented the people, were subject to constant pressure from parties, associations and the interests organised within them.[19] Yet to describe the Reichstag in such terms was, at best, a half-truth. What is missing from Schmitt's account is an understanding that these supposed defects were also steps, however tentative, towards giving parliament a genuine share of governmental responsibility. That a parliament's ethical quality should not rise in proportion to its influence is, alas, a highly unspecific problem with power that could be found to apply to any institution. In the case of parliament, it seems moreover to be inaccurate. The idea of 'government by discussion', which its opponents attribute to the eighteenth-century English form of parliamentary government and to which they make a show of referring as something of the deepest, darkest past, has long been disproved. In fact, wherever it had any power, early bourgeois parliamentarianism was corrupt to a degree that would be utterly unacceptable today.

Schmitt's critique of parliamentarianism gained influence not least by way of Jürgen Habermas's theory of democracy. Although Habermas came to revise his own relationship to parliamentarianism fundamentally, in his early work, he adopted Schmitt's account of an early liberal parliament dominated by speech as the democratic ideal against which the story of the public sphere could be told as one of decline. Later, Habermas rehabilitated parliamentarianism, now considering it a model of public deliberation in a democratic

[18] C Schmitt, *Legality and Legitimacy* [1932], trans Jeffrey Seitzer (Durham, NC, Duke University Press, 2004).

[19] UK Preuß, 'Carl Schmitt and the Weimar Constitution' in O Meierheinrich and O Simon (eds), *The Oxford Handbook of Carl Schmitt* (Oxford, Oxford University Press, 2016) 471, 479–84.

civic society.[20] Both interpretations are, of course, linked by the absence of rule, the manner in which power is systematically rendered invisible. This absence is, for both Schmitt and Habermas, the normative core of parliamentary government, albeit one to which it virtually never conforms. Their political intentions were, of course, entirely different, and Habermas did not simply pit discussion against rule. Yet in his thought, too, the idea of democracy in opposition to parliament remains an ever-present possibility. During the eurozone crisis, Habermas expressed the hope 'that the constitutional court might take the initiative away from the political parties by ordering a referendum on constitutional amendments'.[21]

It should thus come as no great surprise that the German public tends to cherish parliamentary decision-making most over those issues for which the complex institution of parliament is the least necessary. These are the decisions that cannot be reached along party-political lines and hence require little effort of leadership on the part of the governing coalition. Examples that are widely considered to be the great moments of parliamentary culture include the debate over the future capital of the reunited country (Bonn or Berlin?), over the Bulgarian artist Christo's project of wrapping the Reichstag building in the 1990s, or over bioethical questions. These much-vaunted 'matters of conscience' (the reference to Article 38(1) GG is never missing) are supposedly parliament at its best, testimony to the abiding German longing for an absence of politics. The recent decision in favour of 'marriage for all' – no doubt a matter of conscience – was a case in point. As the issue was highly controversial between the coalition parties, the SPD and the CDU/CSU, and even within both of them, nothing happened for a decade. But when Angela Merkel decided to take a more liberal stance on the issue to steal a campaign goal from her opponents in the 2017 election, suddenly a parliamentary majority found itself willing and able to go forward. And yet, as soon as parliament proved itself to be a form of power capable of reaching a decision at short notice, complaints were heard that the whole business was becoming unduly politicised. The Bundestag's truly finest hours meet with scant appreciation among the German public: this is equally true for question times, the budget debates or the pitched parliamentary battles over major acts of legislation. Even a fairly recent best-selling book in Germany, *Das hohe Haus*, by the well-known journalist and writer Roger Willemsen, testifies to a broad lack of understanding of what parliament really produces: not so much political debates as political decisions. Compare this to Sasha Swire's juicy account of the Cameron years in her *Diaries of an MP's Wife* (2020) that implicitly count on the readers' familiarity with the workings of both parliament and a parliamentary government.

Political science has never seriously questioned the false premises on which this theory rests. Modern German textbooks on democratic theory often do not even mention parliamentarianism or the parliamentary system of government. Although German political theory considers democracy and democratisation under all manner of aspects, it fails to address the theoretical problems posed by the German system of government. Germany's constitutional lawyers do no better. One of the discipline's recent flagship projects, the twelve-volume handbook on constitutional law, considers the parliamentary system of government only in passing and the Bundestag as just one out of many 'organs of the state' (*Staatsorgane*). To the extent that constitutional law engages in theorising democracy at all,

[20] J Habermas, *The Structural Transformation of the Public Sphere* [1962] (Cambridge, MA, MIT Press, 1989); J Habermas, 'Volkssouveränität als Verfahren' (1989) 484 *Merkur* 465.

[21] P Bofinger, J Habermas and J Nida-Rümelin, 'Einspruch gegen die Fassadendemokratie' in *Frankfurter Allgemeine Zeitung*, 3 August 2012.

it prefers to do so via the classic authors of the Weimar Republic – who did not have a fully developed system of parliamentary government in the modern sense to consider – or via the importation of American theory. Only there does the separation of powers truly apply, and the legislature hence has a completely different task to fulfil than the German.

III. 1949: Parliamentarianism and the Basic Law

A. The Point of Departure

The Basic Law of the Federal Republic responded to the problems of Weimar-era parliamentary government by raising the status of the federal chancellor, who was henceforth to be elected by and fully responsible to parliament, with no plebiscitary president beside and above him (Articles 63 and 65(1) GG).[22] The 'Parliamentary Council' (Parlamentarischer Rat), Bonn's constituent assembly, was guided by the notion – which historians have since disproved many times over – that one reason for the instability of the Weimar Republic's coalition governments had been the overly strong position of parliament vis-a-vis the executive. Parliament was no longer to be entitled to topple individual ministers by votes of no confidence. A vote of no confidence in a chancellor was henceforth only to be possible in a constructive manner, that is, by simultaneously electing a new chancellor (Article 67 GG). The government was to depend as little as possible on stable parliamentary majorities, since nobody in 1948/49 thought them likely to come about. The experience of a parliament incapable of forming a majority from the last years of the Weimar Republic dominated the deliberations of the Parliamentary Council.

The old institutional separation of parliament and government, however – the constitutional dualism that Weimar had not done away with – was left untouched in the Basic Law too. This is why the Basic Law failed, and continues to fail, to give any full account of how the parliamentary system of government was supposed to function.[23] It is only in the emergency provisions of Article 81 GG that the leading role of government in parliament is expressed by the constitution – in a reference to the Bundesrat as a substitute legislature.[24] But the Basic Law contains no mention of the special treatment in parliamentary procedure usually accorded to government bills in parliamentary systems.

[22] For a concise appraisal, see H Hofmann, 'Verfassungsrechtliche Sicherungen der parlamentarischen Demokratie: Zur Garantie des institutionellen Willensbildungs- und Entscheidungsprozesses' in *Verfassungsrechtliche Perspektiven* (Tübingen, Mohr Siebeck, 1995) 129; the institutional consequences are discussed in S Ganghof and C Stecker, 'Investiture Rules in Germany' in BE Rasch and S Martin (eds), *Parliaments and Government Formation. Unpacking Investiture Rules* (Oxford, Oxford University Press, 2015) 67.

[23] M Jestaedt, *Demokratieprinzip und Kondominialverwaltung: Entscheidungsteilhabe Privater an der öffentlichen Verwaltung auf dem Prüfstand des Verfassungsprinzips Demokratie* (Berlin, Duncker & Humblot, 1993) 313.

[24] The first two sections of Art 81 read as follows:

> (1) If [after a lost vote of no confidence] the Bundestag is not dissolved, the Federal President, at the request of the Federal Government and with the consent of the Bundesrat, may declare a state of legislative emergency with respect to a bill, if the Bundestag rejects the bill although the Federal Government has declared it to be urgent. The same shall apply if a bill has been rejected although the Federal Chancellor had combined it with a [no confidence motion]. (2) If, after a state of legislative emergency has been declared, the Bundestag again rejects the bill or adopts it in a version the Federal Government declares unacceptable, the bill shall be deemed to have become law to the extent that it receives the consent of the Bundesrat. The same shall apply if the Bundestag does not pass the bill within four weeks after it is reintroduced.'

On the contrary, Article 76(2) GG makes government bills subject to a more complicated process of prior consultation in the Bundesrat. Nor does the Basic Law provide for parliamentary interpellations. The senior offices of the Bundestag, its 'speaker' or president (Article 40(1), sentence 1 GG) and the council of elders – the powerful non-partisan body tasked with managing the internal affairs and setting the agenda of the Bundestag – were not developed into institutions that might sustain such a connection. Rather, they were left in a state that had already been outlined in 1915 by the liberal constitutional lawyer Julius Hatschek, author of the first German account of parliamentary law: the 'senior convent' (*Seniorenkonvent*), the Reichstag's equivalent of the modern council of elders, was already an institution stuck halfway to being a cabinet government, partly substituting for it by setting the parliamentary agenda.[25] Unlike the office of the speaker in its US form, impartiality remains a key aspect of the Bundestag president's office. Besides his immediate tasks in running parliamentary business, his role in the German system is similar to that of a second federal president. Questions of procedure are dealt with, in the council of elders, not by majority, but by consensus, according to parliamentary tradition.[26] This impartiality does not, however, go as far as it does in the United Kingdom, where the opposition traditionally does not put up a candidate to oppose the Speaker of the House of Commons in his constituency, where he does not run under the flag of his party but as 'the Speaker seeking re-election'.[27]

The qualifications for government offices laid down by the Basic Law likewise do not follow the strict rules of parliamentary government. Unlike in some state constitutions, which allow the head of government or *Ministerpräsident* to be elected only from the ranks of the state parliament (Landtag), the chancellor need not be a member of the Bundestag. The extent to which parliament is to be considered a recruiting ground for members of government is left open by the constitution. To this day, there is no 'natural' path in the German system of government from leading a parliamentary party to leading the government itself. More often than not, the path has instead been through chairing a *Länder* government as *Ministerpräsident* as was done by Willy Brandt, Helmut Schmidt, Helmut Kohl and Gerhard Schröder. Angela Merkel is a distinct exception in this respect. Nor is the parliamentary party the only arena in which potential ministers commend themselves for office in Germany; *Länder* governments, too, by virtue of their representation in the Bundesrat, are impossible to ignore as what Max Weber called 'a proving ground for political leaders'. It is, however, incumbent on such ministers to win a parliamentary mandate, if belatedly: anyone promoted to a federal ministry from a *Länder* post will, like Peer Steinbrück in 2005, or more recently his successor but one, Olaf Scholz, have to ensure they are elected to the Bundestag the next time around. Genuine novice career changers, such as the public law professor Paul Kirchhof whom Merkel chose for her first shadow cabinet, or Werner Müller, Schröder's first business minister, did not do particularly well.

[25] J Hatschek, *Das Parlamentsrecht des Deutschen Reiches: Im Auftrag des Deutschen Reichstages dargestellt, Erster Teil* (Berlin, Göschen, 1915) 185–91.

[26] P Blum, 'Leitungsorgane' in M Morlok, U Schliesky and D Wiefelspütz (eds), *Parlamentsrecht* (BadenBaden, Nomos, 2016) § 21 ¶ 61, 66. Of particular significance here is the circumstance that all matters of procedure prior to meetings of the council of elders are discussed by the parties' parliamentary managers. On the continuity of this parliamentary institution, see the detailed account of H Franke, *Vom Seniorenkonvent des Reichstages zum Ältestenrat des Bundestages* (Berlin, Duncker & Humblot, 1987).

[27] Erskine May, 25th edn, online, https://erskinemay.parliament.uk, s 4.23.

Parliamentary parties are well advised not to encourage governments to pass them over and allow outsiders to make careers for themselves.

Leaving aside subsequent constitutional developments, one would have no choice but to say that the Basic Law provided not for a government supported by parliament, but rather for an executive able to confront parliament, once elected, as a counterweight to parliament. Above all, the Basic Law adopted from Bismarck's constitution of 1871 the rule – unassuming in appearance, but fundamental in consequence – of Article 43 GG:

> (1) The Bundestag and its committees may require the presence of any member of the Federal Government. (2) The members of the Bundesrat and of the Federal Government as well as their representatives may attend all sittings of the Bundestag and meetings of its committees. They shall have the right to be heard at any time.

There is a spectacular lack of symmetry concealed within these sentences. Whereas section 1 makes parliament's claim on the presence of the members of government dependent on a majority vote – thereby excluding such an eventuality in the normal course of a coalition government – section 2 opens parliament to all members of the executive, both from the political and the bureaucratic level, to an extraordinary degree.

This provision contains an unusually strong negation of the parliamentary system of government, for it denies the distinction, so fundamental to this constitutional model, between the members of the federal government (ie the chancellor and the ministers) responsible to parliament (Article 62 GG) and the bureaucracy *for which* the ministers are responsible, but who are not themselves responsible to parliament. It is an implicit part of parliamentary government that ministers should be allowed to speak in parliament at any time. That lower-ranking federal or *Länder* officials should be entitled to do so – if only duly commissioned by their superiors – is, however, a legacy of Bismarckian cunning, and moreover one that comes with a distinctly anti-parliamentary barb. After all, the members of the federal Bundesrat may be responsible to their *Länder* parliaments, they are not responsible to the Bundestag.

This has led to comic situations in the past. On 26 November 1975 Helmut Kohl, then prime minister of Rhineland-Palatinate and leader of the CDU, made a declaration 'on behalf of my friends in the CDU/CSU' from the Bundesrat benches in the Bundestag (the issue at hand being the German–Polish accords). Herbert Wehner, leader of the parliamentary Social Democrats, objected, and a reprimand from chancellor Helmut Schmidt soon followed: 'Prime Minister Kohl is entitled to speak in this house only in his capacity as member of the Bundesrat, and in no other capacity. (Applause from SPD and FDP – interjection [CDU/CSU]: He certainly has the other capacities!)' Only a year later, following the 1975 elections, did Kohl become a member of the Bundestag.

Since then, interventions from the Bundesrat benches have become a rarity, making more visible the principle that the government, and only the government, is responsible. In August 2002 a far-right figure, briefly senator for the interior in Hamburg whom his admirers called 'Judge Merciless', took advantage of Article 43(2) GG to deliver a rambling speech on his favourite topics of crime and immigration. All parties viewed the incident as an abuse of parliamentary procedure.[28] The Bundestag has also succeeded in substantially reducing the presence of top officials on the government benches. However, the

[28] Plenarprotokoll 14/251, Sten Ber, S 25 443–25 447.

'representatives' mentioned in Article 43(2) GG continue to exert a very strong influence on committee work: meetings of Bundestag committees are generally attended not only by that committee's members, but also by a far larger number of officials, whereas party workers are not admitted.[29] The significance of this provision hence lies less in enhancing government representation than in bringing to bear the full weight and expertise of the bureaucracy. Article 43 therefore adopted into Basic Law the seed of politics relapsing into the rule of bureaucrats or *Beamtenherrschaft*, in Max Weber's phrase, and of the potential predominance of mechanisms of coordination between federal and administrative bodies, bypassing parliament.

B. A Turn Away from the Parliamentary System of Government?

From this state of affairs, the constitutional lawyers of the early Federal Republic drew the widely held conclusion that the Basic Law represented a 'turn away from the parliamentary system'.[30] And it was indeed possible to give the Basic Law an anti-parliamentary interpretation in line with a Gaullist constitutional ideal, in which the chancellor – rather than parliament! – sets the guidelines for policy. The established term soon became *Kanzlerdemokratie*,[31] expressing distance to both parliamentary and presidential forms of democracy.[32] Rüdiger Altmann, a conservative writer, argued that the constitution allowed the chancellor to act largely independent of parliamentary confidence. As far as the relationship between parliament and government was concerned, the Basic Law had 'remained without any great and enlivening ideas. It was more of a reckoning with the past, full of the fear that history might repeat itself.'[33] Early commentary on the Basic Law was dominated by the curious idea of a separation of powers without a democratically elected executive power. Only in 1957 did Ernst Friesenhahn, an influential constitutional lawyer and one of the first justices on the Federal Constitutional Court, hit upon a formula that was to be much repeated later on and which allowed the Basic Law to be given a more strongly *parliamentary* interpretation:

> Parliament may not interfere in the ongoing business of administration, since to do so would conflict with the principle of the rule of law. Yet the political leadership [*Staatsleitung*] is, as it were, by right the joint possession of government and parliament.[34]

Although the unitary control of government policy by the parliamentary head of government was established by the constitution, the basic institutional problems of the German model of government – that is, the strong bureaucratic autonomy of the individual

[29] W Zeh, 'Das Ausschußsystem im Bundestag' in H-P Schneider and W Zeh (eds), *Parlamentsrecht und Parlamentspraxis* (Berlin, De Gruyter, 1989) § 39 ¶ 26; F Schäfer, *Der Bundestag: Eine Darstellung seiner Aufgaben und seiner Arbeitsweise*, 4th edn (Cologne, VS Verlag, 1982) 118.

[30] F Münch, *Die Bundesregierung* (Frankfurt am Main, Metzner, 1954) 159.

[31] FR Allemann, *Bonn ist nicht Weimar* (Cologne, Kiepenheuer & Witsch, 1956) 327.

[32] R Miller, 'Executive Extremes: German Lessons for our Authoritarian Era' (2021) 69 *Jahrbuch des öffentlichen Rechts der Gegenwart*, forthcoming; A Doering-Manteuffel, 'Strukturmerkmale der Kanzlerdemokratie' (1991) 30 *Der Staat* 1.

[33] R Altmann, *Das Erbe Adenauers* (Stuttgart-Degerloch, DVA, 1960) 27.

[34] E Friesenhahn, 'Parlament und Regierung im modernen Staat' (1958) 16 *Veröffentlichungen der Vereinigung der Deutschen Staatsrechtslehrer* 37.

ministries, lacking interconnections between parliamentary parties and government, and the stronger-than-ever interconnection between *Länder* bureaucracies and federal government – remained unresolved. To some extent they were even exacerbated. By virtue of the pronounced bureaucratic independence of each department, ministers now operated independently of any direct parliamentary sanction.

Indeed, the development of the political system in the Adenauer era seemed at first to suggest that the federal republic was not set to develop a parliamentary system of government. This is true not only of the revival of federalism in the 1950s. What is more, Adenauer's relationship with the CDU/CSU parliamentary party was far less close than that of later chancellors. The CDU of that time was more of a loose association of dignitaries, whose commitment to a shared party line was noticeably weaker than the centrifugal tendencies introduced into the governing parliamentary parties by interest groups. The CDU as a modern mass party that was to emerge from the reforms of Helmut Kohl was still a thing of the distant future. Later parliaments were no longer willing to tolerate the limited access to information that Adenauer had granted the Bundestag. Within the government, too, a proclivity to create walled spaces took hold. One example for this is the inception of a 'Security Council' to discuss sensitive issues with the inner cabinet, an institution that met in camera and was not subject to parliamentary control.

C. The House that Adenauer Built (With a Little Help from the SPD)

The emergence of a parliamentary democracy in the Federal Republic is due, without exception, to the development the constitutional system underwent *after* the adoption of the Basic Law. The crucial figure here is Adenauer. His decision not to enter into a grand coalition with the Social Democrats, made at a celebrated conference in Rhöndorf near Bonn on 21 August 1949,[35] inaugurated the dualism of government and opposition 'camps' which was to remain, with a brief interruption from 1966 to 1969, the standard pattern for the Bundestag until 2005, when grand coalitions again took hold: the CDU/CSU was pitched against the SPD, a 'bourgeois' camp against a 'left'. Only under these circumstances did the Bundestag, in its earlier parliamentary terms, begin to develop genuine elements of the government's parliamentary responsibility and a stronger institutional link between parliament and government. The electoral system contributed to this, encouraging the consolidation of the party system by shrinking the number of parliamentary parties from eleven in 1949 to three more than ten years – or rather two and a half, since the small FDP settled at single-digit percentages between conservatives and social democrats.

Political theory nonetheless continued to take a guarded view of all this. With some notable exceptions, German intellectuals evinced no great deal of understanding for the constitutional developments of their times. Indeed, they pronounced parliamentarianism dead during its period of consolidation. The familiar Marxist critique of parliamentarianism

[35] H-P Schwarz, *Adenauer*, vol 1 (Stuttgart, DVA, 1986) 624–5; R Morsey, 'Die Bildung der ersten Regierungskoalition' (1978) 97/98 *Historisches Jahrbuch* 418.

as a form of class rule was now recast and radicalised under a growing welfare state. In his famous book entitled '*The Transformation of Democracy*', which he co-wrote with Peter Brückner and which soon acquired cult status, Johannes Agnoli described parliamentarianism as a repressive structure designed to exclude the majority of the population from power.[36] True opposition had thus to come from outside parliament. As long ago as the late 1950s, a young Jürgen Habermas had seen in the growth of social welfare schemes a danger to oppositional political activity,[37] and his diagnosis resembled that of such conservative sceptics as Ernst Forsthoff and Arnold Gehlen.

Yet opposition as it really existed in the German Bundestag gave the lie to such historically and philosophically loaded accounts of its imminent disappearance. Led by the parliamentary Social Democrats, the Bundestag challenged Adenauer's more Gaullist stance on the constitutional nature of his office. Even without a corresponding provision in constitutional law, the Bundestag established votes of no confidence and of censure, as well as the striking of ministerial salaries from the budget, as admissible means of parliamentary politics.[38] Even in the time since reunification, a total of fourteen votes of censure of dismissal have been held against members of government,[39] though none in the most recent parliamentary term. The parliamentary reforms of 1969 gave parliamentary committees considerable new powers of control. At an informal level, too, the ties between parliamentary party and cabinet became ever closer in the early years of the Federal Republic. The participation of the leaders of the parliamentary governing parties in cabinet meetings became as much a matter of course as the role taken by the chancellor as the 'leader-in-chief' (Hans-Peter Schwarz) of 'his' parliamentary group.[40] Even in the first Bundestag, Adenauer attended thirty-three sessions of the executive committee of the parliamentary CDU/CSU. When important legislation was at stake, he took care to ensure that, conversely, the leaders of the party group took part in cabinet deliberations. Against the objections of his ministers, Adenauer forced through a formal declaration to that effect in April 1951. To this day, the participation of the heads of the parliamentary governing parties in cabinet meetings, which is essential to involving parliament in government policy, is regulated only by coalition agreements.[41] And once again, we find constitutional lawyers decrying this practice, though it has a genuinely constitutional purpose, a being in breach of the separation of powers.[42] Under Angela Merkel's chancellorship, the attendance of the parliamentary party leaders at cabinet meetings has no longer been the norm.

[36] J Agnoli and P Brückner, *Die Transformation der Demokratie* (Berlin, Voltaire, 1967).

[37] J Habermas, 'Zum Begriff der politischen Beteiligung' in *Kultur und Kritik. Verstreute Aufsätze* (Suhrkamp, Frankfurt am Main, 1973) 9.

[38] On this, see U Wengst, 'Ministerverantwortlichkeit in der parlamentarischen Praxis der Bundesrepublik Deutschland' (1984) 15 *Zeitschrift für Parlamentsfragen* 5391.

[39] *Datenhandbuch des Deutschen Bundestages*, online edn, ch 11.4.

[40] H-P Schwarz, 'Die Fraktion als Machtfaktor' in H-P Schwarz (ed), *Die Fraktion als Machtfaktor* (Munich, CH Beck, 2009) 283.

[41] On this, see U Hüllbüsch, 'Einleitung', in Bundesarchiv (ed), *Die Kabinettsprotokolle der Bundesregierung*, vol 4: *1951* (Boppard am Rhein, Harald Boldt, 1988) LXI–LXIII.

[42] M Schröder, 'Kritische Tendenzen im normativen Umriss von Regierung und Parlament' in *Festschrift für Peter Badura* (Tübingen, Mohr Siebeck, 2004) 504; J-P Steuck, 'Die ständige Teilnahme von Fraktionsvorsitzenden an Kabinettssitzungen der Bundesregierung – ein Verstoß gegen das Gewaltenteilungsprinzip?' (1999) 32 *Zeitschrift für Rechtspolitik* 403.

D. The Federal Chancellery as Parliamentary Government Headquarters

Above all, however, the Adenauer era marked the emergence of the first mediating institution between parliament and government: the federal chancellery as we know it today. There is no mention in the constitution of the function it actually fulfils within the political process. Of what does that function consist? Individual departments have responsibilities that are more or less clearly defined by the chancellor's order. The ministry of the interior is responsible for the federal police force, the ministry of transport for supervising the railways, and the ministry of education for ensuring that state authorities implement the federal student assistance scheme correctly. The scope of a ministry's activities accordingly influences the extent of each minister's parliamentary responsibility. Very much in contrast to the chancellor who, according to Article 65 GG, determines 'the general guidelines of policy' (*die Richtlinien der Politik*). The chancellery supports the chancellor in exercising this responsibility; accordingly, it is not an ordinary government department with clearly defined responsibilities. The 'power to determine policy guidelines' is not just another competence, but simply means political leadership. The chancellery hence consists of the advisers who support the chancellor in developing overall government policy.

The full scope of the chancellery's functions can only be appreciated by recalling the fundamental problem of the German model of government: the considerable autonomy of departments and the low degree of their parliamentary scrutiny. Little in the practice of German government is guarded as jealously as the autonomy of departments (*Ressortautonomie*), though constitutionally speaking their 'autonomy' is merely another word for the separation of spheres of action that allows ministers to be responsible for something personally rather than, as in the British case, collectively.

Since the Weimar Republic, the plausible constitutional conclusion to draw from this state of affairs has rightly been considered a failure: to tie the individual responsibility of ministers to the possibility of parliamentary votes of no confidence against individual ministers causes problems of other kind. Meaningful parliamentary interaction between the government and coalition parties requires that government policy is coordinated and coherent to a sufficient degree. The classical model of cabinet government ensures this by means of a cabinet acting in joint responsibility. Since such a model does not exist in Germany, the chancellery takes its place by acting as the ultimate hub of leadership, coordination and planning. It is the headquarters of government[43] and as such corresponds to the White House or 10 Downing Street. Such government headquarters take on a multitude of tasks, from consultation, planning, organisation, control and coordination of departments via appointments to leading positions, representation, public relations and information management to foreign policy. It is led by a chancellery minister who usually has cabinet rank but whose function is closer to a chief of staff and strategy.

Of course, the chancellors of the Weimar era also headed their own departments, but the chancellery was small compared with the powerful ministries – little more, in effect,

[43] On the following, see J Brauneck, *Die rechtliche Stellung des Bundeskanzleramtes: Rechtliche Grenzen für Organisation, Handeln und Kontrollierbarkeit des Bundeskanzleramtes* (Baden-Baden, Nomos, 1994); T Knoll, *Das Bonner Bundeskanzleramt: Organisation und Funktionen von 1949–1999* (Wiesbaden, VS Verlag, 2004); S Bröchler and J von Blumenthal (eds), *Regierungskanzleien im politischen Prozess* (Wiesbaden, VS Verlag, 2011).

than a cabinet secretariat. The Bonn chancellery, too, began in 1949 as a relatively small office with a staff of just over a hundred.[44] If one subtracted the officials responsible for foreign policy, of which Adenauer, who initially did not have a foreign office, himself was in charge, the personnel left for the actual work of coordination was very small indeed. Government headquarters experienced its most rapid growth under Willy Brandt and his chancellery minister Horst Ehmke.[45] The planning staff was significantly expanded. Brandt's vow to 'dare more democracy' (*Mehr Demokratie wagen!*) became the most successful catchphrase of the Federal Republic. At an institutional level, it first of all meant more centralised coordination of government policy. Today, the chancellery has a staff of over a thousand, though the official figure is given as some six hundred. This is due to an organisational trick: the powerful press and information office, which coordinates the government's entire official public relations and also takes to social media in support of government policy is outwardly organised as a government department in its own right, while legally constituting another department of the chancellery. Unlike a minister, its head, the government spokesman (who holds the rank of a permanent secretary), is answerable directly to the chancellor.[46]

In the course of its expansion, the chancellery has taken on the comprehensive coordination of relations between parliament and government. Like 10 Downing Street, it is the institutional hub of parliamentary government. An important function within this system falls to the so-called 'mirror units' (*Spiegelreferate*) conceived in the 1950s by the notorious Hans Globke, who was Adenauer's key aide, but had a dark past as author of a legal commentary of the Nuremberg racial laws. Globke's idea of mirror units was brilliant and is best explained by a look at the organisational chart of the chancellery, in which a miniature version exists of every federal department. The tasks of the important ministry for economic affairs, for example, are mirrored in the chancellery by five small subdivisions dealing with basic issues, competition, foreign trade, innovation and energy, whereas the far less prestigious education ministry makes do with a single mirror unit. Whereas Weimar chancellors had to rely on receiving all relevant information from departments from their respective ministers, federal chancellors have a dedicated staff of their own to understand, coordinate and control the policies of the ministries. This also works extremely well in practice, because the temporary transfer to a mirror unit is usually an important career step, which is why people bring knowledge from their old ministries, but also have a high level of political loyalty to the government headquarters. At the same time, the chancellery is the central clearing house for all formal dealings between ministries and parliament. In that respect, it serves as the central instance of the ministers' responsibility towards parliament.

It should be noted that the functions associated with this are not enshrined in the constitution, but are tucked away in the Bundestag's rules of procedure and in the joint rules of procedure of the federal ministries. The chancellery plans what legislative initiatives

[44] Knoll (n 43) 412.

[45] T Knoll, 'Das Bundeskanzleramt – Funktionen und Organisation' in KH Schrenk and M Soldner (eds), *Analyse demokratischer Regierungssysteme* (Wiesbaden, VS Verlag, 2010) 215.

[46] The official organizational chart of the Federal Chancellery is misleading in this respect, see www.bundesregierung.de/resource/blob/998434/1662408/d95c8a3e27881d9c96a8ae18e56cd21f/2019-08-20-organigramm-bk-en-data.pdf?download=1.

are to be set before the Bundestag and when, and it sets a timetable for the parliamentary process. This procedure is to be observed even when the federal government's leading role in the legislative process is hidden from view. Because Article 76(2) GG demands that the government's bills first be put to the Bundesrat in a time-consuming process, important and time-sensitive legislation is often introduced by the parliamentary governing party though it was in fact drawn up by the government itself.

In Westminster parliamentary procedure, the legal basis of government control is Standing Order No 14, which provides that 'government business shall have precedence at every sitting'.[47] This rule establishing the permanent priority of government bills over other motions has been called the two most important lines of parliamentary law.[48] Largely the same is achieved in German parliamentary law by an entirely informal arrangement between the chancellery and the president of the Bundestag's office. The federal government's power to set the agenda is constitutionally invisible while being firmly established in practice. Hence it is far from being a matter of no concern to find the government contract the drawing up of legislation to big law firms – a circumstance that was hotly debated when a draft bill for a bank bailout at the height of the financial and debt crisis was drawn up by Linklaters' Berlin office at the behest of Karl-Theodor zu Guttenberg, the minister for economic affairs at the time. Of course, regardless of who drafts the text, the ultimate decision continues to rest with parliament.

The chancellery has a share in the decision as to what key political projects are announced by the ministries and when, and by doing so controls the government's political agenda. It passes on the opposition's parliamentary questions to the ministries concerned, ensures that they are dealt with at no great delay, and in the most important of cases simply replies itself. It decides which of the government's papers are to be made available to parliamentary investigation committees. Other tasks are not formally regulated but established in practice. The chancellery can decisively influence which minister is to face government questions in the house every Wednesday at one o'clock during parliamentary sessions. Such a decision can be of considerable political importance depending on whether the minister concerned happens to be in the firing line at the time or is enjoying a run of success. Finally, the chancellery has factual oversight over all the ministries' doings, constantly asks for information on planned initiatives, intervenes when ministries make all too idiosyncratic staffing decisions and mediates in conflicts between ministers.

Organisational links between government, chancellery and parliament can take on a variety of forms – convening the coalition committee, for example, or by inviting the leaders of the coalition parliamentary parties (and possibly experts on a particular topic from within the parliamentary parties) to cabinet meetings.[49] Under Adenauer, this connection was maintained by a simple informal arrangement: the heads of the parliamentary groups, Heinrich von Brentano and Heinrich Krone, were among the chancellor's closest advisers, while coordination between parliament and government lay in the hands of a separate

[47] A thorough discussion of the evolution of agenda rules is J Sharpe and P Evans, 'Finding Time' in P Evans (ed), *Essays on the History of Parliamentary Procedure* (Oxford, Hart, 2017) 227.

[48] BK Winetrobe, 'The Autonomy of Parliament' in D Oliver and G Drewry (eds), *The Law and Parliament* (London, Butterworths, 1998) 20; the seminal work still is GW Cox, *The Efficient Secret: The Cabinet and the Development of Political Parties in Victorian England* (Cambridge, Cambridge University Press, 1987).

[49] V Busse, *Geschäftsordnung der Bundesregierung*, 2nd edn, (Munich, CH Beck), § 2 ¶ 5.

government department with an own minister of Bundesrat affairs at the top.[50] Willy Brandt merged that ministry's tasks into the chancellery, making it clear that coordinating the parliamentary process is a decision at the core of political leadership. In current practice, it is among the tasks of the chancellor's 'minister of state' without cabinet rank (*Staatsminister bei der Bundeskanzlerin*). On the parliament side, coordination with government policy is safeguarded only by a government representative for whom no provision is made in the rules of procedure and who by a permanent yet informal arrangement takes part in meetings of the Bundestag's council of elders.

How 'the government' appears to parliament today is thus largely the decision of the federal chancellery. In doing so, it de facto stands in for the institution absent in the Federal Republic's parliamentary system: a collegial cabinet acting in mutual solidarity and joint responsibility. Decision-making and strategic planning of government as a whole is mostly done outside of any formal institution. The informalisation of government practice that is encouraged by the very institution of the chancellery, and which became proverbial not least through Helmut Kohl's 'kitchen cabinets', is not extraneous to the parliamentary system of government but rather part of its logic.[51]

E. The Chancellor's De Facto Right to Dissolve Parliament

The instrument of the vote of confidence as set down in Article 68 GG is usually referred to as the strongest formal power in the hands of the Federal Chancellor. The clause says that if

> a motion of the Federal Chancellor for a vote of confidence is not supported by the majority of the Members of the Bundestag, the Federal President, upon the proposal of the Federal Chancellor, may dissolve the Bundestag within twenty-one days.[52]

The wording gives only incomplete expression to the chancellor's power to determine policy guidelines vis-a-vis the Bundestag. The chancellor *may* put forward the motion in order to assure himself of the house's confidence. If the Bundestag does not approve the motion, he *may* ask the federal president to dissolve the Bundestag, a request which the president *may* approve, but which he *may* also deny, invoking legislative emergency according to Article 81 GG. What is more, the constitutional court *may* rule on the president's decision if asked to do so by members of the Bundestag (Article 93(1)(1) GG).

The fourfold '*may*' has earned the vote of confidence and the legislative emergency a reputation as paper tigers, since it introduces two powers with veto rights – the president and the constitutional court – besides the chancellor and his parliamentary parties.[53] Yet this formal arrangement in the constitution only proves that the Parliamentary Council had intended the vote of confidence to ensure stable government. Its original purpose indeed was not (or not chiefly) to serve the chancellor as an instrument of parliamentary

[50] Knoll (n 43), 430.

[51] This has first been shown persuasively by Lehmbruch (n 3) 57.

[52] For a comparative discussion of the rules of dissolution, see A Sajó and R Uitz, *The Constitution of Freedom. An Introduction to Legal Constitutionalism* (Oxford, Oxford University Press, 2017) 230–35.

[53] H Döring and C Hönnige, 'Vote of Confidence Procedure and Gesetzgebungsnotstand: Two Toothless Tigers of Governmental Control' (2006) 15 *German Politics* 1.

leadership, nor was it conceived as a licence to make a plebiscitary appeal to voters whenever a government found its parliamentary base exhausted. The original purpose of the vote of confidence was above all to give a minority chancellor the opportunity to free himself from a hostile parliamentary majority, which is why it falls to the president – who is supposed to have an outside view of the state of political play between parliament and government – to adjudicate.

This indicates a marked formal difference between the office of the German chancellor and prime ministerial government as it was until recently practised in the United Kingdom. Since the early twentieth century, one of the UK prime minister's key powers had been the exercise, previously entrusted to the cabinet as a whole, of the royal prerogative of dissolving parliaments.[54] Monarchs invariably complied with their prime ministers' requests to that effect. Prime ministers were also able to tie a vote of confidence to a vote on a particular policy, threatening parliament with dissolution if it did not agree – as John Major did when pushing through the ratification of the Maastricht Treaty.[55] Only the Fixed-term Parliaments Act of 2011, which was passed under pressure from David Cameron's coalition partners, the Liberal Democrats, abolished this power. To call a general election has since required a vote of confidence to be lost in the House of Commons – or for parliament to dissolve itself by means of a two-thirds majority.[56]

This development has somewhat muddied the purpose of the right to dissolve parliament, which originally was not the preserve of the head of a minority government, but could also be wielded by a prime minister who had lost no votes in the commons and had a stable majority. In established practice, the purpose of dissolving parliament was to ensure that voters supported the government and its parliamentary majority in major political decisions. Dissolution, according to Albert Venn Dicey, author of a classic systematic account of English constitutional law in the late nineteenth century, resulted from the exalted constitutional position of parliament. Since sovereignty was vested in parliament, it was imperative to ensure 'sympathy between the action of the legislature and the will of the people' – 'and this security is given by the right of dissolution, which enables the Crown or the Ministry to appeal from the legislature to the nation'. To dissolve parliament thus constituted an 'appeal from the legal to the political sovereign'.[57]

The establishment of a parliamentary system in Germany has brought about a fundamental change in the meaning and application of Article 68 GG. The provision has gradually turned into a corresponding right on the chancellor's part to dissolve the Bundestag similar to the idea of prime ministerial government. Only the premature dissolution of the Bundestag in 1972 could still be explained in terms of the constellation that the framers of the constitution had envisaged: Willy Brandt had narrowly survived the constructive vote of no confidence brought against him by Rainer Barzel, the leader of the opposition, but had lost a stable majority and hence, it seemed, the vote of confidence he had called on 20 September 1972. The situation already looked quite different ten years later. In 1982

[54] C Turpin and A Tomkins, *British Government and the Constitution*, 7th edn (Cambridge, Cambridge University Press, 2012) 384–85.

[55] A comparative overview can be found in JD Huber, 'The Vote of Confidence in Parliamentary Democracies' (1996) 90 *American Political Science Review* 269.

[56] AW Bradley, KD Ewing and C Knight, *Constitutional and Administrative Law* (Harlow, Pearson, 2014) 246–48.

[57] AV Dicey, *Introduction to the Study of the Law of the Constitution* (London, Macmillan, 1923) 429, 433.

Helmut Kohl found himself in the position of a British prime minister who, though he could be reasonably sure of a majority, wanted plebiscitary confirmation of a political about-turn that had been executed in parliament. It should be remembered that Kohl, having defeated Helmut Schmidt in a vote of no confidence, was governing at the head of a CDU–FDP coalition that had not campaigned in the previous election as such. Instead, the FDP had sworn to fight alongside the SPD in the 1980 election to keep away from power Franz Josef Strauß, the extremely polarising yet brilliant head of the Bavarian government then running for chancellor on the CDU and CSU ticket. Kohl had only been chancellor for two and a half months when he announced to the Bundestag:

> In my policy statement … I presented the programme of the federal government supported by FDP, CSU, and CDU and underscored our intention to face the electorate on 6 March 1983 if at all possible. … Having now taken care of the most urgent business, it behoves us to let the electors decide.[58]

Although Kohl invoked 1972 as precedent, Willy Brandt, in the ensuing parliamentary debate, quite rightly reminded him that that situation had been quite different: there certainly was no parliamentary deadlock in 1982.

When this procedure was brought before the constitutional court, it faced – as it would in the summer of 2005, when Gerhard Schröder called a vote of no confidence – one of those seemingly impossible decisions that constitutional courts are sometimes called upon to make. The senate announced its verdict on 16 February, but the election had already been called for 6 March. Should the court have called a stop to campaigning and ordered parliament and government to return to their jobs? The court wound itself out of this dilemma by a decision that favoured Kohl in the verdict, but his opposition in the underlying reasoning.[59] Even the complex interaction of all political institutions in the process as set out by Article 68 GG was not enough 'to guard against any possible abuse'. Of a chancellor calling a vote of no confidence, the court demanded proof of a so-called 'substantive state of dissolution':

> The normative context thus makes it apparent that a dissolution of the Bundestag even by way of art 68 GG must always assume a situation of political instability between the chancellor and the Bundestag, and implicitly requires fulfilment of the condition that the chancellor cannot be sure of the steady parliamentary support of a majority in the Bundestag.[60]

Although the newly formed government had not been defeated in a parliamentary vote, the court was nevertheless satisfied that a substantive 'state of dissolution' obtained, although its reasoning referred mainly to the purported emotional condition of the FDP. In so doing, it defended the vision of the Parliamentary Council against Kohl's interpretation of Article 68 GG as a tool of prime ministerial government and thus provided an argument to those observers who differed in their view of the FDP's state of mind. Sceptics could also take succour from the dissenting opinions of two constitutional justices, Hans-Justus Rinck and Joachim Rottmann, who found the chancellor's actions to be straightforwardly unconstitutional.

[58] Plenarprotokoll Nr 9/141 of 17 December 1982, *Stenographische Berichte*, 8939.
[59] *Dissolution of the Bundestag*, 62 *BVerfGE* 1 (1983).
[60] ibid 42.

The court's solution suffers from a fundamental problem: the criterion of a substantive state of dissolution can always be said to apply and hence is not a criterion properly so-called. This became obvious in 2005, when Gerhard Schröder likewise interpreted the vote of no confidence as a licence to dissolve parliament at will. Once more, the government's ability to find a majority in parliament was not in obvious jeopardy. Again, however the 'Agenda 2010' labour market and welfare reforms had marked a clear political turn within a legislative term. In the light of defeats in *Länder* elections and the formation of a new party which attracted large parts of the SPD's left wing, Schröder no longer considered the result of the 2002 election to give him sufficient legitimacy. This time around, though it gave stronger emphasis to the chancellor's own discretionary judgement in the matter, the constitutional court held to its theory of the 'state of dissolution' and demanded 'facts' from the chancellor, in place of which it ultimately contented itself with reports of severe tensions within the governing coalition.[61] This was likewise a narrow vote on the bench, coming out five to three in Schröder's favour.

One of the constitutional justices dissenting, Gertrude Lübbe-Wolf, offered an opinion in which she fundamentally criticised the role that the constitutional court had arrogated to itself as a controlling instance in this process. Yet she, too, did not appreciate that the emergence of the chancellor's de facto power to dissolve parliament by means of Article 68 GG constituted not only 'deviation' from an original constitutional idea that was open to abuse, but rather a constitutional development that was justified not least democratically. It is precisely in the constitutional provision made for the vote of no confidence that the political link between the federal government and the majority of the Bundestag – and hence the basic idea of parliamentary government – is particularly vividly expressed. For the same reason, the danger of the abuse of this instrument is negligible, as the constitutional history of the past 70 years makes amply clear. The principle of the political connection between parliament and government would not, on the other hand, apply if parliament were to have the right freely to dissolve itself with an appropriate majority. A parliamentary study commission (*Enquete-Kommission*) in 1976 proposed an amendment to Article 39 GG, entitling the Bundestag to vote for its dissolution by two-thirds majority if a quarter of its members requested it.[62] The recommendation was never taken up, and the reinterpretation of Article 68 initiated by Kohl and Schröder and ultimately accepted by the constitutional court makes it unlikely that it ever will be.

IV. 1969: The Normality of Parliamentary Changes of Power and the 'Popular Parties' as Mediating Institutions

The election of Willy Brandt as chancellor finally gave political sanction to the constitutional development towards a genuine parliamentary democracy. In 1969 the promise of making and unmaking governments by electoral majorities was fulfilled by the reversal of

[61] *Dissolution of the Bundestag*, 114 *BVerfGE* 121, 162 (2005).

[62] *Beratungen und Empfehlungen zur Verfassungsreform: Schlußbericht der Enquete-Kommission Verfassungsreform des Deutschen Bundestages*, Teil I: *Parlament und Regierung* (Zur Sache 3/76) 1976, 21.

government and opposition roles in the Bundestag. The significance of this caesura for the democratisation of the Federal Republic has been much emphasised.

What the 1969 change of government meant from a constitutional perspective was the definitive establishment of the *second* mediating institution between parliament and government: the two major parties transformed into centrist mass parties, or 'popular parties' (*Volksparteien*) as they are usually called in Germany. The term is used to describe what the SPD and CDU/CSU have in common as catch-all parties with a streamlined organisation and an inclusive programme, without ties to any particular class or milieu or special interests. At the founding of the Federal Republic, neither of the two main parties was a 'popular party' in this sense; three decades later they both were thoroughly so. After the handover of power from Kiesinger to Brandt, no party could expect to lead a government if it was as organisationally and programmatically inconsistent as the CDU had been before its overhaul by Helmut Kohl. The path is familiar by which the Social Democrats became a catch-all party rather than a party of a particular class: in the Godesberg Programme of 1959, the SPD accepted the core tenets of the Federal Republic's social and economic order, thereby creating for itself a genuine claim to parliamentary power, which it realised in two steps, in 1966, when they entered the grand coalition, and in 1969, when Brandt was elected chancellor.

Less self-evident, but no less crucial, was the thoroughgoing transformation of the Christian Democrats in response to the party's complete loss of power at the federal level. Especially under the party leadership of Helmut Kohl from 1973 on, and his secretary-general Kurt Biedenkopf (who later played a leading role in Saxony after the reunification), it changed from a loose association of dignitaries into a modern, well-organised party with serious programmatic ambitions. At the centre of this reform process stood the kind of professionalisation that turns a party in a parliamentary system of government from an electoral association into a constitutional factor: the closer coordination of programme, parliamentary party and the process of intra-party consensus building. For this to be achieved, however, the party had to be given an organisational form independent of the parliamentary party: a manifest, party conferences with livelier discussions, policy meetings and the recasting of party headquarters as a hub for campaign coordination. It was also Helmut Kohl who gave the role of the parliamentary opposition a visible boost after his party's defeat in the 1976 election by giving up the prime ministership of his native Rhineland-Palatinate and taking the helm of the CDU in the Bundestag. No one before or since has attached such importance to the second most important office of parliamentary democracy, the leader of the opposition. Later unsuccessful candidates for chancellor, Franz Josef Strauß and Edmund Stoiber, by contrast, preferred to keep their office in Munich, though as members of the CSU they would in any case have stood little chance of leading the CDU/CSU joint parliamentary group.

It is this emergence of the popular parties that would appear to mark the principal difference between the *Kanzlerdemokratie* of the Adenauer years and the Federal Republic's later parliamentary governments. The popular parties make a twofold contribution – both personal and substantial – to intertwining parliament and government. For one thing, a popular party is no longer the party of a particular class or milieu and thus is forced to establish compromise between very different groups. As a result, it seeks to govern not with the ideology of a milieu or class, but rather with a programme for government which, paradoxically, must reflect both a close association with and distance from social and economic interest groups. A popular party is thus able to imprint its party line more strongly on the policies of both the parliamentary party and the government. The reverse, however, also applies: in the absence of parties and parliamentary groups on which commitment can be imposed – without, that is, organisations whose members can be made to follow a party line and to vote accordingly – there is no point in making a claim to government.

In the SPD, much like in the Labour Party before Tony Blair, a stronger dependence of the policies of both government and parliamentary party on the party's overall ideological orientation and the trade unions had long been in accordance with the party's self-image as the bearer of a particular *Weltanschauung*,[63] though its chancellors had never shared that self-image. The SPD accordingly had a shorter way to go in its transformation into a popular party. It is hard to imagine that the parliamentary party of the SPD could refuse to obey the party leadership in the nomination of a candidate for chancellor and get away with it – as the CDU/CSU MPs did in 1980 when they chose Strauß against Ernst Albrecht. Much rather, the SPD seems always to have remembered a famous dictum of the Austrian socialist Karl Kautsky: 'The Social Democratic deputy as such is not a free man – ridiculous though it may seem – but merely his party's representative.'[64] The famous legal philosopher Hans Kelsen, another Austrian socialist writing between the wars, was also of the decided opinion that parties should have the right to withdraw deputies from parliament in cases of dissent.[65]

This reveals the true point of the union of party leadership and the chancellor's office, a precedent set by Konrad Adenauer and followed by most of his successors. Anyone forced by his party to depart from that rule – like Gerhard Schröder after 2004 – could not hold onto the chancellery for long. By resigning from the party leadership in October 2018, Angela Merkel openly prepared for her departure from government office too. The only chancellor never to have been leader of his party was the one whose government may have been the most clearly at odds with his party and its parliamentary group: Helmut Schmidt. Of course, this union of chancellorship and party leadership is also a rule of political prudence, since it prevents a rival from using the party to build up a position of power from which to attack the chancellor. Yet one need only compare Angela Merkel's style of government with that of her supposed mentor, Helmut Kohl, to see that more is at stake here. Kohl was the first leader of the CDU/CSU to be a dyed-in-the-wool party man. He maintained that the party leadership was to be dominant over both the parliamentary party and the government. Merkel – on the contrary and to the chagrin of many party members – uncompromisingly placed the *raison d'état* above her leadership of the CDU, in which she was never fully invested. In the Kohl era, chancellor, chancellery, parliamentary party and the CDU's ministers formed a stable unit of political action; the only revolt broke out, in 1989, within the party itself.[66] Merkel, on the other hand, repeatedly had to face down rebellions within her parliamentary party – notably during the euro and refugee crises – which remained politically inconsequential only because the SPD faithfully secured her majority.

[63] For the Wilhelmine era, this has been shown by U Mittmann, *Fraktion und Partei: Ein Vergleich von Zentrum und Sozialdemokratie im Kaiserreich* (Düsseldorf, Droste, 1976).

[64] K Kautsky, *Der Parlamentarismus, die Volksgesetzgebung und die Sozialdemokratie* (Stuttgart, Dietz, 1893) 111.

[65] H Kelsen, 'Wesen und Wert der Demokratie' [1929] in *Verteidigung der Demokratie* (Tübingen, Mohr Siebeck, 2006) 185–86.

[66] Schwarz (n 40) 291.

There is, however, a widespread tendency in the Federal Republic to decry this gradual informalisation of power in the party state. It is the Federal President Richard von Weizsäcker who famously set the tone in his screeds in the later years of Helmut Kohl's government.[67] It is of course easy to present the nexus of party and government as a pathology, a dereliction of political duty, and applause is guaranteed even from politicians whose active careers are behind them. Weizsäcker, himself a product of the CDU, voiced his criticism only after reunification, at a time when the integrative power of the popular parties was already dwindling. Nonetheless, every Federal President is now expected to read the parties the riot act at least once during his term in office. In fact, however, this informalisation – one might also thing of it as relations between parliament and government becoming more constitutionally fluid – is a necessary condition for the functioning of parliamentary government. And it is one of the great achievements of the West German party system.

The reverse of this institutional mediation is a circulation of elites between party leadership, parliamentary party and federal government – a circulation that sometimes leads to an accumulation of offices. Naturally, not all parties are the same in this respect. The Greens always took an ambivalent attitude towards the idea of concentrating power in the parliamentary party, and had long insisted on a separation of party and parliamentary offices that was only recently abandoned for the benefit of the crowd-pleasing Robert Habeck, the most likely frontrunner for the 2021 campaign. It is no coincidence that, with the exception of the former foreign minister Joschka Fischer, the party has barely produced any eminent parliamentarians. Nonetheless, as the product of the integration of the extra-parliamentary opposition into parliamentary politics, the Greens testify to the constitution's ability to bring seemingly opposing political currents into the fold.

In one respect, however, the establishment of the popular parties remained incomplete: electoral law has largely remained in its 1953 form. At the outset of the grand coalition of the late 1960s, the CDU/CSU and SPD agreed in principle to abandon proportional representation in favour of a first-past-the-post system along British lines. Such a reform, which had in Wilhelm Hennis an advocate intellectually equal to the problem,[68] would have had far-reaching and unpredictable consequences for the further development of the German political system. In the short term, it would no doubt have spelled the end of coalition governments. It may also have led to a de-federalisation of the party system, to a changed idea of political representation, or to Germany coming more strongly to resemble the Westminster system. What it would certainly have meant was a greater and more stable dominance of the CDU at the federal level and a weakening of the impetus for innovation arising from proportional representation.[69] The reform never came to pass, and Adenauer's third cabinet (1957–61) has remained the only federal government not to be formed by a coalition. The major parties have continued to have protest, single-issue, milieu-based and special-interest – in short, small – parties to contend with.

[67] '"Wo bleibt der politische Wille des Volkes?" Bundespräsident Richard von Weizsäcker im Gespräch mit Gunter Hofmann und Werner A Perger' in *Die Zeit*, 19 June 1992.

[68] S Schlak, *Wilhelm Hennis: Szenen einer Ideengeschichte der Bundesrepublik* (Munich, Beck, 2008) 123–27.

[69] H Döring and P Manow, 'Is Proportional Representation More Favourable to the Left? Electoral Rules and Their Impact on Elections, Parliaments and the Formation of Cabinets' (2017) 47 *British Journal of Political Science* 149.

A. Parliamentary State Secretaries: Their Uses and Abuses

The link, emanating from the parties, between the government and the elite of the parliamentary parties can only be fully appreciated if one looks beyond the government itself. Cabinets have kept a fairly constant size throughout the history of the Federal Republic. Adenauer began with 14 ministers, Ludwig Erhard had 22, while Angela Merkel today makes do with 15. But such figures are deceptive, for relations between ministers and parliament are to a considerable extent shaped by an institution that was only created in 1967, under the first grand coalition: by parliamentary state secretaries (*parlamentarische Staatssekretäre*). The office is similar to that of ministers of state, parliamentary undersecretaries or secretaries of state but with significant differences: parliamentary secretaries of state in the German system act as intermediaries between government and parliamentary parties. Unlike junior ministers in Westminster parliaments, they are not members of the government, which is constitutionally defined as consisting of the chancellor and the (senior) ministers (Article 62 GG). Their role is described by the relevant law as 'supporting the members of the Federal Government to whom they are assigned in the exercise of their official duties'.[70] It is not immediately apparent what those duties consist of: unlike the (non-parliamentary) state secretaries (*beamtete Staatssekretäre*) who are career civil servants, they are not part of the bureaucratic hierarchy and hence hold little sway within the ministries themselves. The actual task of parliamentary state secretaries is to represent the Federal Government in parliament.

This development, too, appears to have occurred at a sub-constitutional level.[71] But unlike some have argued, its ambivalence is not due to the fact that the 'Federal Government', as the constitution would have it, 'shall consist of the Federal Chancellor and the Federal Ministers'. The law states clearly enough that they are merely 'assigned' to ministers. The problem is rather that the institution effectively divides the office of the minister, which is responsible to parliament, in two. Once again, a comparison with Great Britain reveals the peculiarity of the German model of government: in Britain, too, we find 'junior ministers', not of cabinet rank, but assigned to a department; yet it should be remembered that cabinet responsibility in the British system is organised at the collective, not the individual, level. The junior ministers, too, are thus able to speak for Her Majesty's Government. German ministers are responsible individually, and individual responsibility cannot be delegated, whereas collective responsibility always has delegation in mind. The danger here is of the German ministers delegating their parliamentary answerability more or less completely to their parliamentary aides, thereby causing actual responsibility to be separated from the task of answering to parliament. Ministers who are not themselves members of the house likewise have parliamentary state secretaries, who naturally are much closer to the parliamentary parties than the ministers themselves.

These disadvantages are counterbalanced by the considerable advantages of this office, the most important of which is that it offers, for a significant number of deputies, an institutional link between the politics of their parliamentary party and the logic of government.

[70] § 1, s 2 Gesetz über die Parlamentarischen Staatssekretäre (ParlStG).

[71] An early and influential discussion, addressing the fundamentals of this problem, is E-W Böckenförde, *Die Organisationsgewalt im Bereich der Regierung: Eine Untersuchung zum Staatsrecht der Bundesrepublik Deutschland* (Berlin, Duncker & Humblot, 1964) 232–34.

Thirty-five parliamentary state secretaries are currently working under Angela Merkel's fourth cabinet, which marks a moderate increase from her first cabinet (29), but by no means an all-time high: at one point under Helmut Kohl, the figure was 42. This also leads to a sharp increase in interdependency between parliamentary party and government: between them, the governing parties have 399 seats in the *Bundestag*, only 10 of which – a share of 2.5 per cent – are occupied by cabinet ministers; by adding the parliamentary state secretaries, the proportion of deputies with a part in government responsibility rises to 11.3 per cent.

B. In Praise of Party Patronage

Access to important governments posts such as those of the parliamentary state secretaries gives considerable scope to creating personal links between parliamentary politics and the governing bureaucracy. The fact that this access is regulated by party politics has led to this system being referred to as 'party patronage', with all the implications of political corruption that term entails.[72] Does not the constitution itself clearly state that: 'Every German shall be equally eligible for any public office according to his aptitude, qualifications and professional achievements' (Article 33(2) GG)? Does this not mean that party patronage – the selection of leading staff by party affiliation – is an unconstitutional abuse? In fact, things are a little more complex. The constitutional provisions regarding senior civil service are themselves the historical expression of a proud and infinitely ambivalent independence that the German civil service has maintained vis-a-vis politics and democracy. Civil service laws say otherwise, too: section 30 of the Beamtenstatusgesetz (the law governing the status of civil servants) explicitly states that the most senior civil servants are political appointees (*politische Beamte*) and, as such, must perform their duties 'in continuous accord with the political opinions and goals of the government'.

Contrary to popular opinion, party patronage is not an abuse, but indeed to a certain degree a constitutional necessity. In their departments, ministers encounter a senior bureaucratic staff whose expertise they inevitably lack; as a rule, they have no means of ensuring that their administration will act in accordance with the government's political intentions except for shared party membership. Yet in Germany, the strong autonomy of the bureaucracy means that parties have rather few opportunities to install their preferred candidates in office and thus to impose political commitment on them. This holds true not only in comparison with the United States, where thousands of appointments in the executive branch can be made after an election,[73] but also with other parliamentary democracies. Even among the directors-general (*Abteilungsleiter*), the second-highest rank in the ministries after the state secretaries holding civil service appointments, only about half have a party affiliation.[74] This is due above all to the fact that government bureaucracy is never controlled

[72] For a comparative approach, see P Kopecký, P Mair and M Spirova (eds), *Party Patronage and Party Government in European Democracies* (Oxford, Oxford University Press, 2012).

[73] On the constitutional history of the American civil service, see M Roßbach, *Das Personal der Republik* (Tübingen, Mohr Siebeck, 2021, forthcoming).

[74] P Manow, 'Die politische Kontrolle der Ministerialbürokratie des Bundes: Die Bedeutung der Landesebene' in P Manow and S Ganghof (eds), *Mechanismen der Politik* (Frankfurt am Main, Campus, 2005) 251.

by the Bundestag alone, but also by *Länder* bureaucracies through the participation of the *Länder* governments in federal law-making and their control of implementation. Moreover, the members of the local government enjoy a considerable presence on the federal level through the federal chamber, the Bundesrat, which is not composed of elected representatives of the states like the US Senate but of the governments themselves, more precisely of the prime ministers, ministers and leading civil servants.[75] This leads to a strange kind of federalism in which it is not at all weird but day-to-day business that officeholders on the *Länder* level have a say in matters of national policy.

Americans refer to the 'revolving doors' through which careers pass to and fro between politics and business. German politicians pass with similar frequency between state and federal levels. This interaction between mutually supervisory bureaucracies means that the parties involved at both levels no longer depend on the patronage wielded by the federal parliament. But less party-political patronage by the parliament means less democratic control over the administration. It may in fact be the case that the parliamentary parties have too little influence over the government through appointments. As a result, patronage finds other outlets, often in places where it is a genuine political nuisance such as in municipal services.[76] In the large public broadcasting companies, too, the Federal Constitutional Court has desperately tried to limit the influence of party politics on the boards.[77]

V. The Legal Connection between Parliament and Government Forged by the Constitutional Court

As we have seen, the task of coordinating policy between government and the coalition in parliament falls mainly to the parties, most of all to the popular parties, whereas the political weight and the eminent constitutional role of the federal chancellery reside in the institutional coordination of government action and its responsibility towards parliament and in harmonising it with parliamentary procedure. The Federal Constitutional Court, however, represents a third institution playing a decisive mediating role between parliament and government without being directly involved in their interactions. In this function, too, the constitutional court is not a creature of the constitution itself, but rather of the development it has subsequently undergone.[78] It has often been praised for its contribution to the success of parliamentary democracy, though the nature of that contribution tends to be obscured rather than illuminated by somewhat pathetic notions of the court as a moral authority or an instance of moral and civic education. But what contribution has the court truly made

[75] Art 43(2): 'The members of the Bundesrat and of the Federal Government as well as their representatives may attend all sittings of the Bundestag and meetings of its committees. They shall have the right to be heard at any time.' Art 51(1): '(1) The Bundesrat shall consist of members of the Land governments, which appoint and recall them. Other members of those governments may serve as alternates.'

[76] F Decker, *Regieren im 'Parteienbundesstaat': Zur Architektur der deutschen Politik* (Wiesbaden, VS Verlag, 2011) 92.

[77] *Supervisory bodies of public broadcasting corporations*, 136 *BVerfGE* 9 (2014), ECLI:DE:BVerfG:2014:fs20140325.1bvf000111 (en).

[78] The leading study of the court's genealogy and present constitutional role is now available in English: M Jestaedt, O Lepsius, C Möllers and C Schönberger, *The German Federal Constitutional Court. The Court Without Limits* (Oxford, Oxford University Press, 2020).

to the construction of parliamentary government in Germany? How did its jurisprudence build a government more dependent from parliamentary majorities and more addressable by parliamentary control than the founders of the constitution had envisaged?

A. Limits of Constitutional Review in Parliamentary Democracies

Constitutional courts never simply interpret constitutional law 'as it is'. Constitutional law is political law. Whenever they decide disputes within the political system, constitutional courts themselves are political actors who influence the behaviour of other actors in the political system – even and indeed particularly when they decide according to legal rather than political criteria.[79] The historian Hans-Ulrich Wehler has called Germany's Federal Constitutional Court 'the genuine innovation' of the system of the Federal Republic compared to that of Weimar.[80] The scope of its review is unique compared to any other constitutional court.[81] To consider the compatibility with the jurisdiction of 'Karlsruhe' is an essential part of any due process of parliamentary law-making. The latent presence of the constitutional court's powers pervades the German political system because no other institution can any longer be imagined without the legal form that the jurisdiction of the constitutional court has given it. This is particularly true of the relationship between parliament and government, of which the Basic Law gives only a very incomplete account. Its authoritarian interpretation as a *Kanzlerdemokratie*, with traits of the constitution given by Charles de Gaulle to the French Fifth Republic in 1958, was still plausible in the Adenauer era and was indeed *one* possibility opened up by the constitution. It is not only an achievement of the political institution, but also one of the constitutional court that the Federal Republic eventually took a different constitutional path.

B. A Political Court

Constitutional courts play a role in the political system that is situated between law and politics and consequently is highly ambivalent.[82] A court as such is able to conceive of the interaction between parliament and government only in legal categories, in procedural norms, organisational principles, and set competencies. It is like the legendary King Midas – except that everything it touches turns into law. And Germany's Federal Constitutional Court is not shy of touching political matters; it does so often. There is no such thing in Germany as the *political question doctrine*, under which the US legal system exercises restraint in the political process.

The political role of the Federal Constitutional Court did not stem from the Parliamentary Council. The drafters of the constitution did, however, make it responsible for ruling on

[79] J Collings, *Democracy's Guardians: A History of the German Federal Constitutional Court 1951–2001* (Oxford, Oxford University Press, 2015).

[80] H-U Wehler, *Deutsche Gesellschaftsgeschichte*, vol 5 (Munich, CH Beck, 2010) 6.

[81] C Möllers, 'Scope and Legitimacy of Judicial Review in German Constitutional Law – The Court versus the Political Process' in H Pünder and C Waldhoff (eds), *Debates in German Public Law* (Oxford, Hart, 2014) 3.

[82] C Möllers, 'Legality, Legitimacy, and Legitimation of the Federal Constitutional Court' in Jestaedt et al (n 78).

'disputes concerning the extent of the rights and duties of a supreme federal body or of other parties vested with rights of their own by this Basic Law or by the rules of procedure of a supreme federal body' (Article 93(1) GG), though this constitutional provision alone has remained a German peculiarity.[83] The point of this so-called *Organstreit* process (a dispute between supreme federal bodies) is to protect parliamentary minorities. It is never an abstract dispute over rights and obligations. It allows the defeated party in many political conflicts to further pursue its case by constitutional litigation. In political power struggles, the 'defeated party' usually means the opposition, a minority parliamentary party or individual deputies. Yet the constitution gave no clear indication of how and against what *Organstreit* proceedings were to serve as an instrument of the parliamentary protection of minorities.[84] Only the legislative power and the constitutional court itself adapted the procedure to the institutional conditions of a parliamentary democracy.

C. The Constitutional Enabling of Parliamentary Minorities and of the Parties

In their present form, the Federal Constitutional Court and its procedural law are the creations of the Bundestag.[85] Among other things, section 64 of the Act on the Federal Constitutional Court (Bundesverfassungsgerichtsgesetz, BVerfGG) of 1951 contains an option that lawyers refer to as *Prozessstandschaft*, ie the right to bring a suit on behalf of another applicant: a minority parliamentary group may claim that a particular government measure impinged upon the rights of the Bundestag – and, it should be noted, on the rights of parliament as a whole with regard to the government rather than on the group's own rights as a minority with regard to majority, eg in the legislative process. An important factor here is the constellation, so typical of the parliamentary system of government, in which the majority of the Bundestag fully supports the government's conduct. This is how *Organstreit* proceedings took on what might be called their extroverted character, and it is only through this constellation that the relationship between parliament and government fully became a matter for the court.

For example, it was the constitutional court that invented, once reunification had made deployment of the Bundeswehr more likely, the notion of the 'parliamentary army' or *Parlamentsarmee*. In an answer to a suit brought by the parliamentary opposition (then the Social Democrats), it ruled that the deployment of armed troops required the prior constitutive consent of the Bundestag.[86] The ruling was a sensation at the time. In many situations, parliamentary minorities may claim that the actions of executive institutions impinge on their statutory rights. For this reason, the court was able to rule on the two premature dissolutions of the Bundestag in 1983 and 2005, which had resulted from a vote of no confidence

[83] J Pietzcker, 'Organstreit' in P Badura and H Dreier (eds), *Festschrift 50 Jahre Bundesverfassungsgericht*, vol 1 (Tübingen, Mohr Siebeck, 2001) 587.

[84] In its early years, the constitutional court was more guarded in this respect. See P Cancik, 'Parlamentarismus vor dem Bundesverfassungsgericht – Das Redezeiturteil und die Erfassung der Verfassungswirklichkeit' in F Meinel (ed), *Verfassungsgerichtsbarkeit in der Bonner Republik* (Tübingen, Mohr Siebeck, 2019).

[85] C Schönberger, 'Anmerkungen zu Karlsruhe' in *Das entgrenzte Gericht* (Berlin, Suhrkamp, 2011) 16.

[86] *Military missions out of area*, 90 *BVerfGE* 286, 381 (1994).

being called with the parliament's dissolution in mind – and in which a majority, in both cases, favoured dissolving the Bundestag. And the constitutional court was likewise able to keep the government on its toes on the initiative of a few deputies who were opposed to its policies in the euro bailout – notwithstanding the fact that the government's monetary policy was supported by overwhelming parliamentary majorities.

The second fundamental decision regarding its political role was made by the constitutional court itself. According to settled case law, political parties in an *Organstreit* proceeding may invoke the right to equal opportunity (Article 21 GG). A celebrated judgement of 1976 may serve as an example: the constitutional court found against the government in a case brought by the CDU, that the government had used taxpayers' money on a large scale to fund a campaign for the re-election of the SPD/FDP coalition as such, with the slogan 'We are on the right path. Performance deserves trust. We are securing the future.'[87] Accordingly, in early 2018, the court could find in favour of the AfD and reprimand the federal minister of education for campaigning against a demonstration by that party.[88]

The doctrine on this jurisdiction is ambivalent: while praising its outcomes, scholars of constitutional law are virtually unanimous in considering the admission of parties to an *Organstreit* proceeding to be a mistake, since it means that the court treats political parties in a manner equivalent to the constitutional institutions for which the proceeding was in fact intended. There is, of course, something rather unorthodox about this practice. Parties are not part of the state, and with good reason. What is more, the court's judgment, in which it argues that parties were 'necessary elements of the constitutional structure' and as such performed 'functions of an organ of the constitution … by contributing to the formation of the political will of the people',[89] makes something of leap from that function to a specific legal qualification. Yet in substance, the court accomplished something highly consequential in this judgment: in the German system of government, it is after all the parties, and especially the popular parties, that ensure the parliamentary control of the government for which there is barely any provision in constitutional law. To admit them to the *Organstreit* procedure anticipated the full recognition of this role.

D. The Reservation of Statutory Powers and its Democratic Reinterpretation

However, there are limits to the viability of resolving disputes by *Organstreit* proceedings – not least the fact that, for reasons of time alone, the opposition cannot take every parliamentary conflict to court. Yet the court's key contribution to strengthening the parliamentary aspect of the German system of government seems superficially to have little to do with the relationship between parliament and government. The question here is of the democratic reorientation of the so-called 'reservation of statutory powers' (*Gesetzesvorbehalt*), the reservation of the parliamentary as opposed to delegated law-making. This reservation consists in the constitutional requirement of the specific

[87] *Government campaigning*, 44 *BVerfGE* 125 (1977).

[88] *Neutrality of ministerial communication*, 148 *BVerfGE* 11(2018), ECLI:DE:BVerfG:2018:es20180227.2bve000116 (en).

[89] *Political parties in constitutional litigation*, 4 *BVerfGE* 27, 30 (1954).

enactment of statutes wherever fundamental rights are infringed and in a set of other cases.

In the nineteenth century, this constitutional requirement formed part of the constitutional compromise between the German bourgeoisie and the monarchic state, according to which the monarchy and its administration were not subject to democratic control while having extensive prerogative powers.[90] Only for 'interference with liberty and property', as the standing phrase went, did the executive require parliamentary approval in the form of a law. Hence, in the best tradition of the rule of law, expropriation, taxation, arrest or conscription were permissible only on the basis of a statutory act of parliament.

Over time, the Federal Constitutional Court has increasingly interpreted this principle as expressing the claims of *democratic* legislation, recasting it as a constitutional commitment to the political supremacy of parliamentary legislation. Parliament itself was henceforth to decide not only on infringements of liberty and property, but on everything that is democratically 'essential', which ultimately extends to all political questions: the treatment of prisoners, sex education in schools or the question of whether Muslim teachers at state schools should be permitted to wear the headscarf – to name some cases that have recently come before the courts. What is democratically 'essential'? Anything that touches upon basic rights, is of concern to many or is of broader political significance. The UK Supreme Court presented a similar argument in *Gina Miller v Secretary of State for Exiting the European Union*, when it held that withdrawal from the European Union needed prior parliamentary approval because of its constitutional importance.[91]

To understand this jurisdiction properly, it must first be recalled that, from an ideal type of parliamentary government, it was altogether misguided. After all, the advantage of that constitutional model over the separation of powers is that parliaments are concerned with matters of legislation less rather than more. Instead, it is considered enough for governments to be answerable to parliament for measures enacted by delegated legislation, which is subject to parliamentary scrutiny. Parliament is supposed not to deliberate over laws in detail, but rather to control them by debating and voting on them – which is the reason famously given to this principle by John Stuart Mill.[92] In the United Kingdom, accordingly, by far the larger part of legislation is thus enacted as *delegated* or *secondary legislation*, that is, by executive ordinance subject to parliamentary scrutiny.[93] If the constitutional reservation of statutory powers leaves the Bundestag with a far greater amount of legislative work, it then comes as no surprise that the German parliament has often been criticised for being too concerned with the detailed business of law-making.[94] This is true even though in Germany, too, most bills are of course drafted by the ministerial bureaucracies – a fact that the Bundestag's false friends can also be relied upon to decry.

[90] M Stolleis, *Public Law in Germany: A Historical Introduction from the 16th to the 21st Century*, trans T Dunlap (Oxford, Oxford University Press, 2017) 59–72.

[91] *R (Miller) v Secretary of State for Exiting the European Union*, [2017] UKSC 5.

[92] JS Mill, *Considerations on Representative Government* (London, 1861) ch V.

[93] J Sharpe and P Evans, 'Finding Time. Legislative Procedure since May' in P Evans (ed), *Essays on the History of Parliamentary Procedure* (Oxford, Hart, 2017) 227, 240–46; A Sajó and R Uitz, *The Constitution of Freedom. An Introduction to Legal Constitutionalism* (Oxford, Oxford University Press, 2017) 263–64.

[94] W Hennis, 'Der Deutsche Bundestag 1949–1965: Leistung und Reformaufgaben' [1966] in *Auf dem Weg in den Parteienstaat* (Stuttgart, Reclam, 1998) 21; C Schönberger, 'Der Deutsche Bundestag zwischen Konstitutionalismus und parlamentarischer Demokratie: Historische und vergleichende Variationen auf ein Thema Gerhard Loewenbergs' in Schöne and von Blumenthal (n 2) 45–46.

The approach adopted by the Federal Constitutional Court has nonetheless been proved right by time. In Britain, too, the idea has taken hold that parliamentary control of delegated legislation is largely an illusion.[95] Given the scope for action at the disposal of a modern executive, the 'premiums' on the legal possession of power – as Carl Schmitt has put it[96] – are so high that they can be anchored in parliament only by a fairly detailed involvement of parliament in decision-making. As the German national parliament since the days of the Bismarckian empire had developed a strong institutional tradition of legislative work, the jurisdiction of the German constitutional court turned this path-dependency into a strength and encouraged the growth of the republic's institutions in such aspects as were already strong. The jurisdiction had the desired effect and strengthened parliamentary influence on government. It assigned the Bundestag a more active role where its strong suit as a parliament lay: in its tradition as a legislative chamber. The Reichstag, too – for want of political alternatives – had thought of itself as a legislative body, and this self-understanding is carried on by the *Bundestag*.[97]

In the considerable extent to which juridical regulation took over the administrative state, the court took particular advantage of the long-term development of Western welfare states since World War II. The need for regulation in the welfare state grew steadily for reasons that had nothing to do with the system of government. It thus took only the extension of legislation (and thus parliamentary statutes) into such realms as business, environmental, consumer or social law – in brief, into the areas subject to regulation, control and intervention by the welfare state – for parliamentary influence on government to be strengthened.[98] The dynamisation and functionalisation of the concept of law inevitably demanded much closer coordination between proposed legislation and parliamentary consultation. In an industrial welfare state such as the Federal Republic, government policy has for a very long time essentially been made along the lines of great projects of legislation: the Equalisation of Burdens Law (*Lastenausgleichsgesetz*, one of Adenauer's signature achievements that provided for a fair distribution of the losses and damages during the war), dynamic state pensions, no-fault divorce, co-determination in the workplace and university reform.

Moreover, having influence over legislation that extended much further across all areas of government policy than before provided parliament with an ally in the form of those social and economic interest groups that, in a neat architectural metonymy, are referred to as lobbyists. The greater a parliament's influence not just in matters of filling senior posts and deciding basic issues of policy but, as in the case of the *Bundestag*, also in the detail of legislation, the more important it becomes for associations to secure influence on legislation for themselves. It is no coincidence that the formalisation of the involvement of interest groups in the legislative process through a register of interest groups initially dates back

[95] R Fox and J Blackwell, *The Devil Is in the Detail: Parliament and Delegated Legislation* (London, Hansard Society, 2015).

[96] Schmitt (n 18) 31–32, 35–36.

[97] The problem is accurately described by C Schönberger, 'Das Parlament: Geschichte einer europäischen Erfindung' in M Morlok and D Wiefelspütz (eds), *Parlamentsrecht* (Baden-Baden, Nomos, 2016) § 1 ¶ 55.

[98] The connection between the policy imperatives of the welfare state and the German model of parliamentarization is also made by P Badura, 'Die parlamentarische Demokratie' in J Isensee and P Kirchhof (eds), *Handbuch des Staatsrechts*, vol II (Heidelberg, CF Müller, 2004) § 25 ¶ 8–9; H Schulze-Fielitz, *Theorie und Praxis parlamentarischer Gesetzgebung, besonders des 9. Deutschen Bundestages (1980–1983)* (Berlin, Duncker & Humblot, 1988) 4–8.

to a time when the Federal Republic was making the greatest strides towards a parliamentary system of government. A *Lobbyregistergesetz* providing for a significantly more formal regulation of pressure groups has been introduced by the governing majority (albeit under considerably public pressure) and is currently in the legislative process of the Bundestag.

The Bundestag's increased focus on the work of legislation, reinforced by the jurisdiction of the constitutional court, has therefore always been ambivalent. On the one hand, it burdens parliament with a task which, according to the constitutional structure of parliamentary government, it would not even need to perform and which detracts from the Bundestag's capacity for dealing with other matters, in particular with parliamentary control. The Bundestag has remained a 'working legislature'. This was the price exacted by a jurisdiction for the immense influence it acquired in the process of the juridical elaboration of the welfare state.

E. Parliament as an Agency of Legalisation and a Machine of Legislation

Since the 1980s, the Federal Constitutional Court has fleshed out the idea guiding its jurisdiction as a general and abstract constitutional principle. Under the decisive influence of Ernst-Wolfgang Böckenförde, who was himself a justice at the court from 1983 to 1996, it has come to an understanding of parliamentary democracy as a system of graduated democratic 'legitimation'. The court conceives democracy as a cyclical process in which the individual institutions are connected by so-called 'chains of legitimacy'.[99] By their choice as voters, citizens set up and legitimise parliament, the pivotal institution of democracy, which in turn imparts legitimacy to all other institutions and holders of public office by the rule of law, by electing a chancellor and exercising control over government.

This theory brings about a heavy and far-reaching juridification of the notion of democracy in German constitutional law. It makes it possible for the institutional anchoring of government in parliament to be discussed in terms of constitutional law even where the constitutional reservations of legislative powers must fail, because what is at stake is not legislation, but rather other government decisions or organisational decisions. The democratic principle in Böckenförde's interpretation is, as it were, the meta-organisational norm that serves the constitutional court as a means to supplement the organisational law of the parliamentary system of government – of which the Basic Law contains the mere rudiments – as it sees fit. The court has since taken advantage of this in elaborating parliamentary co-determination in European policy, in involving the Bundestag in addressing the financial crisis, or in elaborating parliamentary oversight.[100]

Intuitively, this is of course reasonable: parliament is directly elected, but the government proceeds from parliament. But what does this entail? The constitutional institutions

[99] Böckenförde's key text on the constitutional law of democracy ('Demokratie als Verfassungsprinzip') is missing in the two volumes of selected writings that are now available in English; see, however, E-W Böckenförde, 'The Constituent Power of the People: A Liminal Concept of Constitutional Law' in *Constitutional and Political Theory. Selected Writings I* (Oxford, Oxford University Press, 2018) 168.

[100] A Voßkuhle and C Bumke, *German Constitutional Law. Introduction, Cases, and Principles* (Oxford, Oxford University Press, 2019) 321.

that stand outside the cyclical process – the *Länder*, the Bundesrat, the European Union – do not even feature in this model. Nor does the theory seem to correspond directly to the idea system of parliamentary government: the formation of a government is not the transfer by parliament of a power that is originally its own, but rather a particular means within constitutional law of making appointments to public office. The government is not parliament's executive committee, nor does it proceed from parliament in its entirety – only the office of the chancellor does. If we were to believe this theory, he would have to enjoy greater legitimacy than the ministers who depend on him. Article 65 of the Basic Law, however, says the very opposite: the standard case of government action under parliamentary responsibility is action by the individual minister.

Böckenförde's theory of democracy is not just any old theory, it is a theory – indeed, *the* constitutional theory – of the social-liberal era. It is the institutional structure of the old Federal Republic given constitutional form. It naturally relied on a reasonably clear idea of how, in the parliamentary system under the Basic Law, legitimation is politically and institutionally produced: by national elections, popular parties ready to govern in parliament, a government dependent on parliament, consistent political control of the ministerial bureaucracy – in short: by a national welfare state with a working legislature.

It is the constitutional model of a parliamentary system in the making – one that, as Böckenförde hoped, was yet to break free of the shackles of administrative federalism. This has not come to pass. Accordingly, his theory of legitimation is a future past rather than our present. The constitution retained its dual structure; the inertia of the federal system had evidently been underestimated. Meanwhile, the political function of the concept of legitimation has undergone a complete change in constitutional jurisdiction, the court having turned it into a formula to be invoked whenever the issue of transferring competencies to the European Union is at stake.[101]

It seems increasingly apparent that by means of its legitimation-based jurisdiction and the theory of democracy it entails, the court is not so much interpreting the system of government established by the Basic Law as in fact normatively remaking its very core. In its verdict on financial aid to Greece in September 2011 – to give just one example – it concluded, from the principle of democracy, that not only was the Bundestag's budget committee charged with overseeing the decisions of the finance minister, but also that the federal government in certain cases was obliged to secure approval from the budget committee in advance.[102] This jurisdiction can barely be reconciled with the principle of the government's responsibility to parliament. While the federal minister of finance is responsible in parliament to all members of the Bundestag for making so far-reaching a decision as accepting guarantees for the purchase of government bonds, this does not apply to the members of the budget committee who, equipped as they are with a free mandate, are not responsible to the house in any meaningful legal sense.

This is not the last word on whether legitimation-based jurisdiction is the appropriate answer to the problem of the constitutional court's oversight of processes of parliamentary

[101] For the first time in *Maastricht Treaty*, 89 *BVerfGE* 155 (1993); the foundational text of this jurisdiction's intellectual progenitor is P Kirchhof, 'Der deutsche Staat im Prozeß der europäischen Integration' in J Isensee and P Kirchhof (eds), *Handbuch des Staatsrechts*, vol VII (Heidelberg, CF Müller, 1992) § 183 ¶ 57–61.

[102] *Greek bail-out*, 129 *BVerfGE* 124, ¶ 141 (2011), ECLI:DE:BVerfG:2011:rs20110907.2bvr098710 (en).

decision-making in an ever more complex institutional environment.[103] All it demonstrates is what function the theory of democratic legitimation can no longer fulfil today: that of a conceptual shorthand for that peculiarly German form of parliamentary government that emerged largely beneath the organisational purview of the Basic Law and at the centre of which stand the three genuinely new institutions of the postwar era: the popular parties, the constitutional court and the federal chancellery. After having looked different for a while, the parliamentary democracy of the Federal Republic of Germany is now once again a constitution without theory.

[103] Questions to the constitutional court arising in this context are put by C Schönberger, 'Identitäterä' (2015) 63 *Jahrbuch des öffentlichen Rechts* 42.

4

What is the Bundestag? Political Representation in a Working Legislature

I. What is Parliamentary Representation?

Throughout all the constitutional changes parliamentary democracy has undergone since the founding of the Federal Republic, its key question for Germany has remained unanswered: from where or what does parliament derive its claim to be the highest instance in the constitutional realm? The usual and most frequent answer is: by representation. Members of the Bundestag, according to the standard expression in German constitutional history, are 'representatives of the whole people' (*Vertreter des ganzen Volkes*). But what does that actually mean?

Western political theory has framed two fundamentally different answers to this.[1] Each grasps a core aspect of the constitutional meaning of parliamentary representation, though neither does so in full. Liberal concepts, following in the tradition of Thomas Hobbes, conceive representation as authorisation. Although sovereignty may reside with the people, the exercise of the rights following from sovereignty – above all, that of legislation– is monopolised by certain bodies.[2] The populace has a political existence only in this body, not directly on its own. Representation, in this sense, is an entirely abstract answer to the problem of legitimacy of rule as such. Yet parliamentary representation is only one possible form of representation. To Hobbes himself, the question whether the rights associated with rule were delegated to a monarch or an assembly was ultimately of secondary importance.[3] As a monarch's absolutist form of representation could be captured in the phrase *rex est populus*, Hobbes by the same token declares the sovereign representation of an assembly to be *omni obligatione libera* – free from all obligation. It was rather the people, though it may only have elected the assembly once, who were henceforth bound by its decisions, for they had vested in it all civil power (*tenebantur inde ad factum populi transferentis jus civitatis in optimates*). In this view, too, the people existed politically only in the institutional bearer of its sovereignty; in the moment of electing such a ruling assembly, the people had effectively dissolved itself (*ea electa, populus simul dissolvitur*).[4]

The constitutional principle of parliamentary government would be unthinkable without this notion of representation as authorisation.[5] What we mean today by parliamentary

[1] M Brito Vieira and D Runciman, *Representation* (New York, Polity, 2008).

[2] A fascinating reappraisal of this intellectual tradition is offered by R Tuck, *The Sleeping Sovereign* (Cambridge, Cambridge University Press, 2016).

[3] Q Skinner, 'Hobbes on Representation' (2005) 13 *European Journal of Philosophy* 155.

[4] T Hobbes, *De cive*, ch VII, 9.

[5] A Sajó and R Uitz, *The Constitution of Freedom. An Introduction to Legal Constitutionalism* (Oxford, Oxford University Press, 2017) 99–103.

representation is first of all parliament's authority to exercise civil rule, to make decisions that are binding on the citizenry, which it derives from election. Representation in this sense is made possible by the free and independent status of the representatives, the so-called 'free mandate', which the constitution describes in terms that are part lyrical, part bureaucratic, and hence distinctly German: members of the Bundestag are 'not bound by orders or instructions and responsible only to their conscience'. The free mandate is a necessary condition of parliamentary rule, for only by excluding any notion of deputies acting under instruction from their voters is the concentration of power in parliament possible in the first place. The members of the ruling assembly must not themselves be subject to any rule. As Edmund Burke famously framed it in his *Speech to the electors of Bristol* of 1774:

> Parliament is not a Congress of Ambassadors from different and hostile interests; which interests each must maintain, as an Agent and Advocate, against other Agents and Advocates; but Parliament is a deliberative Assembly of one Nation, with one Interest, that of the whole; where, not local Purposes, not local Prejudices ought to guide, but the general Good, resulting from the general Reason of the whole. You chuse a Member indeed; but when you have chosen him, he is not Member of Bristol, but he is a Member of Parliament.[6]

If the constitution addresses the deputies as representatives of the 'entire people', this no longer implies a holistic notion of a higher common good as opposed to party politics – as a misconception particularly popular in Germany would still have it. The representation of the entire people rather than of a certain group or party testifies first and foremost to an institutional necessity of the parliamentary system.

A quasi-absolutist idea of representation as authorisation is, of course, unlikely to convince anybody in modern constitutional democracies. Rather than being bearers of sovereign rights, modern parliaments are institutions of constitutionally bound rule. Ever since the United Kingdom adopted constitutional review, this holds true in principle also for the Westminster Parliament with its traditional notion of parliamentary sovereignty. The idea of representative democracy also considers the representative body as answer to a practical conundrum: the direct self-government of the people is a fine idea, but impractical in execution, which is why the people must consent to being represented by institutions. This understanding usually comes with a corollary: that deputies should be guided by the true interests of those they represent.

To another current of political theory, which goes back largely to Hanna F. Pitkin, representation is a substantial form of active responsibility, of 'acting for' others.[7] Within political institutions, representation thus denotes a particular form of the possibility of articulating external concerns that has both an outward and in inward dimension. This makes representation extraordinarily complex at the conceptual level: since voters do not develop preferences with regard to most alternatives on which decisions are to be made, a deputy of the people must act according to a well-founded notion of the voters' good. Where voters do indicate a preference, their representatives are expected to be responsive. This does not answer the question of who is even being represented: the voters, the citizenry, the population, constituencies, social groups or particular interests?

In short, the problem with this notion is that it eludes any attempt at being captured in a constitutional norm. For what (if anything) representatives stand for is difficult to

[6] *Select Works of Edmund Burke*, vol 4 (Indianapolis, Liberty Fund, 1999), 11–12.
[7] HF Pitkin, *The Concept of Representation* (Berkeley, University of California Press, 1967).

control and ultimately remains vague. Their constitutional immunities and privileges make it impossible to enforce any legally binding demand for substantial representation. While adequate recompense, and, to some extent, rules governing supplementary income and other activities, can reduce the risk of parliamentarians acting as paid representatives of particular interests, the exclusion of any imperative mandate precludes any positive obligation to advocate any specific cause.[8]

There are, however, rules in a democracy that create a link between these different aspects of representation – rules that, on the one hand, prescribe the process by which the ruling body is authorised by the people, and, on the other, make it more or less likely for certain interests or causes to find expression in the political process. The electoral law is one such set of rules. By mediating between the two aspects of parliamentary representation, electoral law is constitutional law of the highest order. It achieves this mediation by means of a third aspect of representation, one that is aesthetic in nature: to symbolise a relationship of absence. A parliament elected by proportional representation – composed, that is, in accordance with each political group's share of the vote – is something of a mirror image of the people as a whole. A parliament elected according to a first-past-the-post system, consisting of the deputies of individual constituencies, likewise offers an image of the nation in miniature, albeit by other means.[9] The principle of representation as such does not contain a preference for one form of representation of the other, nor does it have anything to say regarding the size of parliament, constituency boundaries, communications and feedback between voters and members, the issue of allowances, or the question the representativeness of representatives – that is, the parliamentary visibility of minorities. Yet it is on the electoral law that the political and constitutional meaning of representation depends.

A. Representation without Decision?

German electoral law lacks any specific theory of representation. The idea of popular or parliamentary representation tends to be seen as something either very solemn or highly banal. Parliament is regarded as part ritual, part town hall meeting, part complaints office. The Latin term itself conveys a sense of solemnity, of representation and hence politics finding its consummate form, if not in the ceremonial opening of parliament, then at any rate in free discussion of questions of principle. A more banal imaginary is implied in the German *Volksvertretung* or 'popular assembly', which seems to suggest that its members should exercise the political representation of their voters in much the same way as a shop steward represents workers' interests to management. But while the so-called will of the people is not something that emerges free from political influence, to represent particular interests is considered somehow unseemly.

These two prevailing notions of parliamentary representation have one thing in common. They deliberately hide from view the element of decision around which it all revolves, and in doing so conceal the essential purpose of democratic parliaments: the decision of the voters, structured by the electoral law, and the decisions produced by the institutions of

[8] *cf* Sajó and Uitz (n 5) 108–10.

[9] G Conti, *Parliament the Mirror of the Nation. Representation, Deliberation, and Democracy in Victorian Britain* (Cambridge, Cambridge University Press, 2019).

parliamentary democracy, whose legitimation is at issue. To think of representation as an ideal in the terms set by Carl Schmitt and others, as an image of a higher notion of political existence, is to negate the claim to rule which that term encapsulates – as do the proponents of an 'identitarian' notion of popular representation.[10] In fact, Carl Schmitt's celebrated claim that parliamentary representation was built on the ideal of 'government by debate' within the bourgeois public sphere, and in which the better argument deserved to carry the day,[11] was founded on the negation of parliamentary decision in favour of an exclusive decisionism on the part of a plebiscitarian executive.

The extent to which the political meaning of parliament is far from self-evident permeates even the language of the Bundestag. The very word for its members, *Abgeordnete*, or 'delegates' – in which the Basic Law follows the German constitutional tradition – tends to obscure rather than clarify the matter. After all, members of parliament are not 'delegated' by the electorate for a particular task[12] – as officials might be by their superiors – but rather are elected representatives authorised to make decisions. Constitutional language continues to deny this. It persists in referring to the 1977 Gesetz über die Rechtsverhältnisse der Mitglieder des Deutschen Bundestages ('Members of the Bundestag Act') by the abbreviated form of *Abgeordnetengesetz* or 'Delegates' Act, while its official title and the official job title of 'Members of the German Bundestag' (*Mitglieder des Deutschen Bundestages*, MdB) give a correct account of the matter: membership in the highest decision-making body, the German Bundestag, confers upon each of its elected members an equal share in parliamentary rule by virtue of representation.

Nor do the rules of parliamentary conduct traditionally contribute to revealing the character of parliamentary representation as rule. The members of the House of Commons tend to refer to and address each other by their constituencies (eg 'the member for Sevenoaks'), and are referred to accordingly in transcripts of debates and other official documentation. Yet they define their electorate not primarily in geographical terms, as in the German electoral district or *Wahlkreis*, but rather by the political unit that constitutes their power: the constituency. Meanwhile, the president of the Bundestag calls speakers to the rostrum as 'Ms Deputy Schulze of the CDU group', and members address each other as prosaically as possible – as 'colleagues' (*Herr Kollege, Frau Kollegin*).

Yet the historical ballast of ideas with which the German idea of representation is burdened has not escaped scholarly attention.[13] In the nineteenth century, German political thought came to situate the political authority to rule not in the institutions of the constitution themselves, but rather in the 'state' as an abstract subject. From this is derived the notion of *Staatsgewalt*, which means rather more than its literal translation as 'state power' would suggest. According to this idea, the 'organs' of the state merely discharge 'competencies' *for* the state. In so doing, they act only as organs of the state, they act in its name. Legally, their actions are considered to be those of the state. But 'organs' that represent the abstract state

[10] A foundational account is still H Hofmann, *Repräsentation: Studien zur Wort und Begriffsgeschichte von der Antike bis ins 19. Jahrhundert* (Berlin, Duncker & Humblot, 1974).

[11] C Schmitt, *The Crisis of Parliamentary Democracy*, trans E Kennedy (Cambridge, MA, MIT Press, 1988).

[12] On the genesis of this idea, see especially G Loewenberg, *Parlamentarismus im politischen System der Bundesrepublik Deutschland* (Tübingen, Wunderlich, 1969) 73–74.

[13] The ground-breaking intellectual history of this ambiguous tradition is C Neumeier, *Kompetenz. Zur Entstehung des deutschen öffentlichen Rechts* (forthcoming, 2021); an excellent reconstruction of the related concepts of state and constitution is M Loughlin, 'In Defence of *Staatslehre*' (2009) 48 *Der Staat* 1, 5–14.

in such a manner cannot simultaneously represent the people: there is a conceptual barrier here to democratic representation. Nearly one hundred years ago, Carl Schmitt's pitiless gaze already perceived that this was the anti-democratic twist in the tale of nineteenth-century constitutional public law.[14]

B. Constitutional Problems of Representation

A glance at recent discussions on constitutional politics or the jurisdiction the Federal Constitutional Court will suffice to demonstrate the continued virulence of the question of parliamentary representation, which remains unsettled in German constitutional law. This can be seen, for instance, in the treatment of the parliamentary right-wing AfD under constitutional and parliamentary law. What positions must its deputies be accorded in the general assembly, in the chair and committees, they too being, after all, elected members of the Bundestag?[15] The more strictly the idea is adhered to that parliament and all its organs ought as faithfully as possible to represent the electorate in its party-political composition, the harder it becomes for the majority to keep members of parties at the margins of the political spectrum out of the presidium of the Bundestag, as well out of such sensitive operational departments as the Parliamentary Oversight Panel in charge of scrutinising the intelligence agencies. By using the concept of representation in its jurisdiction in order to impose on parliament the rules of political processes, the constitutional court has further complicated this situation. This tendency goes back to rulings concerning the composition and processes of the Mediation Committee (Article 77(2) GG). At the time, the court took the principle of democratic representation to demand that parliamentary seats in that committee must be filled strictly proportionately to reflect the strength of the parliamentary parties, and on no account by a majority vote of the governing parties in the Bundestag.[16]

Yet the court itself displayed a fundamental disagreement in its understanding of representation when, in 2007, it was called upon to rule on the private additional income of deputies.[17] The question cut to the very nature of the job. Were they to be considered public officers of a kind, whose sidelines were rightly subject to strict regulation? Or were they rather independent citizens, whose parliamentary office should not restrict an independent citizen's right to have a profitable occupation? A variety of factors came to play in the ensuing debate. One was a blinkered resentment of parliamentarians having any outside earnings at all, usually as members of the liberal professions (lawyers most of all) – only farmers seem to escape this public grudge. Then there was the problem of a parliament that was increasingly made up of party functionaries, civil servants and public-sector employees, for whom financial transparency rules were also a means of safeguarding their social

[14] C Schmitt, *Die Diktatur: Von den Anfängen des modernen Souveränitätsgedankens bis zum proletarischen Klassenkampf* (Munich and Leipzig, Duncker & Humblot, 1921) 138–42. An English translation of Carl Schmitt's first and most important contribution to constitutional law (*On Dictatorship*) is in preparation with Polity Press.

[15] C Schönberger and S Schönberger, 'Die AfD im Bundestag' (2018) 73 *Juristenzeitung* 105.

[16] *Mediation Committee*, 112 *BVerfGE* 118 (2004).

[17] *Additional income of members of the Bundestag*, 118 *BVerfGE* 277 (2007), ECLI:DE:BVerfG:2007:es20070704.2bve000106 (en).

position. Among other considerations were the institutional problem of lobbyism and the shameless manner in which some members took advantage of their position to receive fees for speaking, consulting and similar jobs requiring little actual work. In a rare instance of a four-to-four stalemate, the justices ruled in favour of enhanced transparency requirements, thus paving the way for deputies increasingly coming to resemble duty-bound functionaries.

The concept of representation also has a key role to play in the jurisdiction of so-called 'overhang seats' (*Überhangmandate*). These occur when a party wins more seats by direct election ('first vote') in a particular state than that party could expect to receive on account of its overall share of the vote ('second vote'). Since they would appear to distort the will of the people by preventing parliament from directly reflecting the result of the second vote in its composition, the court finds these seats to be of constitutional concern.[18] Meanwhile, the principle of parliamentary representation has taken on an altogether different meaning in rulings on the limits of European integration, in which it is interpreted as prohibiting the transfer of certain functions of the state to the European level and thereby removing them from parliamentary control.[19] The principle of representation likewise serves the court in striking down the surveillance of members of the Bundestag by the Federal Office for the Protection of the Constitution (*Verfassungsschutz*): to impede parliamentary work was to interfere with the balance of power within parliament and thus with the principle of parliamentary representation itself. On this understanding, representation – suddenly – takes on the meaning of communication.[20] More recently, the court has further amplified the principle that the make-up of parliamentary committees must reflect that of parliament as a whole. At the same time, the principle was clarified and used to limit the transfer of decision-making powers to committees: 'In principle, the German Bundestag exercises its function as a body of representation in its entirety and through the participation of all its Members, not through individual Members, a group of Members or the parliamentary majority.'[21]

It seems unlikely, however, that the constitutional concept of representation that underlies these judgements really can bear quite so much weight. Even the postulate of the 'mirror of the people', the principle of reflectiveness, which the court deduces somewhat abruptly from the principle of democracy, is anything but a postulate of democracy in its development and systematic meaning. It is first and foremost an aspect of making appointments along party lines, the roots of which can be traced back to the institutions of the old *Reich*, and then, more specifically, a consequence of proportional representation. Even in a parliament lacking a democratic executive – as did the pre-1919 Reichstag, in which all parties were to some degree in the minority vis-a-vis the government – the parties' equitable share in the political process was the guiding principle of the parliament's work. But the organisational principle of parliamentary government is not the equitable distribution of posts according to party-political criteria, but rather the distinction between majority and

[18] *Overhang seats*, 131 *BVerfGE* 316 (2012).

[19] *Maastricht Treaty*, 89 *BVerfGE* 155, 182 (1993); more recently *Lisbon Treaty*, 123 *BVerfGE* 267, 359 (2009) ECLI:DE:BVerfG:2009:es20090630.2bve000208 (en).

[20] *Observation of a member of Parliament by intelligence services*, 134 *BVerfGE* 141, 172 (2013) ECLI:DE:BVerfG:2013:rs20130917.2bvr243610 (en).

[21] *European Stabilisation Mechanism*, 130 *BVerfGE* 318 (2012) ECLI:DE:BVerfG:2012:es20120228.2bve000811 (en).

minority, government and opposition. Yet this distinction is absent from the concept of representation assumed by the constitutional court.

The mirror-of-the-people-principle of intra-parliamentary representation as it has developed in the constitutional law of the Federal Republic of Germany reflects the coordination of majority and minority in parliaments at federal and *Länder* level, which, after the concentration of the West German party system in the 1950s, were for many decades essentially concerned with loyal oppositions that did not fundamentally question the system of parliamentary democracy. The more recent polarisation of the German party system, and the polarisation of parliamentary debate that has followed on its heels, confronts parliaments with the question of whether this tradition of a pronounced culture of proportional representation requires careful correction. For the German type of working parliaments with a pronounced committee culture, proportional distribution of parliamentary agenda powers and strong minority rights has developed without strong constitutional impulses in the parliamentary culture in the Federal Republic. Much rather, it was driven by the absence of anti-system parties and significant parliamentary obstruction. A working legislature, however, is much more susceptible to parliamentary tactics of obstruction and can be discredited much more easily by anti-system parties.[22] This is why parliamentary democracies can and must constantly readjust the right balance between the principle of majority rule and the protection of minorities, between the governing majority's agenda control and scrutinising powers of the opposition, between safeguarding stability and ensuring dynamics. For this reason, too, parliaments must be given a broad and constitutionally legitimate scope for institutional self-evolution. This sovereignty of the parliament over its own institutional development is the substantive core of the constitutional autonomy of parliament.[23]

II. The Constitutional Importance of the Electoral System

The German electoral system on the federal level (equally practised in most of the *Länder*) has been described as 'personalised proportional representation'. It is something of a synthesis of principles, of first-past-the-post at constituency level and proportional representation via *Länder*-level lists. These state-level lists in turn bring a third principle, the federal principle of representation, into play. Its advocates praise the system for combining the best elements of all systems. And this German system of personalised proportional representation does indeed have undeniable advantages.

One of the greatest problems of the majority or first-past-the-post voting system as it is practised in the United States consists in gerrymandering, that is, the tendency on the part of state legislatures to draw constituency boundaries in such a manner as to enhance the electoral prospects of one party. If, on the other hand, constituencies won outright are brought into proportion with the overall share of the second or list vote – as in Germany – there

[22] M Koß, *Parliaments in Time. The Evolution of Legislative Democracy in Western Europe, 1866–2015* (Oxford, Oxford University Press, 2018).

[23] F Meinel, *Selbstorganisation des parlamentarischen Regierungssystems. Vergleichende Studien zu einem Verfassungsproblem der Bundesrepublik Deutschland* (Tübingen, Mohr Siebeck, 2019).

is far less scope for gerrymandering. In any case, the issue of constituency boundaries is barely politicised at all in Germany. By law it is entrusted to a commission, nominated by the Federal President, which is made up of the president of the Federal Statistical Office, a judge on the Federal Administrative Court and five other members, who are usually drawn from state interior ministries. Moreover, keeping the selection of constituency candidates at the local level serves to counterbalance, at least in part, the power of the party leadership to place candidates on state lists.

Whether personalised proportional representation really offers the best of all possible worlds is no longer a question that is much discussed, nor does anyone really wonder why the system is not adopted throughout the world.[24] If it is considered a tried-and-tested recipe in German political life, then this is due in large part to the simple fact that all the actors have adapted their tactics accordingly. Moreover, its very complexity contributes to the German electoral system going largely unquestioned. In Germany, the principles of parliamentary representation are a matter for a handful of specialists, a fact due not least to the complexity of calculating the relationship between party lists and overhang seats, which must – according to the constitutional court – in turn be compensated for by 'levelling' or 'adjustment' seats (*Ausgleichsmandate*) to ensure an overall proportionality of party seats. Notwithstanding all parliamentary reform efforts to the contrary, this jurisdiction has led to an inflation of the Bundestag in recent years. In the current 19th parliamentary term, Wolfgang Schäuble in his new capacity as President of the Bundestag has made a valiant attempt to shrink it back to size. This move has largely been frustrated. Under pressure from both opposition parties and the press, the governing coalition has agreed on a minimal reform that leaves all essential parameters as they are for the 2021 election. Later in the future, a reform commission is to consider a more fundamental reform of the electoral law. The more technical these debates over the electoral system became, the less its political consequences were questioned. But the fundamental political problem of this electoral system is no longer whether there should be more of fewer constituencies, let alone optimising its standards of justice within the framework of the existing system. It goes much deeper. Political science refers to the German electoral system as 'mixed-member proportional representation' (MMPR), which aptly describes the heart of the matter, which is that this electoral system produces two kinds of parliamentarians: one elected on a local and personal basis, the other through a party list. In the first case, the concept of representation is personal at least in principle: constituency X has elected Mr Müller. In the latter, it is party-political: Ms Schulze represents not a constituency, but the manifesto of party Y that has received a certain share of the vote.

What are the consequences of this for the system of government? The consequences of the two systems which together form that personalised proportional representation are reasonably well known and diametrically distinct. The first-past-the-post system promotes a two-party system and promises easier formation of governments. Under normal circumstances, it encourages concentration, there being little incentive to form extremist or breakaway parties. It also (at least in theory) corresponds to a relatively low degree of influence of party leaderships over the selection of constituency candidates, and a relatively

[24] For a comparative account, see MS Shugart and M Wattenberg (eds), *Mixed Member Electoral Systems* (Oxford, Oxford University Press, 2001).

high level of individual members' independence with regard to their parliamentary parties. Proportional representation, on the other hand, almost inevitably leads to coalition governments. Yet there is also stronger enforcement of the party line within parliamentary groups, since party leaderships can exert pressure through their control of party lists.

Taken by itself, each of these principles embodies a reasonably consistent theory of parliamentary representation: in the case of the majority voting system, what is represented are territorial units or constituencies which, taken together in parliament, are considered to represent the people as a whole, while proportional representation is based on the idea of representing the nation in its political – that is, its ideological or social – composition. A modern way of putting would be that the spectrum of opinion within the electorate is represented. Dicey made a memorable distinction between the 'representation of persons' and the 'representation of ideas'.[25] But the first-past-the-post system certainly understands itself to represent the nation, but at a regional level and hence somewhat selectively where extreme positions are concerned. Dicey himself, after World War I, thought it absurd that an ideology like anti-Semitism should merit parliamentary representation simply by virtue of having a sufficient number of adherents. After all, parliament was not a 'debating society': '[W]here a body of men such as constitute the House of Commons are at all concerned with government, unity of action is of more consequence than variety of opinions.'[26]

By combining the two approaches, by having both principles work in tandem in the German federal electoral law, the resulting concept of representation comes to appear curiously diffuse in constitutional law. The sweeping rhetoric typical of party leaderships, which would have us believe that a particular policy was supported by so and so many million voters, is only ever half true, at any rate for the Bundestag. The parliamentary parties in the Bundestag more strongly represent those states in which their share of the second vote was disproportionately high, and parties in whose ranks are many directly elected candidates tend to reflect local considerations more strongly than those recruited entirely from party lists. This may be the most fundamental political problem in the current electoral system in Germany: in the current Bundestag, the chancellor's party, of whose 246 deputies 231 were directly elected by their constituencies, has a virtual monopoly of local representation. Smaller parties are virtually excluded from constituency-level representation. Meanwhile, parliamentary parties that benefit from a large number of levelling seats – all parties, that is, other than the CDU/CSU – may in a certain sense be said to exercise representation only in fiction.

It may be objected that such distinctions are irrelevant in parliamentary practice – as indeed they are. On his website Heiko Maas, the current foreign minister, presents himself as 'Member of the Bundestag for Saarlouis and Merzig Wadern (district 297)', though he failed to win that constituency against his fellow minister, Peter Altmaier, in 2017 and entered the Bundestag only as first-placed candidate on the SPD's party list for the Saarland. Yet candidates elected through party lists nonetheless maintain constituency offices and do constituency work – not least with a view to the next election.[27] Conversely, even members

[25] AV Dicey, *Introduction to the Study of the Law of the Constitution*, 8th edn (London, Macmillan, 1923) lxixlxx.

[26] AW Bradley, KD Ewing and C Knight, *Constitutional and Administrative Law*, 16th edn (Harlow, Pearson, 2014) lxix.

[27] This is very vividly described in D Schindler, 'Die Mühen der Ebene: Parteiarbeit der Bundestagsabgeordneten im Wahlkreis' (2013) 44 *Zeitschrift für Parlamentsfragen* 507.

directly elected by their constituencies are first and foremost party politicians. Even deputies who enjoy strong local support, and hence can claim a degree of independence from the party leadership, tend to enjoy the safety net of a place on their party's state list, and are expected to demonstrate the appropriate degree of loyalty. In practice, then, the type of mandate held by a politician tends not to influence parliamentary activity in any meaningful way. For instance, there is no evidence for directly elected candidates being more involved in local issues.[28]

The crucial result of all this is that the mixed German system has barely profited at all from the advantages of the first-past-the-post system. Backbenchers – politicians who hold no government office and hence are able to go against their party's line – are virtually absent from the Bundestag, while doing so much to enliven the Westminster Parliament. Parliamentary party leaders exercise a comparatively high level of control over the legislative initiatives and the voting behaviour of both directly elected and party list candidates.[29] And while there is no pejorative connotation to the English term 'backbencher', there certainly is to its German translation, *Hinterbänkler*, which suggests biddable lobby fodder. Only directly elected members who enjoy strong local support in safe seats – of which there are fewer and fewer – can enjoy the luxury of relative independence. The best-known individuals of this rare species are now retired (Peter Gauweiler, Wolfgang Bosbach, Hans-Christian Ströbele).

The lack of backbenchers in the British sense of the word is of course the effect of certain traits of the German political system, which at every level selects in favour of a type of politician who is loyal to the party line and can hence be expected to act with similar loyalty within the institutions of the state. This is primarily an effect of election by party lists and is a key contributor to that system's success. Yet the institutional structure of the Bundestag as a working legislature tasked primarily with law-making further encourages members' loyalty towards their parties and parliamentary groups. Why is that the case? One reason may once again be the electoral system. Party lists on the *Länder* level yield the sub-organisation of parliamentary groups in powerful regional caucuses. Although these so-called *Landesgruppen* provide for a considerable degree of political diversity within political parties, they tend to remain outwardly invisible. A member of parliament seeking to carve out a position independent of the parliamentary party leadership would be well advised to pursue the path of specialisation rather than voicing divergent opinions. Even within the parliamentary governing parties, only recognised experts on certain policy fields with access to the mass media are hard to whip into line – not least because they may harbour a grudge for having been passed over in the selection of the cabinet minister in their field. The model of the working parliament also offers advantages to members who might not be cabinet material at all. While the rhetorical traditions of the House of Commons favour a confrontational debating style, the Bundestag allows a wider spectrum of temperaments to be heard. Although the Rules of Procedure of the German Bundestag explicitly prescribe the contrary, it is not unusual for entire speeches to be read out, which allows for the participation of members who might find it difficult to speak freely for a quarter of an hour.

[28] P Manow, 'Mixed Rules, Different Roles?' (2013) 19 *Journal of Legislative Studies* 287; P Manow, *Mixed Rules, Mixed Strategies: Candidates and Parties in Germany's Electoral System* (Colchester, ECPR Press, 2015) 178–180.

[29] See eg F Decker, *Regieren im 'Parteienbundesstaat': Zur Architektur der deutschen Politik* (Wiesbaden, VS Verlag, 2010) 66.

And indeed, the highly developed division of labour within this working parliament encourages the development of hierarchies within parliamentary parties, which in turn is strongly conducive to integration and discipline. The rules governing the Bundestag as a whole and its parliamentary parties contain a multitude of offices and functions: as chair or head of a committee, in the party leadership, as parliamentary secretaries, as legal advisers, as heads of party working groups or in the different caucuses such as the party's youth or women's wing. Even in a large parliamentary party, more than a quarter of deputies – which means, in effect, all those with ambitions – can thus be placed in some position or other of responsibility. This may also be one of the reasons why even parties with independent and opinionated *Länder* organisations – notably the Greens – have not divided along regional lines, though the drawing up of *Länder* lists falls within the domain of state party organisations and hence outside the direct influence of the federal parties.

This results in a peculiar simultaneity of functional differentiation and political non-differentiation. While members of parliament tend to specialise, the political elites are not bound to choose between a career at the *Länder* or the federal level, but are able to move between them. Members of a state government thus have an interest in the party loyalty of federal deputies from their state, since they hope to benefit from that loyalty when they themselves occupy federal office.[30]

A. Is there a Democratic Precedence of Proportional Representation?

In Germany, at any rate, commonplace political feeling accords precedence to proportional representation. 'The second vote is the vote for the chancellor!' (*Zweitstimme ist Kanzlerstimme!*) is an axiom that many voters have internalised. The principal consideration here is the representation of parties. Accordingly, the political meaning of the 'first vote' at constituency level is a power of substitution, by which voters may express their preference for their constituency candidate over the list candidates. That leads to a paradox if voters cast their votes for a constituency candidate from a different party to that which they vote for with their second vote.

This interpretation has been spearheaded by no less an authority than the constitutional court itself, which has grown increasingly critical of the moderating effects exercised by the representation of persons over the representation of opinions. From the fact that constituency results are factored into the list vote – and not vice versa – the court has long deduced the precedence of proportional representation in constitutional law. Although it has repeatedly stated that the legislative instance was 'in principle free' to formulate electoral law as it sees fit,[31] its rulings show the exact opposite. For some time, the Federal Constitutional Court has subscribed to the theory of *Erfolgswertgleichheit*, ie the equality of the chance of a vote contributing to success. This principle holds that not only must each vote be counted equally – one would expect no less in a democracy – but also that each vote must contribute equally to, ie have the same impact on, the final result, ensuring that 'each valid vote cast

[30] I owe this argument to Philip Manow.

[31] Most recently *Party lists*, 131 *BVerfGE* 316, 334–35 (2012).

must be entered into the calculation bearing equal weight …, each as it were having an equal part of success'.[32] Only thus could it be ensured that parliament really was an image of the people in miniature. Yet this obviates the legislature's freedom and portrays proportional representation as the better and more constitutional electoral system. For only a system of pure proportional representation with unitary national party lists would offer *Erfolgswertgleichheit* to its fullest degree. Meanwhile, any deviation from this jurisdiction must, as limitations on the democratic principle, be justified by arguments concerning the political system's ability to function.

B. The Political Consequences

The court justifies its jurisdiction in the highest terms possible, namely in those of the principle of democracy enshrined in Article 20(2) GG.[33] But does the precedence of proportional representation really conclusively follow from constitutional law, and what notion of parliamentary representation does it imply? The idea of constituency representation of the first-past-the-post system is, from the outset, no less democratic than that of proportional representation. The idea of representation reflected in the constituencies spread out evenly across the country is more centralist, that of the *Länder* lists rather federal.

Under the aspect of parliamentary government, too, the court's line of argument seems questionable. In contrast to the centrifugal arithmetic of proportional representation, the centripetal forces of the majority voting system stand in close functional relation to the parliamentary system. Overhang seats having produced, in 2002, a governing majority that was slightly larger than perilously close, this might have been appreciated as the underlying cunning of the electoral law: in an age of increasing party fragmentation, it contains safeguards that benefit the larger parties, which win direct seats and which support the government. Should it thus not be seen as an expression of the idea of the parliamentary government to set up the electoral law in such a manner so as to create strong incentives to being a governing party while maintaining the principle of equal opportunity?

One may of course dismiss this argument as an ideology of the structural majority of the conservative CDU[34] in constituency representation or as a post facto rationalisation of an accidental phenomenon: after all, overhang seats are the result purely of contingent effects of constituency boundaries and the discrepancy between first and second votes. But the very design of the compromise between proportional and majority voting systems was guided by the idea of restoring the link between members of parliament and their constituencies by means of local representation.[35] Is that much less democratic than the idea of the proportional representation of parties? Is this aspect of the majority voting system – in a world in which the local is held up for its transparency and closeness to

[32] ibid, ¶ 61.

[33] ibid, ¶ 52: 'The right of citizens equally and freely to determine, by elections and other votes, the composition and policies of the civic power, is an elementary component of the democratic principle. The principle of an equal vote expresses the equality of citizens assumed by the democratic principle.'

[34] On the question of a structural bias and majority representation, see H Döring and P Manow, 'Is Proportional Representation More Favourable to the Left? Electoral Rules and Their Impact on Elections, Parliaments and the Formation of Cabinets' (2017) 47 *British Journal of Political Science* 149.

[35] Loewenberg (n 12) 94–95.

citizens' lives – not rather a significant contribution to bridging the gap between society and professional politics? The electoral system in its present state lacks any convincing justification for local representation.

The Federal Constitutional Court here somewhat surprisingly seems willing to rule in the interest of the party leaderships, which in other areas – eg in party finance – it is prepared to restrict: success at the constituency level is flagged as politically questionable and in need of large-scale correction by constitutional law. This kind of jurisdiction was bound to remain without political consequences as long as parliament was divided into two political camps. But its effects in the 19th *Bundestag*, two decades into the twenty-first century, are very troubling indeed. With each new party that enters the Bundestag and with the corresponding losses of the old popular parties, the number of levelling seats rises sharply. Germany already boasts the world's second-largest parliament – after the Chinese National People's Congress.

C. The Eternal Question of Electoral Reform

What is to be done? Are there alternatives to the system as it stands?[36] The reintroduction of the first-past-the-post system is a matter for frequent debate in Germany, in which elder statesmen, retired presidents of the constitutional court and liberal commentators are wont to praise the supposedly simple process of securing a majority in Britain.[37] But neither is the situation there as simple as all that, nor can it be reproduced in the Federal Republic. The right moment, the *kairos* for introducing a majority voting system, would have been the time of the first grand coalition, which lasted from 1966 to 1969. Today, with 47 per cent of votes in the 2017 Bundestag election having been cast for parties other than CDU/CSU and SPD – while they continue to hold 291 of 298 constituencies – even an attempt to change the system would result in political disaster. The other parties in the Bundestag – the Left (*Die Linke*), AfD, Greens and FDP – could hardly be expected to attach themselves as wings to the two remaining parties at short notice.

In fact, the German electoral system has already realised other aspects of the majority voting system. One of its key differences from the UK system is the fact that the Bundesrat already exists as an instance of regional representation at the federal level. What is more, the centralism of proportional representation is already somewhat modified by the federal structure of the parties and the system of state lists. And not least within the Bundestag itself there is a strong element of local representation, embodied by the powerful *Länder* caucuses within the parliamentary parties – notwithstanding the fact that they do not hold public meetings, make no formal decisions and hence tend to exercise a rather less visible influence.

[36] Reform options are discussed in J Behnke, F Decker, F Grotz, R Vehrkamp and P Weinmann, *Reform des Bundestagswahlsystems. Bewertungskriterien und Reformoptionen* (Gütersloh, Bertelsmann Stiftung, 2017).

[37] The usual political arguments can be found, for example, in C Schwennicke, 'Deutschland braucht ein Mehrheitswahlrecht', *Cicero Online*, 29 August 2013, www.cicero.de/innenpolitik/plaedoyerdeutschland-brauchteinmehrheitswahlrecht/55576. Detailed references to the constitutional discussion are provided by H Pünder, 'Wahlrecht und Parlamentsrecht als Gelingensbedingungen repräsentativer Demokratie' (2013) 72 *Veröffentlichungen der Vereinigung der Deutschen Staatsrechtslehrer* 213.

Nor is the opposite extreme – a purely list-based electoral system founded on party representation alone – a plausible strategy for reform. The proportional system will in any case never be 'pure' as long as the 5 per cent threshold makes its indispensable contribution to safeguarding viable majorities.[38] The principal consequence of proportional representation – the strengthening of party leaderships both inside of parliament and out – is already highly developed in Germany. In the local autonomy of constituency associations in selecting candidates there is still at least a counterweight to the power of party leaderships.

III. The Tasks of Political Theory

Although there may at present be little chance of renewing the principles of parliamentary representation through reform of the Bundestag electoral law, the question remains: is there a different theoretical way of imagining parliamentary representation in the German political system? Yet as soon as that question is asked, it comes up against that peculiar effect of the German electoral system, which seems to evade any consistent idea of popular representation. Accordingly, the attempts of modern political theory to give new life to the concept of representation find no tangible object in the German parliamentary system. This is a problem not least because the two principles on which the German electoral system is based grew from historical circumstances that can no longer be treated as self-evident.

Historically, the first-past-the-post system is the older principle of representation, that most closely identified with the bourgeois notion of representation. In its ideal-typical form, it constitutes an assembly of free and equal members that is imagined as depicting the equality of bourgeois society. And since Emmanuel Sieyès, the great constitutional theorist of the French Revolution, this idea of representation has been founded not least on the idea of the division of labour: by institutionalising professional politics, bourgeois society relieves its citizens of the burden of constant political activity in a polis that has grown too complex. The idea that party preferences should be reflected, on the other hand, is a product of the development of modern democracy, of the extension of the franchise and the lifting of property qualifications around the turn from the nineteenth to the twentieth century. It follows a fundamentally different idea of representation and is based on the idea that various groups among the population – classes, social groups or milieus, religious denominations, ideologies, etc.) should be represented by organisations.

To put it briefly: the idea of representation at the heart of the majority voting system is based on civic equality and the division of labour, that of proportional representation on the political articulation of group interests in 'organised modernity'. There is no road back to either model in its pure form. Not to the bourgeois idea of first-past-the-post, because this kind of parliamentarianism, with the free member as its principal figure, is not conducive to forming the governing parties able to impose discipline on their members that are essential to the parliamentary system of government. Even in Great Britain, the parties naturally exercise control over the selection of candidates in constituencies. We are now also well aware that the representation of persons was based on exclusion: the representation of minorities

[38] C Schönberger, 'Lob der Fünfprozenthürde', *Verfassungsblog* (27 September 2013) https://verfassungsblog.de/lobfuenfprozenthuerde/.

is the strongest argument in favour of proportional representation. Yet its theoretical plausibility declines along with a society's degree of organisation. As long ago as 1950, Dolf Sternberger, a key figure of postwar political science in West Germany, argued that the basic problem with representative democracy was the latent 'outrage of the non-organised'.[39] This resentment on the part of consumers to membership of social organisations – with churches, trade unions, and other clubs and associations often mentioned in the same breath – has long also affected parties qua organisations. The groups that act as agents of social conflict today are no longer organised in political parties as they would once have been.

This is not to say – contrary to a widespread conservative critique of modernity – that such conflicts are altogether incapable of representation. There is, however, good historical and sociological evidence for a connection between societies lacking the ability to organise social group interests in a political form and the tendency to develop the Caesarist idea of representation that only the kind of plebeian presidentialism embodied by Donald Trump can satisfy. A society that increasingly comes to think of itself in terms of decline and multiple crises comes to think of social media filter bubbles as its defining organisational form, and a society that thinks cohesion and loyalty can be bought only by welfare state munificence will almost inevitably develop a preference for authoritarian figures. Parliamentary representation will indeed soon come to look like an absurdity under such conditions, as the populists know full well.

How can political representation be organised today? The impression given to society by incessant political communication based on feedback loops and user-generated content is the very opposite of professional politics. What it suggests is rather that the division of labour between government and society has broken down, while the disintegration of social milieus and groups weakens the forces of party formation at an elementary level.

A revived interest in these questions can be found in the international political theory of recent years.[40] In it, the question of political representation in a supranational polity has become as virulent as the problem of non-democratic forms of representation, for instance by NGOs. Above all, however, constitutional theory has grappled with the question of how to represent the increasing heterogeneity of democratic societies. Nobody would any longer call the Federal Republic of Germany – as Helmut Schelsky, a conservative sociologist of the postwar era did – a 'levelled middle-class society' (*nivellierte Mittelstandsgesellschaft*). The representativeness of representation is now a question concerning the visibility of people without degrees, women, families with many children, first-time voters, non-voters, old-age pensioners, immigrants or future generations.[41] The representativeness is no longer the concern of parliamentarianism alone. As early as 1944, the political scientist John Donald Kinsley coined the term 'representative bureaucracy'. It is today self-evident that the representation of women, and increasingly also of immigrants, is a question of the highest political

[39] D Sternberger, 'Berufspolitiker und PolitikerBerufe' (1950) 5 *Die Gegenwart* 9.

[40] A useful summary is M Brito Vieira and D Runciman, *Representation* (New York, Polity, 2008); more recently M Brito Vieira: 'Introduction' in M Brito Vieira (ed), *Reclaiming Representation* (New York, Routledge, 2017) 1; N Urbinati, *Representative Democracy. Principles and Genealogy* (Chicago, University of Chicago Press, 2006); A Rehfeld, *The Concept of Constituency: Political Representation, Democratic Legitimacy and Institutional Design* (Cambridge, Cambridge University Press, 2005).

[41] S Boysen, 'Repräsentation und Repräsentativität. Geschlechterfragen im internationalen Demokratiediskurs' in M SchulerHarms (ed), *Gleichberechtigung und Demokratie* (Baden-Baden, Nomos, 2019) 85.

importance when it comes to forming governments.[42] And when it comes to parliament, the gender balance is now a highly political question. After the French National Assembly had become the first of the major world legislatures to adopt a 'parity law' that provides for equal representation of men and women on party lists, electoral gender equality became a constitutional issue in Germany too.[43] Parity laws were first adopted in two East German *Länder* where representation of women is stronger anyway, but in the case of Thuringia was struck down as unconstitutional by the regional constitutional court. Reforming electoral law on the federal level to create incentives for more women on party lists and constituency ballots will be a major issue in the parliamentary term.

All these debates cast the principle of mirror-image representation by party, which German constitutional jurisdiction may by now be said to fetishise, in a strangely provincial light – not least because it casts a polite veil over the quality of the representatives themselves. It used to be taken for granted that the right people would rise to the top within the parties. Indeed, at the beginnings of the modern theory of representation, among the American founding fathers, the mirror-image idea of representation stood for the selection of the best.[44] As the American political scientist Hanna F. Pitkin once remarked, few people truly believe the best legislators to be typical and average in every possible respect, 'including intelligence, public spiritedness, and experience'.[45] Meanwhile, critics such as Peter Sloterdijk loudly decry the 'oligocratic structures' of a political class performing 'the monologue of a club of autists' only, in the same breath, to inveigh against 'mobocracy', ie the low intellectual level of politics as represented in the media.[46]

Aside from discussions over quotas for women, in which the Bundestag engaged in a manner both dour and truculent, none of this has yet really registered in Germany. The only attempt to develop a political concept of parliamentary representation on the foundations of the Basic Law was made by the jurist Gerhard Leibholz, who had returned to Germany after the World War II from exile in Great Britain. He found the institutional dualism of personal and party-state modes of representation to be resolvable only in favour of party and proportional representation, with all the constitutional consequences: the de facto absorption of the parties into the state, the legal incorporation of parliamentary parties into their party organisations, and the end of the free mandate.[47] A great deal might of course be said against all this. But academic public law in Germany has been content simply to denounce Leibholz's so-called 'party state doctrine' as an unconstitutional assault in the free mandate or otherwise to ridicule it, by means of superficial arguments, as a theory of party rule. What it failed to see was that Leibholz was the only scholar even to draw attention to the Bundestag's lack of an institutionally acceptable idea of representation.

[42] M Linden, *Einschluss und Ausschluss durch Repräsentation: Theorie und Empirie am Beispiel der deutschen Integrationspolitik* (Baden-Baden, Nomos, 2014).

[43] A series of relevant contributions has been published as a special issue of *Verfassungsblog* on 'Gender Equality in Parliaments', https://verfassungsblog.de/category/debates/gender-parity-in-parliaments-debates/.

[44] J Adams, 'Thoughts on Government' [1776] in CS Hyneman and DS Lutz (eds), *American Political Writing During the Founding Era*, vol 1 (Indianapolis, Liberty Fund, 1983) 401.

[45] Pitkin (n 7) 76.

[46] P Sloterdijk, 'Von pseudonymer Politik' in FW Graf and H Meier (eds), *Die Zukunft der Demokratie* (Munich, CH Beck, 2018) 171; the phrase '*Monolog eines Autistenclubs*' is to be found elsewhere, in P Sloterdijk, 'Der verletzte Stolz', *Der Spiegel* 45/2010.

[47] G Leibholz, *Das Wesen der Repräsentation und der Gestaltwandel der Demokratie im 20. Jahrhundert* (Berlin, DeGruyter, 1966).

From the vantage point of constitutional law, this is as hard to implement as calls for women's quotas. As long as there are geographically defined constituencies, it will hardly be possible to prescribe their selection of candidates – less still whom they elect. This means that any question of quotas is off the table as far as the party with the largest share of the second vote is concerned – and hence, for reasons of fairness, also for all other parties. Of course, it would be possible to imagine constituencies defined in different terms – by ethnic, social or other identity – though it is hard to imagine such an idea not deepening already existing rifts in society, not to mention the matter of multiple identities. A more consistent idea would be of an American political scientist, Andrew Rehfeld, who proposes the creation of 'random constituencies', each consisting of a random sample of voters.[48] This proposal, which takes to an intellectual extreme the abstract and indeed artificial aspect of any modern (ie supported by a highly complex society) notion of a constitutional relationship of representation, also reveals the dilemma of what Carl Schmitt called the 'intellectual-historical state': the transition from the nineteenth-century liberal idea of parliamentarianism based on free constituency representation to the mass-democratic model of organised group representation could be accomplished only once. It cannot be repeated for the representation of contemporary societies, whose political organisation is no longer party-based, without placing representatives under some sort of legal obligation to their constituencies. This would mean the end of the free mandate and with it of the constitutional principle of parliamentarianism. In this respect, parliament is an institution of civic liberalism in a post-liberal age.

[48] Rehfeld (n 40) 209.

5

The Crisis of the Mediating Institutions

I. The Abiding Peculiarity of Parliamentary Government in the Federal Republic

German discussions about constitutional developments all too often confuse genealogy with pathogenesis. The Weimar constitution had to succumb to its structural flaws. Failure to build a political union in the 1950s inexorably led to today's crisis of the European project. Conversely, it was by remedying the flaws of the Weimar constitution that the Basic Law succeeded in securing the future of the Bonn Republic. But things are seldom as straightforward as that. The connection between the emergence of a constitution and its subsequent development tends rather to be indirect and far more subtle. And yet, with the previous considerations in mind, certain peculiarities in the constitutional setup of the Federal Republic of Germany's political and constitutional system can be identified: the government's dependence on parliament was established retroactively against a government that was already fully formed and organisationally shielded from parliament. A political idea of representation – one, that is, that refers to the system of government – was unable to emerge under the electoral law of the Federal Republic. Like no other, the German constitutional system is distinguished by the insufficient degree to which parliament and government are linked by the constitution. The basic question of how the system of government can be organised to ensure the institutional realisation of the government's responsibility to parliament on the one hand, and the parliamentary majority's self-awareness as supporting the government's political agenda on the other has *not* been solved in *constitutional law*. For a state that is so concerned to understand itself primarily in terms of its constitution, there is something of an irony in this.

The cross-bracing, as it were, that keeps the structure standing has evolved at the sub-constitutional level in the mediating institutions that the constitution did not envisage, or at least not in the functions that they have assumed: the popular parties, the Federal Constitutional Court and the Federal Chancellery. For this reason, however, the parliamentary system of government that thus came into being has remained but one aspect of the constitutional order. It embodies only one potentiality of a German system of government that in many of its aspects has preserved traits of the order from which it emerged – an order in which parliament, by virtue of its diligently fulfilled task of legislating, had an important part to play, yet without being the bearer of a democratically responsible government.

This peculiarity is not only the source of many legal and political misunderstandings. It is also at the heart of the present-day German constitutional problem. The cross-bracing has ceased to function in the accustomed manner. The transmission between parliamentary politics and government action is not running as smoothly as it might. The parliamentary and government institutions have to a certain degree – and perhaps irreversibly so – been left once more to their own devices. Thus, the constitutional system realises its other potentiality and in its constitutional substructure relapses into an earlier state that it was thought to have left behind. Why this should be so has very different reasons for each institution concerned.

II. The Creeping Decline of the Popular Parties as a Constitutional Factor

A. The Limits of Culturalist Explanations

The party systems that emerged in the postwar period are in all Western democracies in a state of deep structural weakness, or in any case are undergoing rapid change. Germany is no exception. Since reunification, the major parties have lost around half their members. Between 1990 and 2015 their recruiting rate, defined as the share of actual party members among those eligible to join, has declined from 3.65 to 1.71.[1] Small spikes in recruitment – notably following the election of Donald Trump as President of the United States – did nothing to stop this long-term trend. Even the last genuine popular party, the Bavarian CSU, has fallen victim to this development, albeit more slowly. The social milieus that supported the parties have eroded, whether based around the churches or the labour movement. Voter loyalty and retention have likewise dwindled as the number of floating voters has increased. In a last-ditch effort to win over these floating voters, parties have increasingly resorted such fundamentally apolitical campaign slogans as 'The new centre' (the SPD in 1998) or 'For a Germany in which we live happily and well' (the CDU in 2017). Opportunities have increased for parties with a relatively poor organisational base and a limited range of issues – most notably the AfD. German party law, however, seems still to stand in the way of a development like that seen in France, where Emmanuel Macron's 'La République en Marche' won an overall majority in the 2017 parliamentary elections, having only months earlier been little more than the hashtag used in its founder's victorious presidential campaign. Donald Trump's rise to power has likewise been narrated as the hostile takeover of a major party in crisis by a successful media campaign. However, the charge brought against the 'establishment', against the 'old' parties, is itself an old hat donned by every hopeful new party until it, too, comes of age. Yet resentment against established parties can still be mobilised profitably enough, as the AfD has recently demonstrated.

It would be too easy, however, simply to interpret the crisis of the popular parties as a sociocultural phenomenon – though it certainly is that too – without also considering its consequences for the constitutional system. The rise of populism itself can be understood only incompletely as a cultural phenomenon. Populism has an economic underpinning too.[2] But the decline of the popular parties also has tangible institutional consequences,

[1] O Niedermayer, 'Parteimitglieder in Deutschland: Version 2017', *Arbeitshefte aus dem OttoStammerZentrum*, no 27 (Berlin, Freie Universität, 2017).

[2] P Manow and A Gattig, 'The Distributional Context of Populist Protest' (2020, unpublished, on file with the author).

since the parties were an essential support of the system of government without that role being recognised in constitutional law. 'The contradiction between the general disdain in which the parties were held and their virtually indisputable necessity for democracies could', as Christoph Möllers has put it, 'be concealed for as long as parties could promise at least a share in power. Their poor reputation in Western democracies today is due not least to nobody believing that promise anymore.'[3]

B. In Praise of Lobbyism, or: The End of West German Corporatism

The institutional causes of this decline are largely familiar: the disdain felt by large portions of the electorate for membership of organisations of any kind deprives the parties of the foundation on which they could claim to be arenas for the negotiation of political compromise. Accordingly, the political relevance of party conference resolutions and the commitment they impose grow ever weaker in parties that are dominated by functionaries. Official opinion polling, conducted by the Federal Press Office, allows the government to develop its approach in line with public attitudes before a serious debate within the party can even occur.

Where the parties' loss of power in the parliamentary sphere in particular is concerned, it is necessary to consider a development that is often ignored or misunderstood in its significance. Parliaments that, like the Bundestag, focus strongly on legislation have a clear advantage when functioning within an interventionist welfare state. Their influence over the detail of economic and social legislation naturally attracts economic and social interest groups. The successful integration of the major lobbying organisations, which was accompanied by an extraordinarily low degree of corruption, is one of the German Bundestag's major institutional achievements. Indeed, these associations might be ranked alongside the parties, chancellery and constitutional court as the fourth mediating institution, but this would leave their relationship with the popular parties unclear.

Alas, it is an ineradicable commonplace in the German understanding of politics to make a scandal of this fact. Carl Schmitt's 'unmasking' of parliamentary government as window-dressing for organised interests has proved enduring in this respect, too, and was perpetuated not only in Jürgen Habermas's celebrated phrase about 'the arcane politics of the interest groups'. Such judgements invariably testify to an inward reservation against parliamentarianism as a form of rule. Anyone hoping to gain power will need allies – that is a truism. Who would make useful allies to members of parliament and their parties if not forces that can be used to put pressure on the government? These forces are the notorious associations or pressure groups. What is more, the relationship between deputies and their parliamentary parties on the one hand, and the lobby on the other, is reciprocal. Anyone lacking good relations with the interest groups relevant to their chosen field of policy will have to depend on the media to find out what is new. If the parties serve the interests organised in associations as mediating institutions, this is enhancing the powers of parliament rather than weakening it. Contrary to a prejudice that permeates even political science, the integration, by means of the parties, of organised interests into the parliamentary system

[3] C Möllers, 'Wir, die Bürger(lichen)' (2017) 71 (818) *Merkur: Deutsche Zeitschrift für europäisches Denken* 7.

is among that system's great achievements in the Federal Republic and indeed a political precondition of its institutional strength.

One thing that powerful organisations accomplish is to enhance the prestige of those whom they approach with their concerns. A well-documented example is the parliamentary CDU's health policy. After the party had lost power in 1969, its members of parliament shook off the direct influence that associations had had in the Adenauer era and instead succeeded in integrating organised interests into its own decision-making processes – that is to say, in mediatising them through parliamentary politics.[4] Something similar, of course, also holds true not just for parliament, but for the government. The joint rules of procedure (*Gemeinsame Geschäftsordnung*) of the federal ministries contain rules for involving interest groups in framing legislation at an early stage. For that reason, too, parliament would be well advised to keep abreast.

These connections become amply clear when it comes to former relations between the Catholic Church and the parliamentary CDU/CSU, or between the trade unions and the SPD. The SPD's parliamentary weakness is a consequence not least of the dramatic decline of trade unionism. In 2009 the German Trade Union Confederation (Deutscher Gewerkschaftsbund, DGB) for the first time did not endorse the Social Democrats in a Bundestag election. Beginning in the 1990s, the ties between the parliamentary SPD and social policy interest groups have loosened, a trend that can be explained in terms of increasing conflicts of interest within the associations.[5]

But other interest groups and parties have much the same issues to contend with. A glance at the lobby registry – which its rules of procedure oblige the Bundestag to make publicly available – will suffice to correct the impression that it is dominated by sinister corporate interests.[6] The great industry bodies are, of course, present, but the number of organisations is nearly 7,000, and they are concerned with every possible policy area and from every imaginable angle. Of course, these associations are not all equally powerful or well organised, but in that respect they barely differ from other forms of social power.

What is really of concern should thus not be the attempt to bring power to bear at the sub-parliamentary level. It would rather be genuinely worrying if associations were to begin losing interest in the parties active in parliament. The problem of the Weimar-era Reichstag was not that interest groups were too strong, but that their connection to parliament was too weak. The desolation of the German *Landtage*, or state parliaments, illustrates just how weak parliamentarianism is in the absence of lobbies. What is critical about the current situation is how specialised the representation of interests had become compared to an age when a handful of organisations – trade unions, industry associations, churches, welfare bodies – between them largely covered the field of social interests. Their articulation was in turn the result of compromise and hence compatible with the politics of parliamentary parties. There can be no doubt that the osmotic relationship between corporatism and the party state, as it obtained in the old Federal Republic, was a stabilising factor in parliamentary government that is lacking today.

[4] P Manow and M Döhler, *Strukturbildung von Politikfeldern: Das Beispiel bundesdeutscher Gesundheitspolitik seit den fünfziger Jahren* (Wiesbaden, VS Verlag, 1997) 49.

[5] C Trampusch 'From Interest Groups to Parties: The Change in the Career Patterns of the Legislative Elite in German Social Policy' (2005) 14 *German Politics* 14.

[6] Annex 2 to the Rules of Procedure of the German Bundestag. The list is kept up to date on www.bundestag.de/parlament/lobbyliste.

Among the reasons for the organisations' differentiation of lobbying are the corresponding processes of social differentiation on the one hand, and tendencies to address matters at the European or international levels on the other. After all, if all the Bundestag has to do is to implement European legislation, there is little point in trying to persuade it. Even where this is not the case, the particularisation of interest groups is highly unequal in its effects when confronted with the specialised bureaucracies of the government ministries on the one hand and the parliamentary parties on the other. For instance, it seems plausible to imagine that the department in the Federal Ministry of the Environment responsible for packaging regulation might be able to exchange information effectively with the seven interest groups registered in this field of packaging alone. The members of parliament who take an interest in environmental policy, and thus also have to deal with such matters as sewage, fracking, wind energy and conservation, will find such communication impossible to maintain.

The same also holds true for the cross-beams connecting interest groups and political parties at the extra-parliamentary level. A popular party may maintain sub-organisations of employers or the self-employed, of Christians or senior citizens, which reflect broader currents within the party and can express their views to the party leaders. But a deeper level of differentiation comes at the risk of irrelevance. Nor have parties so far formed ethnically defined sub-groups.

C. There are No Small Parties Any More

The institutional weakness of the popular parties in the political system is also demonstrated by the fact that even the formerly so-called small parties are forced to reconsider their strategies. Consider, for instance, the liberal democrats: as the representative of a particular socioeconomic group – broadly, small businesses and the liberal professions – the FDP acted as a stabilising factor within the political system by preventing its larger coalition partner from veering too far to the left or right. Its voters appreciated this, and by campaigning largely for the second vote, it stabilised the parliamentary dualism of the two major camps. Since the late 1990s, however, under the leadership first of Guido Westerwelle, then of Christian Lindner, the FDP has sought to reinvent itself in the image of protest party for the post-political *jeunesse dorée*, and its political tactics have accordingly shifted away from parliament to unconventional form of media campaigns. It was a profoundly transformed FDP that caused some of the crises of the second Merkel government (2009–13) through rude behaviour and failed internal coordination. It later was the present party leader, Christian Lindner, who coined one of the most fatal phrases in recent years after coalition talks with CDU and Greens broke down in late 2017: 'Better not to govern at all than to govern wrongly' ('*Besser nicht regieren als falsch regieren*').

The Greens, meanwhile, having sloughed off the separation between parliamentary and party office as the last reminder of their early, anti-parliamentary stage, had a distinct parliamentary orientation especially in the decade of potential or actual cooperation with the Social Democrats (1994–2005). Since that time, their participation in a large number of state governments has given them, via the Bundesrat, a strong federal power base which they have been able to leverage, for instance during the refugee crisis in negotiations over the safe third-country rule or in nominating constitutional court justices. It is hardly overstated to say that the Greens have succeeded in adapting to their ends the opportunities for influence that the German Bundesrat system offers a typical conservative party: a party, that is to say, with a strong social base throughout the bureaucracy and a high proportion of university graduates among its members. Today, the Greens are – besides the AfD – the only party with a consistent programme and a voter base to support it. There is no predicting whether that state of affairs would endure renewed participation in a federal government which is widely expected to happen in 2021.

D. At the Borders of Government and Opposition

Together with the pluralisation of the party system, the growing inability of the popular parties to build government policy through parliamentary politics has also contributed to altering the rationale of the parliamentary opposition. As we have seen, the idea of the opposition as a government in waiting, familiar from the Westminster model of parliamentarianism, never corresponds to the reality of proportional representation, since politically divided opposition parties may be more hostile to each other than towards the government.[7] This is particularly true for the Bundestag. The German parliament has never maintained such a stark division between minority and majority; the opposition is always involved in some form of cooperative parliamentary co-government – by heading committees and sitting on controlling bodies, but especial at an informal level, in negotiations on legislation that involve the Bundesrat. But it ranks among the achievements of the constitutional system that the opposition has at times nonetheless been able to establish itself as a competitor to the government. This was true not only for the Social Democrats from Kurt Schumacher to the first grand coalition. On taking over the party leadership in 1973, Helmut Kohl turned the CDU into a strong parliamentary force directed against the government,[8] and when he became chancellor was himself faced with vigorous parliamentary opposition, culminating in the blockading policy that crippled his last term in office (1994–98). Under Wolfgang Schäuble, Friedrich Merz and Angela Merkel the parliamentary CDU/CSU acted no differently during the years of the red–green coalition.

All that has changed since 2005. In view of increasing polarisation at the fringes, the established parties seem to be huddling together. As the number of parties represented in the Bundestag has increased, so has the need for coordination and compromise to prevent the increased veto opportunities from being exploited. A key appointment like that of the president of the constitutional court, requiring as it did two-thirds majorities in both the Bundestag and the Bundesrat, in November 2018 took not just the agreement of the coalition partners, but also the involvement of the Greens and the FDP. The complex decision-making process that resulted lasted for nearly a year.

For this reason, the policy of the parliamentary Social Democrats cannot simply be explained by their willingness to put country before party, though it is remarkable how willingly it offered its weight to the chancellor during the most recent coalition of CDU/CSU and FDP between 2009 and 2013. Also to be considered is the near-permanent

[7] A Sajó and R Uitz, *The Constitution of Freedom. An Introduction to Legal Constitutionalism* (Oxford, Oxford University Press, 2017) 247–48.

[8] Assessments of this achievement vary; see H-P Schwarz, *Helmut Kohl: Eine politische Biographie* (Munich, DVA, 2012) 166; P Bahners, *Helmut Kohl: Der Charakter der Macht* (Munich, CH Beck, 2017) 51.

crisis of the European Union, which creates pressure to have in reserve, at all times, the majority required for constitutional change, since Article 23(1) GG provides that changes to the EU treaties and comparable regulations shall be subject to the rules of constitutional amendments. This pressure imposed by the need to react to unforeseen crises structurally prevents the formation of a consistent parliamentary opposition. It is, therefore, far from certain that the SPD, had the Federal President not forced it to join the government by invoking the spectre of a crisis of state in 2018, would really have had an opportunity for political renewal in opposition.

E. Forming Governments I: Why do Coalition Talks Take Longer and Longer?

Meanwhile, coalition talks keep taking longer and getting more complicated. After the election of 2017, half a year elapsed before a new government under the old chancellor was formed.[9] The blame, as a rule, goes to parties and their calculations over, indeed obsession with, power. In truth, the exact opposite is likely to be the case: longer and longer coalition talks are probably another symptom of the increasing difficulty of translating party policy into government policy through the parliamentary governing parties. In the early years of the Federal Republic, written coalition deals were the exception, and a joint working programme was expressed in the government's policy statement (the equivalent of a Queen's Speech), which was of course carefully worded and agreed on by the coalition partners. Written coalition treaties became the norm later on, though even that on which Helmuth Kohl's first government was based was only eight pages long, and 1987 saw a return to individual agreements without a formal treaty.[10] The coalition treaty of the current ruling grand coalition, which was agreed upon in 2018, is 175 pages long – and more narrowly spaced than Kohl's eight. It sets out in great detail the policy objectives, programmes and intentions for four years of government work in virtually all policy areas.

There may be many reasons for this increasing tendency to set as much as possible in a public document,[11] but what is certain is that they do not bespeak a decline of 'trust' and the concomitant need to have everything in black and white. It is well known that chancellor Kurt Georg Kiesinger did not trust his Social Democratic deputy, Willy Brandt, very far at all. Nor can it really express a belief in the possibility of setting out four years of government work in full detail. During the coalition talks of 2013, for instance, many key participants were sure that the coming parliamentary term would be dominated by energy policy and ecological transformation. Accordingly, Sigmar Gabriel, the head of the SPD at the time, who could have demanded virtually any department for himself, chose economic affairs and energy – a mistake, as events were to show. Halfway through the government's term, the

[9] On the negotiations of 2017 and 2018, see S T Siefken, 'Regierungsbildung nach der Bundestagswahl 2017' (2018) 49 *Zeitschrift für Parlamentsfragen* 407.

[10] An archive of the coalition agreements under CDU governments is available at www.kas.de/de/web/geschichte-der-cdu/koalitionsvertraege, those under SPD-led governments at www.fes.de/bibliothek/koalitionsvereinbarungen-der-spd-auf-bundesebene.

[11] For the full text of the 2018 coalition agreement, see www.cdu.de/system/tdf/media/dokumente/koalitionsvertrag_2018.pdf?file=1. An English abstract is available at www.kas.de/c/document_library/get_file?uuid=bd41f012-1a71-9129-8170-8189a1d06757&groupId=284153.

refugee crisis came to dominate public debate. Long-distance cables over- or underground? Offshore wind farms or co-generation plants? Nobody cared any more.

Why, then, do coalition talks require so much time today? Part of the answer may lie in the simple fact that the parties – including representatives of their state organisations – are far more closely involved in negotiating coalition agreements than they are in the work of government. After all, coalition treaties are signed by the party chairmen while the government has to be supported by the work of their parliamentary leaders. The parliamentary parties nonetheless play an important de facto role in forming a government, since there is often overlap between the party leadership inside and outside of parliament or, at any rate, close coordination between the two levels. This is what allows even policies that find scant support among members of parliament – like the motorway toll for foreign vehicles, which has brought Germany virtually nothing but a lot of noise – can nonetheless be enshrined in a coalition agreement.

What is more, coalition agreements usually require the approval of party conferences. The influence exercised by parties over coalition agreements would thus seem to be a form of exerting control over the contents of the government's working programme by parties that have lost confidence in their own internal processes of opinion formation. The fact that the SPD has now made a permanent feature of direct votes by party members – previously a means of last resort – and hopes by this quasi-plebiscitary process to give the impression of democratic process within the party, testifies to an even higher degree of disillusionment.

This, however, weakens the position of the parliamentary parties. During coalition talks, the public is told what it wants to hear, namely that the guiding concern is issues, not the allocation of offices. One would do well not to believe this – or even to wish it were so, unless one had a particularly low opinion of parliament. For of course the claim of leading parliamentary politicians to important government posts is, from the parliamentary perspective, what forming a government is all about. Successfully staking their claims secures the influence and prestige of parliamentary parties even while the government is still being formed. To the extent that parties form the impression that their parliamentary representatives were trying to evade their political influence or, conversely, that parliamentary parties find their organisations reluctant to commit to supporting a government, the parliamentary party's claim to fill cabinet posts is in jeopardy. It might then occur to a chancellor instead to give so-called 'experts' or other career changers a chance, disregarding the ambitions of parliamentarians. Such ministers are invariably dependent entirely on the good will of the chancellery.

F. Forming Governments II: Intervals of the Political System

In terms of constitutional law, it is not the negotiations that matter, but what they delay. A new Bundestag convenes no later than 30 days after the election. This event brings the term of office of the chancellor and all her ministers to an end, as prescribed by Article 69(2) GG. At the same moment, a diffuse constitutional situation occurs. On the morning of that very day, before the constituent meeting of the Bundestag, a messenger delivers to the chancellor's office a letter from the Federal President, in which the chancellor is asked to 'continue to manage the affairs of his office until a successor is appointed' as the constitution allows (Article 69(3) GG). The purpose of this exercise is to avoid a hiatus without an acting chancellor. On the afternoon of that day, following the constituent meeting of the Bundestag, there follows a brief ceremony, open to the press, in which the members of the federal government are officially relieved of their duties.

This seemingly sober bureaucratic procedure in fact fundamentally alters the constitutional situation. From this moment on, constitutionally speaking, the government no longer depends on parliament and on the confidence of the parliamentary majority, but solely on the head of state's request to remain in office as the acting government. As such, it is subject to parliamentary control within the framework of the existing institutions; it is accountable and answerable to the Bundestag and thus 'responsible' in a non-political sense. In the absence of the confidence of a parliamentary majority, however, it is not *responsible to parliament* in the true constitutional sense of the term. From this point on, as the example of the long-drawn-out change of government (from the FDP to the SPD as the CDU's coalition partner) in 2013 shows, the government no longer needs to gather a parliamentary majority behind it. The acting government has all the powers of a government – which, constitutionally speaking, it is – but it is not a *parliamentary* government. To be exact, this is a 'presidential cabinet'. Historical reasons prevent the term, which was coined for a series of governments, including Hitler's, in the late days of the Weimar Republic, from ever being uttered in Germany, but it accurately describes the constitutional situation.

The president is under no constitutional obligation to ask the incumbent to continue in her duties; he may also choose not to do so if he does not trust her or wishes to exert pressure on parliament to form a majority. The acting government, in short, is in office only by the decision of the head of state. If coalition talks are concluded by the time the newly elected Bundestag convenes, this is not a problem, because the acting government will be in office for only a matter of days. If, however, nearly half a year passes between elections to the Bundestag and the Bundestag's election of the chancellor – as was the case from September 2017 to March 2018 – this represents a significant interval in which there is no parliamentary government.

Although both variants are permissible under Article 69(3) GG, the established practice in such cases is for the president not to ask the individual ministers to continue in their duties, but rather to limit this request to the chancellor, who in her turn makes the request of her ministers. If the chancellor wishes to dismiss a minister who is merely acting in that capacity – as was almost the case with Christian Schmidt, minister of food and agriculture, in 2017, who took half the government by surprise when he arbitrarily voted in Brussels to extend the authorisation of a controversial pesticide – she needs merely to withdraw her request to the minister to remain in office. Yet the constitution only allows ministers to *remain* in office as acting ministers, but not for '*new*' acting ministers to be nominated. This is bound to cause difficulties when several ministers move out of the cabinet for political reasons. In 2017 the finance minister, Wolfgang Schäuble, became president of the Bundestag; the minister of labour and social affairs, Andrea Nahles, became the parliamentary leader of the SPD; and the minister of transport, Alexander Dobrindt, became the leader of the CSU caucus. Yet Article 69(3) GG prohibits these ministers from being replaced. The government rules of procedure here come into play, according to which a cabinet colleague is to take over the running of the vacant ministry.

Depending on the ministry concerned, this can have far-reaching consequences: while Europe was debating the Emmanuel Macron's proposals for 're-founding' Europe, the German ministry of finance was headed by a caretaker, Peter Altmaier, the chancellery minister – in other words, it was politically out of action, even though the francophile Altmaier did more to ensure that the talks at the working level progressed than anyone else in his position probably would have done. The fact that there was nevertheless no German response to Macron during this period is also due to the political constellation of the coalition talks: the partners Merkel courted, the FDP and the Greens, held exactly opposite views on the French president's economic ideas. Since the Chancellor was only 'acting' at the time, she had no political mandate to take the lead on the issue.

The osmotic connection between parliament and government in the German system of government is seldom demonstrated quite so impressively as it was during this transitional period. Since the remit of the committees depends on the exact definition of the individual portfolios, the Bundestag puts the formation of select committees on hold until the government has been formed. Draft legislation cannot be debated during this time, for the government does not propose any. Yet the Bundestag has been forced to recognise that the committees have an important role to play as controlling instances in this interval. In 2013, a single committee of leading parliamentarians of parties was considered sufficient to deal with the most urgent business. An attempt to repeat this in 2017–18 was stopped by the opposition, which insisted on the specialist committees being reinstated according to the portfolios as they had been defined in the previous Bundestag and hence also to those of the acting government. The consequence of this procedure, however, is something of an optical illusion: the analogy between the ministries and the committees is normally an expression of the ministers' parliamentary responsibility, which is expressed through the controlling function of the committees. If the committees reform under a merely acting government, they suggest normality whereas, in fact, the principle of parliamentary responsibility has been suspended.

G. Forming Governments III: The Latency of the Presidential Factor

The increasingly complicated task of forming a government means that other aspects of constitutional practice that seemed to have been settled are once more called fundamentally into question. This holds true even of the position of the Federal President in the parliamentary system. A consensus had been reached that the parties' practice of contesting federal elections with a candidate for chancellor rendered obsolete the Federal President's principal constitutional right, which is to nominate a chancellor for election by the Bundestag (Article 63(1) GG). The same applies as for the choice of the British prime minister by the monarch: although the form has been maintained, the candidate to be nominated is de facto chosen by parties and voters. This has allowed the conviction to take hold that the president performed something of a purely civic functioned, endowed with moral authority but otherwise powerless.

Whereas this might once have been taken for granted, it has been made doubtful by the loss of power experienced by the parties. This development is confirmed by the key political role performed by President Steinmeier in the restoration of the grand coalition in 2018. After Merkel's attempt to build a coalition of her CDU with the free-market-liberal FDP and the Greens had collapsed for reasons nobody even remembers today, President Steinmeier very early and decidedly refused to countenance the calling of a new election. In cases where the Bundestag fails to elect a chancellor with an absolute majority, this is what the constitution allows for.[12] Without the significant pressure he then put on his SPD, it is highly unlikely that a new grand coalition government would have been formed, since the SPD had demonstratively reiterated the decisions of its own governing bodies to find a new role in opposition just before. These events for the first time have suggested the abstract possibility of a presidential government stepping into the breach.

What if a president, with parliament neither willing nor able to govern, simply insisted on the continuation of coalition talks, meanwhile refusing to nominate a candidate for election as chancellor by the Bundestag according to Article 63 GG? To proceed in such a manner would suit not least the institutional interests of an acting chancellor who wished to remain in power and who would then be free to draw out coalition talks at will, leaving parliament condemned to passivity. Yet in a situation of crisis, the question might become virulent in an altogether different manner: what if a president disloyal to a new parliamentary majority refused to nominate the *Spitzenkandidat* of the strongest parliamentary party for election by the Bundestag? It is far from clear how the roles would be assigned in such an eventuality. Let us consider the hypothetical situation of a Social Democratic president after the electoral victory of the AfD – an AfD, moreover, that has kept moving further to the right. What if he were to ask the previous government to remain in office as the acting government, agreed upon certain policy guidelines with this acting government, and otherwise did nothing? Would political responsibility fall to the constitutional court, at the request of the AfD, by means of *Organstreit* proceedings to force the president to make a nomination or to impeach him according to Article 61 GG?

For it is only by the president making his nomination that the complicated constitutional process of forming a government is triggered. If he fails to do so, an unprotected flank of the Basic Law is exposed. The constitutionally decisive question here is whether the Bundestag is then empowered – as would befit the leading position of parliament in a parliamentary system of government – to take the initiative and elect a new chancellor according to Article 67(1) GG. It is worth recalling its provisions:

> The Bundestag may express its lack of confidence in the Federal Chancellor only by electing a successor by the vote of a majority of its Members and requesting the Federal President to dismiss the Federal Chancellor. The Federal President must comply with the request and appoint the person elected.

The scholarly commentaries on the Basic Law deny this possibility. Their reasoning is correct as far as it goes: they argue that since the acting government, following the election, had never enjoyed the confidence of parliament, parliament was also in no position to withdraw its confidence. The instrument of the vote of no confidence simply did not apply in such a situation. The chancellor, too, was thus barred from calling for a vote of no confidence as provided for by Article 68 GG.

Yet this argument is questionable not only politically, but also from a systematic perspective. The phrase 'only by' in Article 67 GG was clearly chosen with Article 54 of the Weimar Constitution in mind and intended to preclude a 'simple' vote of no confidence. That aside, it contains only the most basic constitutional feature of a parliamentary democracy, notably that parliament is entitled to replace one government with another. Accordingly, the notion

[12] Art 63(4)(3) GG: 'If the person elected does not receive such a majority, then within seven days the Federal President shall either appoint him or dissolve the Bundestag.'

of confidence does not really have an autonomous meaning in Article 67 GG. The better arguments instead favour the possibility of the Bundestag electing a chancellor of its own accord if the president fails to adhere to the sequence, as laid down in Article 63 GG, of nominating a chancellor after the elections to the Bundestag. In the comparable situation of a government not enjoying parliamentary confidence the Bundestag is likewise entitled to elect a new chancellor without the federal president having first to nominate a candidate (Article 68(1)(2) GG).

However, this interpretation would appear to be contradicted by Article 63(3) and (4) GG. As a rule, it is only when the candidate proposed by the Federal President fails to be elected that the Bundestag may elect another candidate (Article 63(3)) or choose instead to follow the path of a minority government and new elections (Article 63(4)). If the *Bundestag* were permitted to take the initiative in forming a government, for instance by a quarter of its members signing a motion to elect the candidate of the largest parliamentary party as chancellor according to parliamentary rules of procedure, these provisions would be effectively void. This could be justified only if the election had been so recent that Article 63(3) and (4) GG barred the way via Article 67 GG. The thought experiment of this extreme case shows that, in the absence of a clear government alternative dominated by two major parties, it is far from clear whether, in a crisis, the parliamentary system or the reserve powers of the Federal President would retain the upper hand.

III. The Dilemma of the Federal Constitutional Court

The development of the second mediating institution, the Federal Constitutional Court, cannot be narrated as a tale of decline. On the contrary, the court's authority in domestic politics is uncontested, and its popularity is such that other political institutions can only dream of it. Why this should be so has recently been the subject of much fundamental debate. Is it a deep-seated German longing for non-partisan decisions? Or is it faith in the law, another distinctly German trait that is not shared throughout Europe? Or is it the cultural memory of a country formerly riven by religious conflict that has instilled in its people a distrust of the majority principle, the boundaries of which are institutionalised by the constitutional court?[13] The result, in any case, is truly remarkable. Even such eminently political judgments on the court's part as those on the euro bailout or the matter of same-sex marriage are widely accepted as a matter of course. Even the question of the court's loss of importance through European integration,[14] which was debated quite passionately some time ago, now seems to have subsided. While there are judgements such as the one on the European Central Bank (ECB) in May 2020 that led to fierce political controversy, the European Union's permanent crisis seems to be generally bolstering the court's sceptical position.

At a systematic level, it is hard to reconcile parliamentary government and a fully developed constitutional jurisdiction. This point has already been made. After all, the heart of

[13] On these questions, see the contributions in M Jestaedt, O Lepsius, C Möllers and C Schönberger, *The German Federal Constitutional Court. The Court Without Limits* (Oxford, Oxford University Press, 2020).

[14] C Schönberger, 'Karlsruhe: Notes on a Court' in Jestaedt et al (n 13) 28.

the constitution is not an institutional frontier between executive and legislative bodies, but rather the institutional fusion of government and parliamentary governing party, which cannot be thought of in terms of fixed legal competencies. It is no surprise, then, that the institution of the constitutional court should have reached a comparable state of development in the United States, a democracy based on the separation of powers. There, however, the Supreme Court itself is a branch of government, whereas the German constitutional court carefully cultivates the impression of itself as a neutral referee rather than an active participant in the political process.[15] The court's historic achievement was hence to have ensured the anchoring of the government in parliamentary opinion formation without interfering too directly in the political process.[16] This was accomplished by the democratisation of the constitutional reservation of statutory powers, by means of which the court used the growing need for legislation in an industrial welfare state to advance the cause of parliamentary government, later using it to develop a general constitutional theory of the effective democratic legitimation of state actions.

This is no longer the case today, and the function of the constitutional court's jurisdiction in the parliamentary system of government has fundamentally changed. In more and more fields, the court has come into increasing conflict with the governing majority: electoral law, European integration, euro bailouts, parliamentary rights to information, mediation procedures. Politically, too, a chill has entered into communications between the constitutional court on the one hand and the world of politics on the other. Its professional observers often criticise the court's jurisdiction fundamentally while leaving its systematic role unquestioned.[17] More legal protection and more juridical control tend always to be considered desirable in Germany. Perhaps that is why the fundamental change has been overlooked. This change, in simplified terms, has seen the court move in recent years from exercising indirect control over the parliamentary system of government to a far more direct form of control.[18] There are two possible explanations for his.

A. The Temptations of the Grand Coalition

The first explanation is connected to the court's changed role under conditions of a grand coalition, which have obtained – though technically interrupted – since 2005. As such, the conflicts that have arisen between the Karlsruhe court and the political realm are far from new, but rather show the constitutional court in the role that it has grown into over the course of decades and to which it owes a good deal of its authority. It has often been remarked that the constitutional court envisages its role, albeit very cautiously, as a corrective to the governing majority of the day. Its spectacular rulings of the Adenauer era – notably that prohibiting what would in effect have become a government-run television broadcaster – helped sharpen the court's profile as a constitutional institution in its

[15] C Möllers, 'Legality, Legitimacy, and Legitimation' in Jestaedt et al (n 13) 155.

[16] See ch 2 above.

[17] J Collings, *Democracy's Guardians. A History of the German Federal Constitutional Court 1951–2001* (Oxford, Oxford University Press, 2015).

[18] I have discussed the Federal Constitutional Court's more recent stance on the democratic process in more detail in F Meinel, 'Das Bundesverfassungsgericht in der Ära der Großen Koalitionen: Zur Rechtsprechung seit dem Lissabon-Urteil' (2021) 60 *Der Staat*, 37.

own right. If its detractors saw in these rulings a leftward bias, its judgments during the years of the SPD/FDP coalition pointed in the opposite direction: its rulings on abortion, co-determination and universities, or the so-called 'new Ostpolitik' with the GDR tended to reflect opposition concerns. This is inevitable and appropriate for a court that is intended to preserve the constitutional boundaries of majority rule and safeguard the rights, and particularly the basic rights, of social and political minorities.

Yet in addition to this, the constitutional court has often thought of itself as an instance of counter-representation. It seeks to ensure a hearing for interests that would otherwise be unable to find suitable expression within the political system. It seeks, in other words, to remedy so-called deficits of representation. This is evident in a variety of instances dating back to the early 1980s. When the peace movement first held large-scale demonstration against the construction of nuclear power stations, the Greens were not yet represented in the Bundestag. Since all parties represented in the Bundestag at the time were pro-nuclear, the opposition view was not yet able to be expressed within the parliamentary system. The court hence raised the status of the freedom of assembly to an 'indispensable functional element' of parliamentary democracy. As a 'political early warning system', it helped draw attention to undesirable developments, thus ultimately serving to stabilise the political order.[19] By the same token, in its rulings on party finance, the court has interpreted its role as that of a mouthpiece of an interest not represented in professional politics and has been accordingly strict in controlling decisions made by political parties in their own interest.

Such constellations can naturally be expected to increase under a grand coalition, when the constitutional court almost by default is made to assume the role of an externalised opposition against the consensus of the major parties. This is most impressively demonstrated by the court's jurisdiction on the constitutional limits of European integration. In view of the two-thirds majority required in order to make changes to the constitution, the policy of European integration has always been pursued by a tacit grand coalition, leaving the court to step into the breach as a 'substitute opposition' in matters of European policy.[20] From the outset, and particularly since the quantum leap marked by the Maastricht Treaty of 1992, European policy was supported by overwhelming majorities in the German Bundestag. Until the rise of the AfD, no party fundamentally critical of the European project had ever been represented in the Bundestag, with even the Left Party objecting to the manner of integration rather than its basic principles. In order to do justice to this part that had fallen to it, the constitutional court interpreted the franchise guaranteed by Article 38(1)(1) GG in spectacular fashion: as the right of citizens to be protected against any transfers of power to the European Union that threatened to erode this democratic right of participation by compromising the 'substance of the democratic ability to shape policy'.[21] In the bailout and sovereign debt crises, too, the court gave a voice not least to

[19] Å Doering-Manteuffel, B Greiner and O Lepsius, *Der Brokdorf-Beschluss des Bundesverfassungsgerichts 1985: Eine Veröffentlichung aus dem Arbeitskreis für Rechtswissenschaft und Zeitgeschichte an der Akademie der Wissenschaften und der Literatur Mainz* (Tübingen, Mohr Siebeck, 2015).

[20] C Schönberger, 'Die Europäische Union zwischen "Demokratiedefizit" und Bundesstaatsverbot: Anmerkungen zum Lissabon-Urteil des Bundesverfassungsgerichts' (2009) 48 *Der Staat* 557.

[21] *Maastricht Treaty*, 89 *BVerfGE* 155, 171–72 (1993); *Lisbon Treaty*, 123 *BVerfGE* 267, 340–41 (2009), ECLI:DE:BVerfG:2009:es20090630.2bve000208 (en).

those who were not yet able to raise their concerns in the Bundestag. The court hearings received tremendous media attention and served as a substitute arena for a conflict that was not carried out in parliament. Only now were the critics of the bailout policy heard prominently, and only now was the political role of the ECB – notably in the form of its purchasing programme – subjected to the scrutiny of a German constitutional organ. This fact alone will have worked in favour of the democratic acceptance of the decisions reached by parliament and government, though it will have done so rather less where the Bundestag's democratic acceptance is concerned.

There can be no doubt, however, that this kind of jurisdiction entails a latent and self-reinforcing problem: that of supermajorities. The governing majority is institutionally obliged at all times to retain the possibility of constitution-altering majorities, not least to be able to respond to crises in the European Union. And at the same time, the court's jurisdiction has assumed a position against this latent supermajority by taking on a task it has called the review of 'constitutional identity'.[22] In its ruling on the Lisbon Treaty, the constitutional court reserved judgment on whether a change to the European treaties passed with a constitution-altering majority according to Article 23(1)(2) of the Basic Law infringed upon 'the identity of the liberal constitutional order'.[23]

In this manner, the constitutional court has compensated from the outside for an antagonism absent from the parliamentary system in a key question – even against a two-thirds majority in the Bundestag. But even beyond the question of European integration, the court's rulings on electoral law and the constitutional limits of overhang seats can also be understood as articulating a position opposed to the major parties' consensual interest in the preservation of these seats – and hence in their own advantage. Indeed, this is a particularly apt expression of the court's self-conception as an instance setting rules in the political process: the question confronting the court here was just how many overhang mandates were still compatible with the principle – which the constitutional court itself found to be deducible from the constitution – of the equality of the chance of a vote to contribute to success (*Erfolgswertgleichheit*). The surprisingly concrete answer was: fifteen. 'The number of fifteen overhang mandates', argues the court, 'as an act of the judicial specification' (*richterliche Normkonkretisierung*) could not be fully accounted for.

> Yet in the present case it is the task of the Federal Constitutional court to specify the demands made on the system of allocating seats in such a manner as to allow the legislature to frame electoral law on a reliable constitutional basis, thereby minimizing the risk of the Bundestag being dissolved as a result of electoral complaint proceedings.[24]

Particularly intense conflict between parliament and the constitutional court arose over the question of the statutory election threshold in European elections. After the court, in 2012, had initially declared a 5 per cent threshold – as it applies in *Bundestag* elections – to be unconstitutional, the legislature responded by lowering the threshold for entry into the European Parliament to 3 per cent. The constitutional court, however, cashiered this

[22] *Lisbon Treaty*, 123 *BVerfGE* 267, 354 (2009), ECLI:DE:BVerfG:2009:es20090630.2bve000208 (en).

[23] For a comparative critique of the concept and its use by European constitutional courts, see F Fabbrini and A Sajó, 'The Dangers of Constitutional Identity' (2019) 25 *European Law Journal* 457.

[24] *Overhang seats*, 131 *BVerfGE* 316, 370 (2012).

ruling too.[25] In doing so, it paved the way to the European Parliament for German deputies representing the Animal Rights Party (Tierschutzpartei), the satirical 'Die Partei' – and the full-fleshed Nazi party, the National Democrats (NPD).

B. Europe and the Difficulties of Bringing Back in Parliament

The second explanation for the increased claim to direct control made by the Federal Constitutional Court is of a more fundamental nature. It concerns the institutional options for action open to a court which, in order to constitutionally secure the government's anchoring in parliamentary processes of opinion formation, must involve itself far more directly in the institutional questions of the system of government than would previously have been the case. A number of recent decisions on the scope of parliamentary rights to information and control the organisation of committees in the Bundestag, or its involvement in the legislative procedures of the European Union may serve as cases in point. Today, it is no longer enough to make all important political decisions dependent on a parliamentary vote by means of a democratically interpreted reserve of statutory powers (*Gesetzesvorbehalt*).

This is, in the first instance, also linked to many legislative competencies being transferred to the European Union. Whenever the European Council and Parliament pass legislation in the form of guidelines, this legislation must then be implemented in German law within a prescribed period. Although the legislature has some room for interpretation, it remains, inasmuch as European law is unambiguous, bound by it. Yet if the constitutional court's rulings depict this transition principally as a *loss of legislative power*, they give only an incomplete picture. No less important are the indirect consequences for parliament's relationship to the government. The parliamentary system ensures their interdependence by charging parliament with the legislative implementation of the government's political agenda, to which extent parliament must stand in a political relationship to the government. Every decision on proposed government legislation is, as it were, a miniature vote of confidence. This is certainly not the case where the implementation of European legislation is concerned and where the Bundestag is faced with an instance against which it can bring no meaningful sanctions to bear. Within the overall constitutional framework of the European Union, the German government, too, always pursues two legislative agendas simultaneously: one in the Bundestag, and the other in collaboration with the European Commission in the council. It hence also has a second addressee besides the Bundestag.

Not only constitutional lawyers, but also many political practitioners agree that the Bundestag being inundated with implementing legislation is an inevitable development in a multi-level system like that of the European Union. Yet this view is mistaken. European law does not demand that guidelines always be implemented by parliamentary legislation; as a rule, their implementation by a legislative decree issued by the government is sufficient. The Bundestag's close involvement in implementing legislation is rather the outcome of German constitutional law, with Article 80 tying executive regulations to detailed and specific legislative authorisations. The constitutional court's jurisdiction certainly demands that decisions that infringe on basic rights and other key decisions be

[25] *European Parliament election threshold*, 129 *BVerfGE* 300 (2011); 135 *BVerfGE* 259 (2014), ECLI:DE:BVerfG:2014:es20140226.2bve000213 (en).

made only by law.[26] This case law has never been questioned in principle and in political practice only during the corona virus crisis, when the Bundestag amended the Infection Protection Act by an almost unlimited general authorisation allowing the Minister of Health to issue emergency regulations of all sorts.[27] In many of its rulings – that on the European Arrest Warrant of 2005 is particularly well known[28] – the court has required the legislature to exercise greater diligence in fulfilling its duties deriving from the implementation of EU law.

However, it should be borne in mind that Article 80 GG assumes that the government, charged with secondary legislation, is bound by a decision by parliament, rather than both parliament and government being bound by the decision of a third party. Any decision for which the government might be held responsible to parliament remains, within this arrangement, invisible to parliament, having as a rule been made much earlier: by the agreement of the German representative on the EU Council to the passing of the European legislative act. However strong the involvement of the Bundestag in framing the implementing legislation may be, it nonetheless has no influence over the antecedent actions of the ministries and their representatives in the Council. The real problem of how to incorporate European policy into the parliamentary system of government thus remains unresolved.

For that reason, Article 23(3) GG points a different way: the Bundestag is entitled to give 'opinions' on the European legislative process, which the government may then 'take into account' when casting its vote in the Council. Opinions on the effectiveness of this instrument markedly diverge. Moreover, it only serves to move the problem of the Bundestag being overburdened to another level; and the Bundestag, pressed for time as it is, can ill afford to form an opinion on every relevant legislative initiative at the European level. Moreover, the instrument of the 'opinion' structurally uncouples the decision made at the European level from the institution that makes it, namely the federal government. If, in the European Council, it is the governments of the Member States who decide on legislation, it might be more in keeping with the parliamentary system of government if they were also to take a stronger hand in its implementation by legislative decree, for which they would be held responsible by parliament. That this is not in contradiction to the parliamentary system of government can be seen in the British case, where the implementation of European law was to a much higher degree possible by means of delegated legislation. Whether this would be politically viable in Germany, and whether the courts would accept it, is another matter. It should, however, be noted that the constitutional court's broad definition of the statutory provision achieves the opposite of its political aims when it comes to implementing European law: parliament ends up taking on the government's work rather than supervising it.

C. Formalising the Informal: A Juridical Dilemma

We know that Europe cannot be blamed for everything, and hence it can be held only partly responsible for the creeping de-parliamentarisation of the executive body. The constitutional

[26] Details are given by B Remmert in T Maunz and G Dürig (eds), *Grundgesetz* (Munich, CH Beck, 2013) Art 80 ¶ 113.

[27] J Kersten and S Rixen, *Der Verfassungsstaat in der Corona-Krise* (Munich, CH Beck, 2020) 36–42.

[28] *European Arrest Warrant*, 113 *BVerfGE* 273 (2005), ECLI:DE:BVerfG:2005:rs20050718.2bvr223604 (en).

court's method of ensuring parliamentary involvement by means of expanding the scope of legislation can only work where previously autonomous bureaucratic realms are first made subject to legal regulation, thereby falling under the remit of parliamentary politics. Once these fields of governmental and administrative action are placed on a legal foundation, their juridification cannot endlessly be pushed further. Since the 1980s, awareness of the unintended consequences of juridification has grown, and too much rather than too little parliamentary regulation has come to be seen as the political problem. It may stand to reason why parliament should legislate on the penitentiary code, the introduction of sex education at schools or questions associated with the Muslim headscarf. It seems less self-evident, however – to adduce only two random examples from recent jurisdiction – why it should concern itself with a maximum age for candidate for public-sector jobs but not with orthography reform.[29]

Meanwhile, other fields have seen a tendency towards the increased informalisation of executive action that structurally eludes control by means of parliamentary legislation. A case in point is the practice of 'legislation by pact', which first came to constitutional attention under Gerhard Schröder's government. The issue at hand was the gradual phasing out of nuclear energy, and a draft bill had been agreed in advance between the government and the energy companies. This bill was then introduced as a package and its details were closed to scrutiny. An even bolder instance of such informal action could be observed in a celebrated press conference in October 2008, when Angela Merkel and her finance minister, Peer Steinbrück, promised savers that their deposits were safe. In so doing, they hoped to prevent a further worsening of the financial crisis. The constitutional court had already addressed two such instances of informal statements of government policy in 2008. The government had warned the public of cults preying on the young and of traces of toxic substances to be found in certain wines – informal executive actions with potentially far-reaching consequences for those concerned. The court here seemed suddenly to turn away from its democratic reading of statutory powers and instead delivered a convoluted verdict which, on close inspection, appears to grant nothing less than general executive privilege for speaking through the mass media:

> The assignment of a task in principle entails an empowerment to carry out information activity in the framework of the implementation of this task, even if this may bring about indirect factual impairments. The proviso of legality [ie the reserve of statutory powers] does not demand the legislature to provide any particular authorisation going beyond this.[30]

The tendency on the court's part, more pronounced in recent years, to intervene in parliamentary matters – notably the marked increase in decisions on parliamentary rights to information[31] – is surely another aspect of the crisis of the older, indirect mechanism of control and a testament to its increasing dysfunctionality. Yet the role of the constitutional court as the advocate of parliament inevitably remains paradoxical. By juridifying the exercise of oversight functions, the court gives renewed emphasis to the antagonism between parliament and government. In other words, it formalises something that in a parliamentary

[29] *Orthography reform*, 98 *BVerfGE* 218 (1998).

[30] *Public warnings*, 105 *BVerfGE* 279, 303 (2002), ECLI:DE:BVerfG:2002:rs20020626.1bvr067091 (en).

[31] J von Achenbach, 'Parlamentarische Informationsrechte und Gewaltenteilung in der neueren Rechtsprechung des Bundesverfassungsgerichts' (2017) 48 *Zeitschrift für Parlamentsfragen* 491.

democracy is normally informal, and in so doing contributes to the legal dissociation of parliament and government.[32]

IV. The Chancellery Unchained

This leaves only the Federal Chancellery unchallenged in its powers among the mediating institutions of the parliamentary system of government. What is more, the relative weakness of the party system and of the constitutional court means that it has outgrown its status as a mediating instruction and for some time already has been *the* super-institution of the German political system. The chancellery now stands as the visible symbol of that system's increasingly presidential character. This refers not to matters of style, though the present chancellor, in the early years of her tenure, was often described as 'presidential' on account of her preference for compromise solutions and avoidance of sharp confrontation with the opposition. Yet from a constitutional perspective, this 'presidentialisation' presents a more complex phenomenon, at the heart of which stands not the chancellor herself, but rather the Federal Chancellery, by the largest government headquarters in the world in terms of staffing, proudly residing in one of Berlin's architectural landmarks, the Bundestag.

A. What Matters when it's a Matter for the Boss

The drastic extension of its powers and responsibilities demonstrates the transformation towards an 'imperial chancellery'. The chancellery tends to communicate newly acquired competencies by stating that this or that matter was accorded top priority, was now, as the German goes, *Chefsache* – a matter to be made the personal concern of the boss. Such announcements seem to solicit praise, giving as they do the impression of responsibility being assumed. From the perspective of constitutional law, however, there is little cause for enthusiasm. That the chancellery should abstain from concerning itself with any particular department or policy portfolio (its so-called *Ressortfreiheit*) is among the organisational principles of a government with parliamentary responsibility. By law, the chancellery is limited to the role of a government headquarters, tasked with planning, coordination, communication, and supervision, but not with matters of policy that fall within the remit of individual ministries.

That ministers, while being subject to the chancellor's right to set policy guidelines, should be in charge of their respective departments (Article 65 GG) is an indispensable precondition for the individual responsibility of ministers as enshrined in German constitutional law. The federal government is thereby compelled to divide the totality of its activity into particular fields, in other words, to form ministries, for each of which a particular member of the federal government is held politically responsible. It is far from inconsequential whether this member is a minister or the chancellor. Only when a specific government policy remit is subject to ministerial control can its dependence on parliamentary responsibility be kept

[32] I have argued this in more detail elsewhere. See F Meinel, 'Confidence and Control in Parliamentary Government' (2018) 66 *American Journal of Comparative Law* 317.

separate from the continuance of the government as a whole. This intermediate level disappears when the chancellery itself takes on government tasks. Only by bringing down the government can parliamentary responsibility then be brought to bear. What is more – and this will come up again – only that part of the government's actions that is divided along departmental lines is subject to the direct control of the relevant specialist committees. Meanwhile, there is no committee that is charged with supervising the chancellery. The chancellor's responsibility is an overall responsibility that includes every single department but does not replace theirs. Even though this rule does not exist in the United Kingdom, where the prime minister can hold ministerial office concurrently with his duties as head of government, nevertheless, he, too, assumes an overall parliamentary responsibility for all matters within the concern of the members of his cabinet, formally by stating before answering the first of the 'Questions to the Prime Minister': 'This morning I had meetings with ministerial colleagues and others. In addition to my duties in this House, I shall have further such meetings later today.'

From the beginnings of the Federal Republic, there was one major exception to the rule that the chancellery must be free of any departmental responsibilities (*Ressortfreiheit*): the Federal Intelligence Service (Bundesnachrichtendienst, BND). Building a foreign intelligence service was a highly sensitive matter so soon after World War II – all the more so given that it was entrusted to Reinhard Gehlen, who had been chief of the 'Foreign Armies East' military intelligence service in the Wehrmacht general staff. Rather than passing it on to one of his ministers, Adenauer hence preferred to keep responsibility for this service in the chancellery.[33] For a long time, this remained the only exception.

Today, the principle of *Ressortfreiheit* is a thing of the past. It all began with Gerhard Schröder who, in 1998, declared the development of the former GDR to be his *Chefsache*, which he placed in the hands of a special commissioner attached to the chancellery. The Federal Government Commissioner for Culture and the Media is likewise a creation of the red–green coalition. This policy of integration did not, however, end with Schröder's departure. Although the Federal Government Commissioner for Integration had originally been attached to the ministry of labour and subsequently to that of families, Angela Merkel situated it in the chancellery upon taking office. Other and more important policy areas were to follow. The permanent state of crisis of the European Union has seen European policy largely shift from the foreign ministry to the chancellery. At the peak of the refugee crisis, Merkel removed important responsibilities from the ministry of the interior, which previously had been responsible for the matter, and created a staff position for refugee policy with Peter Altmaier, the chancellery minister, as 'refugee coordinator'. Digitalisation followed when a new government was formed in 2018, again with a federal commissioner in the chancellery in charge. This, however, seems to have been something of a cosmetic measure designed largely as a gift to the CSU. The organisational plan of the federal chancellery reveals that the Directorate-General responsible for Digital Policy and Strategic IT Management is not even in charge of the Federal Government Commissioner for Digital Affairs. This constant shifting of tasks to the chancellery is not solely a matter of internal concern for the government, but directly affects the government's relationship with the Bundestag. Under Angela

[33] Unabhängige Historikerkommission zur Erforschung der Geschichte des Bundesnachrichtendienstes (ed), *Die Geschichte der Organisation Gehlen und des BND 1945–1968* (Marburg, 2014).

Merkel's chancellorship, for example, the practice of having the leaders of the governing parliamentary parties take part in important cabinet meetings fell out of use. Instead, these meetings are now attended by the department heads of the chancellery.

B. The Creeping Unitarisation of the Executive

Of course, international crises and key policies have always demanded that the chancellor rise to the occasion. There was never any doubt that rapprochement with the East under Willy Brandt and reunification under Helmut Kohl would be decisively managed by the chancellery. Yet the ministers concerned retained their institutional responsibilities, and Walter Scheel and Hans-Dietrich Genscher certainly carried political clout of their own. The sheer multiplication of trouble spots in recent years may be one factor that makes coordination between the chancellery and the ministries, or even between ministries, seem unwieldy and virtually forces a concentration of decision-making powers. The principal factor, however, is surely the extreme shortening of executive decision-making processes, which in turn results from an imperative to respond to crises at ever shorter notice. At the same time, it seems to be getting harder and harder for individual ministers to assert themselves politically without being considered a threat to the chancellery's dominant position. It is surely no accident that, under Angela Merkel, it was above all the ministry of finance under Wolfgang Schäuble and, albeit less, his successor Olaf Scholz that once more managed to shape policy.

Is there any recourse under constitutional law against this creeping unitarisation of the government's organisation? Ministers' ability to defend their departments is of course primarily a political question, one in which ministers will as a rule come out second best. Even the proud ministry of the interior found itself worsted in the refugee crisis. Any impulse for change must hence come from parliament. If the Bundestag were to insist on government tasks being discharged in the constitutional manner by the ministers responsible to it, the process of further centralisation might at least be impeded. It might also be worth considering whether the opposition, too, can invoke the principle of ministerial rather than headquarters' responsibility. The constitutional court has so far refused to countenance this possibility. Its jurisdiction assumes that the allocation of tasks within the federal government falls within a 'core of autonomous executive responsibility' and moreover that, as far as 'the legal relationship with the German Bundestag and its members' was concerned, it was immaterial where within the government organisation a decision was made as long as it could clearly be ascribed to the federal government.[34] If one were indeed to content oneself with such a formal view – rather than seeing the very point of Article 65 GG in assigning *parliamentary* responsibility to ministers – the unitarisation of the executive would be a done deal. From the viewpoint of constitutional history, this may evoke painful memories. If it follows its present course, the organisation of the German government at its highest level is set once again to resemble the monocratic model of a highly powerful chancellor and subordinate officials – a model identified with a problematic predecessor, namely Bismarck.

[34] *Arms exports*, 137 *BVerfGE* 185, 236–37, 239 (2014), ECLI:DE:BVerfG:2014:es20141021.2bve000511 (en).

6

Potentials and Weaknesses of Parliamentary Control

When, on 16 December 2015, after the regular government questions session held on Wednesdays at one o'clock, Angela Merkel was expected to deliver a government declaration on the European Council in the Bundestag, she did not turn up. She had been told, she later explained, that she had better leave the government benches, 'because otherwise I might have been asked a question, too'. Norbert Lammert, the president of the Bundestag, acidly replied: 'It seems rather far-fetched that anyone should ask you, having accidentally attended government questions for once, to leave the government benches.' To which the chancellor retorted: 'It wasn't anyone in parliament, but someone on the government benches. In any case, it seemed better to be off.'[1] Yet even being present need not entail an obligation to answer questions. When, on 15 June 2018, the *Bundestag* held a debate on a matter of topical interest (*aktuelle Stunde*) – at the request of the FDP – on some migration plan by the interior minister Horst Seehofer, which was still unknown to the public, speakers included members of all parties in parliament. Yet the minister himself remained seated on the government benches, silent to the very end.[2]

That the members of a government responsible to parliament should respond to questions *from* parliament is far from being a matter of course in Germany. Yet nothing seems to better illustrate the position of parliamentary government in constitutional law. After all, what responsibility means above all is to be answerable for one's conduct in office. Many commentators accordingly regard a parliament that scrutinises the government more closely and publicly as the solution to the current crisis of parliamentary government.[3] Transparency, scrutiny and responsibility are the shibboleths of good governance. Parliamentary scrutiny appears to be the order of the day. Yet at the same time, the discourse of transparency signals a lack of trust in institutions: ever since the idea was successfully propagated that democracy was above all about transparency, deficits of transparency, scrutiny and responsibility seem to be discovered everywhere. But how does parliamentary control actually work? It will become apparent that its strengths and weaknesses are distributed in an extremely unfavourable manner: what works well, namely non-public scrutiny in select committees, remains largely invisible. What works badly, on the other hand, namely the public accountability of government for its policies in parliament, is very much on display.

[1] Plenarprotokoll 18/145, 14 279.

[2] Plenarprotokoll 19/40, 4006–24.

[3] A Tomkins, 'What Is Parliament For?' in N Bamforth and P Leyland (eds), *Public Law in a Multilayered Constitution* (Oxford, Hart, 2003) 74.

The constitutional court's recent jurisdiction, at any rate, would seem to suggest that parliamentary scrutiny has emerged as a constitutional problem of the highest order. Whereas, well into the 1990s, there had been – aside from two leading decisions on the rights of parliamentary committees of inquiry[4] – barely any rulings on parliament's supervisory functions, they seem to have occurred regularly in recent years. For instance, the constitutional court was called upon to decide on whether files on the lists of US National Security Agency (NSA) search terms should be made available, on parliamentary scrutiny of the surveillance of Bundestag members by the domestic secret service, on parliamentary scrutiny of the euro bailout and of arms exports, on parliament's right to be informed with regard to operations of the Federal police and emergency deployments of the military abroad, on parliamentary supervision of the railways and the financial markets regulator, and on whether the opposition – which, in the eighteenth Bundestag, consisted only of the Green and Left parties – was constitutionally entitled to further rights of scrutiny.[5] And those are only the major cases, important enough to engage the attention of the Karlsruhe court. At a lower level, too, parliamentary practice was confronted with entirely new challenges: how, for instance, was a parliamentary committee of inquiry to operate if its key witness – Edward Snowden – could not be brought to attend?

It is hard to pinpoint the individual factors contributing to the increasing level of conflict in this area. Is parliament intensifying scrutiny, or is it rather the government that is increasingly concerned to avoid scrutiny? Or does this phenomenon instead testify to what organisation theory has come to call the 'paradox of scrutiny': the more intense the scrutiny is, the more its blind spots emerge. However, the increasing insistence of opposition parties on rights to information would seem also to be linked to the strategic weakness of a competing opposition under a grand coalition.

I. What is Parliamentary Scrutiny?

The idea that parliament controls the government by demanding information, giving its political assessment and opinion, and thereby making it public, is old and, some might say, hopelessly old fashioned. The famous case of *Stockdale v Hansard*, in which the British High Court referred to parliament as 'a great inquest of the nation', was brought before the court in 1839.[6] At the time, parliament's ability to bring before the tribunal matters, as it were, of public opinion constituted a considerable source of legitimacy. Today, by contrast, parliament competes with other supervisory bodies and seldom comes out well by comparison. Audit offices, NGOs, the media – they all seem ahead of parliament in both speed and expertise. It is no accident, then, that the focus of parliamentary scrutiny is increasingly shifting to those areas in which the state acts under cover of secrecy. On the other hand, this means that scrutiny is extended to fields of policy that were long left to themselves, largely free of parliamentary oversight. Yet what this also means is that the Bundestag finds

[4] *Investigation committee 'Flick'*, 67 *BVerfGE* 100 (1984); *Investigation committee 'Neue Heimat'*, 77 *BVerfGE* 1 (1987).

[5] For a comparative account of this jurisprudence, see F Meinel, 'Confidence and Control in Parliamentary Government' (2018) 66 *American Journal of Comparative Law* 317.

[6] (1839) 9 Ad & Ell 96.

itself pushed to exercise its scrutiny in the few remaining areas in which, by virtue of its privileged access to government information, it still has an in-built advantage over competing actors.

One would do well, however, not to imagine the constitutional purpose of parliamentary scrutiny of the government as residing in a set of rights to information, but as being above all about access to knowledge. This distinction is best made by comparing parliament to other forms of oversight. Governments are subject to scrutiny from many instances: audit offices look for cases of waste, courts try to ensure that they operate within the law, journalists ask critical questions and, ideally, may work with informers to throw light on questionable decisions, and lobbyists confront it with the effects of policy on their respective fields. What is more, government oversight has been, since 2006, what lawyer's call an 'everyman's right': according to the German freedom of information act, everybody is entitled to access to official information of all kinds without having to give reasons. Research is made easier by such websites as fragdenstaat.de ('ask the state'), the legal, if slightly less exciting, alternative to Wikileaks. So what does parliament still do when scrutinising the government?

A. Trust and Scrutiny

Obtaining information and safeguarding transparency are at most indirect purposes of parliamentary scrutiny of a government responsible to parliament. It is also less concerned with compliance with legal or budgetary standard than with ensuring that the executive body remains in touch with the parliamentary process of opinion formation.[7] As exercised by the right to ask questions and receive information, parliamentary scrutiny is a key means of ensuring that the executive and legislative functions are performed in tandem. Accordingly, parliamentary scrutiny is not something passive, designed only to review government action after the fact, but rather is intended to put parliament in a position to exercise continuous influence on the political running of government.

Parliamentary scrutiny is thus intimately tied to the government's foundation in the confidence of parliament, for the confidence of the parliamentary majority is not an attitude of tacit general approval, but rather a process of ongoing communication about shared policy objectives between members of the government and the majority in parliament. The parliamentary system of government thus entails a notion of parliamentary control that implies the involvement of members of government in the process of parliamentary opinion formation. It also implies, but is not limited to, that abuses are subject to sanction.

Parliamentary scrutiny may therefore appear in a variety of guises, depending on whether it is exercised by the government or the opposition in parliament. Since confidence is founded on the close political association between the majority parliamentary parties and members of government, the majority can be largely discounted when it comes to exercising the legally formalised rights of scrutiny. Of course, it too may employ the means of

[7] See A Le Divellec, 'L'Articulation des pouvoirs dans les démocraties parlementaires européennes', (2012) 143 *Pouvoirs* 134; P Cane, *Controlling Administrative power: An Historical Comparison* (Cambridge, Cambridge University Press, 2016) 151–53.

scrutiny to stabilise the government, especially when regular members of the parliamentary governing parties do so. Yet in the German system, they hardly ever do so in the way that backbenchers do in the House of Commons, but rather through less formalised channels: within their own parliamentary groups, parties and specialist bodies. By these (albeit less visible) means, the parliamentary majority is involved in parliamentary scrutiny. For instance, we may one day find out to what extent Angela Merkel's about-turn on refugee policy in 2016 was forced upon her by the parliamentary CDU/CSU. After all, ministers do often participate in the plenary meetings of the governing parliamentary parties and of the relevant working groups. Sometimes they may even prefer to face committees, where the presence of opposition deputies is likely to ensure the loyalty of their own party's representatives. In intra-party working groups, by contrast, they can often expect to be openly challenged. Adenauer is said to have found having to face his own parliamentary party to be 'purgatory'.[8] Constitutionally and empirically, this makes the scrutiny exercised by the parliamentary majority hard to pin down, whereas scrutiny and supervision of government action constitute the key and visible functions of parliamentary opposition.

B. The Dialectic of Ministerial Responsibility

Yet the opposition's own rights of parliamentary scrutiny also serve the purpose of stabilising the system: they are the means by which the opposition tests the level of political accord between the parliamentary majority and the government personnel responsible. A minister able to parry opposition attacks effectively will bolster his authority within his own party, whereas a poor response to questions or requests for information is liable to weaken his position. Accordingly, the rights of parliamentary scrutiny enshrined in German law – major and minor interpellations, question time and individual written questions, debates on matters of topical interest – are closely connected to the principle of ministerial responsibility. They serve to ensure the commitment of the political leadership to political goals rather than the general scrutiny of the executive. This is evident not least from the attitude of the ministerial bureaucracies, which are not part of the political alliance of majority parties and members of government, and whose members tend to view answering frequent parliamentary questions as a waste of time: if they did not again have to explain one thing or another to the Bundestag, they might get on with their important duties. And parliamentary scrutiny indeed is a political, not an administrative matter.

The consequences of its systematic connection with ministerial responsibility are twofold. First, parliamentary scrutiny cannot be forced, not even by the conditional court. Second, to state that parliament scrutinises the government is a mere banality as long as it is left open just who is actually involved in this process. Although parliament and government do not confront each other as separate entities, the manner in which various members of parliament may interact with various members of the government may differ significantly, and the forms taken by parliamentary scholarship will differ accordingly. The scrutiny exercised by individual members of parliament, by committees, government or opposition

[8] Quoted in H-P Schwarz, 'Die CDU/CSU-Fraktion in der Ära Adenauer' in H-P Schwarz (ed), *Die Fraktion als Machtfaktor* (Munich, CH Beck, 2009) 14.

parliamentary parties, and the house as a whole may be directed at individual ministers, the entire government or at bodies at a lower level, for instance the secret services or the railways.

However, there is one respect in which all these forms of parliamentary scrutiny differ from parliament's other work, notably in legislation. Control over the agenda of scrutiny, over its thematic focus and its timeframe – control that is of tremendous political importance – lies with parliament to a much greater degree than it does with the government. Whereas the government largely sets the legislative agenda – and rightly so – it is parliament that sets the agenda for parliamentary scrutiny. The decisive point, then, is that *the agenda for scrutiny is set by the scrutiniser, not the scrutinised.* Scrutiny therefore works in a way that is diametrically opposed to that of legislation.[9] Whereas the opposition's legislative initiatives tend largely to be ignored, its supervisory rights allow it to force committees or the house as a whole to confront the hot topics of the day. This might be called the rule of balance in the parliamentary agenda, though this is more of a theoretical model than a description of practice. In reality – and this is a major and perhaps even the fundamental problem of parliamentary scrutiny – this balance simply does not exist.

C. Who is the Federal Government? or: The Object of Scrutiny

German parliamentary law continues largely to conceal the inner connection between parliamentary scrutiny and ministers' parliamentary responsibility. The traditional architecture of parliamentary procedure under the Basic Law deprives parliamentary scrutiny of its political punchline. For the instruments of parliamentary scrutiny – major and minor interpellations, individual written questions, etc – are directed not at the ministers responsible but, according to the Bundestag's rules of procedure, always against the Federal Government as such. Yet Article 65 GG expressly and unambiguously states that the government as such is not constitutionally responsible. The responsibility lies with its individual members. Nevertheless, while members of the House of Commons will always address their questions to the prime minister, the home secretary, etc, their German counterparts always ask 'the federal government'.

The direct political consequences of this arrangement follow not from the Bundestag's rules of procedure, but from those of the government. The head of the chancellery decides who is to respond to parliament – a particular ministry or the government as a whole. This organisational question is far from being a mere technical detail. Its purpose is to allow the government itself to decide in which institutional form to confront parliament: that of a collegial cabinet or a particular minister, or represented by a parliamentary state secretary, or under the guise of a bureaucracy that submits its answer in writing. All these forms are admissible under the rules of procedure, which thereby conserve, at a crucial point, the constitutional dualism of parliament and government. This is far from constitutionally plausible, since Article 43(1) GG only mentions the Bundestag's right to 'require the presence of any member of the Federal Government', but not the government as a whole.[10] This makes it

[9] An in-depth discussion of these aspects is given by M Koß, 'Time Rules and Time Budgets in Legislatures' in KH Goetz (ed), *The Oxford Handbook of Time and Politics* (Oxford, Oxford University Press, 2019).

[10] Accordingly, and with good systematic reason, the SPD in the joint commission on constitutional reform set up after reunification sought to regulate the parliamentary right of interpellation in a new Art 43(1)(2) GG, which

all the more baffling that the constitutional court, which in its earlier jurisdiction had rightly expressed the opinion that parliamentary rights of scrutiny imposed a constitutional obligation to respond on 'the *members* of the Federal Government',[11] in its more recent decisions, speaks consistently of 'the government's' obligation to do so.[12]

II. Functions and Limits of Plenary Control

'As an institution, parliament today can only be justified by what it does in in its plenary proceedings.' In these words, written in 1969, Wilhelm Hennis condensed his critique of two decades of postwar parliamentarianism. What he was referring to was mainly parliamentary scrutiny.[13] He had in mind the example of the United Kingdom: ministers facing the House of Commons and the public, and being answerable for the government's policies, as well as heavy hitters on the opposition benches with a knack for revealing the government's weak points. In his *Considerations on Representative Government*, John Stuart Mill, the great English liberal who was himself briefly a member of the House of Commons in the 1860s, provided the classic foundation of this idea: in view of the complex tasks of regulation required by a modern industrial society, no parliament could be expected to take on the full burden of legislation. Instead, then, of getting bogged down in detail and legal technicalities, the lower house would be better off reimagining itself as a 'controlling assembly'.

A. Questions of Style, Rules of Procedure

For a variety of reasons, the Bundestag never completed this transition to a controlling assembly. At a time when the complexity of the government's activities might still have been manageable in the plenary, the Reichstag had no rights of scrutiny. Later, the Bundestag, for several reasons, was unable to give up its legislative power. Mill's observation, brilliant as it was with regard to Victorian Britain, was barely accurate in Hennis's time. For some time now, the German parliament has had a manifest and well-known problem with government scrutiny in the plenum, that is, by the house as a whole. The idea of parliamentary scrutiny seems to have fallen out of style politically, and this has often been remarked on with regard to the chancellor. Angela Merkel is known to prefer such journalistic formats as the summer press conference, the summer interview, the citizen dialogue or – most embarrassingly of all – a 'town hall meeting' (the English phrase was used) under the heading 'Living Well in Germany'. This latter occasion was memorable chiefly for the chancellor's hapless reaction to Reem Sahwil, a young Palestinian girl who broke down in tears at being told she would

was to read: 'Parliamentary interpellations and questions put by individual members of the Bundestag are to be answered without delay and in full' (BTDrucks 12/6000, 91). This solution was not adopted. The commission regarded it as a threat to the 'separation which the constitution draws in principle between parliament and government, that is, between the executive and legislative organs'. Unfortunately, that kind of reasoning is symptomatic of the intellectual level of this last great attempt at constitutional reform in the Federal Republic.

[11] *NPD*, 57 *BVerfGE* 1, 5 (1981) (emphasis added); similarly *Parliamentary questions*, 13 *BVerfGE* 123, 125 (1961).

[12] *Parliamentary information on EU affairs*, 132 *BVerfGE* 195, 242 (2012), ECLI:DE:BVerfG:2012:rs20120912.2bvr139012 (en).

[13] W Hennis, 'Rechtfertigung und Kritik der Bundestagsarbeit' in W Abendroth (ed), *Festschrift für Adolf Arndt zum 65. Geburtstag* (Frankfurt am Main, Europäische Verlagsanstalt, 1969) 151.

have to leave the country. Faced with critical situations, minsters, too, prefer to enter into a 'dialogue' with 'those directly affected', while being notable by their absence at government questions.

None of this is really new. Earlier chancellors, too – unlike British prime ministers in the House of Commons – did not make themselves available to the Bundestag for questioning. Nor are television talk shows, which sometimes re-enact debates of the kind one might expect to find in parliament, a new invention. Yet such journalistic formats, in which the fetish of the authentic supplants the institutional distinction between government and opposition, become increasingly problematic in proportion to the distinction becoming increasingly blurred in parliament too. This raises the question of the means remaining at the Bundestag's disposal to exercise its parliamentary scrutiny. Even though the Bundestag has reformed the rules on parliamentary questioning as recently as 2019 to make them slightly more favourable to the opposition, the key problems remain. This is not principally because the rules in their existing form are deficient; the difficulty seems to be mainly with applying these rules. The reality of the Bundestag, as its former president, Norbert Lammert, put it in his farewell speech, in this respect 'falls somewhat below the minimum standard to which a self-confident parliament must hold itself'.

B. The Lack of Rhetorical Culture

Take, for instance, interpellations, both major and minor. Whereas a major interpellation is always put to discussion in the plenary session, minor interpellations, as a rule, never are. Leaving aside for the moment the stumbling-block of interpellations not being answered by the minister concerned but rather by an entity known as 'the federal government', these instruments – for all that the speed and precision with which they are handled by individual departments may vary – appear largely funcitonal.

The deficits are to be found rather with the oral forms of scrutiny. Parliamentary law makes provision for three forms of non-written questioning. One that is surely superfluous is question time (§ 195 and Annex 4 GOBT), which requires that members' questions be submitted, in writing, in advance. Consequently, the level of spontaneity is zero, and many questions cannot even be discussed in the session because the members asking them do not even bother to attend. Since the government usually has parliamentary state secretaries represent its own ministers, the benches of the governing parliamentary party are empty, and the tone between those answering questions and those replying tends to be unduly chummy. And since many members who raise questions are in any case referred to written answers, the spoken form is mere window-dressing and politically ineffective.

An altogether different matter is the questioning of the federal government on 'questions of topical interest' (*Regierungsbefragung*). When the Bundestag is in session, this question time is held – interestingly, half an hour later than PMQs in Westminster – on Wednesdays at noon in the plenary chamber.[14] Their principal flaw is a procedural rule that makes life very comfortable indeed for the government. Topics are chosen not by parliament, but by the chancellery, which also decides on the ministers sent to face parliament.

[14] The details are set down in Annex 7 to the Rules of Procedure of the German Bundestag.

Since the criterion tends to be to deflect heat from the government, ministers tend to be chosen mainly for their ability to avoid public embarrassment. By thus evading scrutiny, the government makes a mockery of the whole instrument. On 13 June 2018, at the height of the conflict over asylum policy within the CDU/CSU, the government decided to make its climate protection report for the previous year the topic of the day. It sent Svenja Schulze, the minister for the environment, to answer the house's questions – a politician who, at the time, was new in office and had not yet introduced policy initiatives of any kind. The opposition had no recourse against being treated with such condescension. The government's handling of this instrument still betrays its historic roots in a session in which the government would unilaterally present parliament with the results of its work. In early 2018, it seemed as though government question time was about to be completely redesigned. In the months during which it hung suspended between government and opposition, the Social Democrats had made this demand, which the Greens in particular had pursued for years, their own and forced the CDU to concede the point in the coalition treaty. The core of this reform – the chancellor's regular attendance – has since been fulfilled by the reformed rules of procedure. Angela Merkel first faced parliamentary questions in June 2018 and has continued to do so ever since three times a year.

C. The Complicity of the Opposition

Yet the opposition is not in a position to make too much of a fuss about this unsatisfactory state of affairs, as it is a consequence of its own priorities its own priorities. It too seems to treat government questions as a chore best left to its backbenchers. The weakness of these oral forms of parliamentary scrutiny thus can be found to reside not only in the government's behaviour, obstructive though it may be, but also in the opposition's own frequent lack of interest in this format. One might go so far as to speak of a 'disengagement compact' between government and opposition in matters of plenary control: the opposition does not expect ministers to be present for questions; what it expects instead is the government's cooperation in the bargaining systems of the parliamentary committees and federal institutions. In return for this consideration, the government need not fear being questioned by the opposition's heavy hitters. If the opposition did not leave the questioning of the government and the conduct of topical debates to its second-, third- and fourth-tier MPs but rather put in the hands of the leadership, the government could not get away indefinitely with sending in ministers chosen for their likelihood of being met with indifference or having general questions fielded by parliamentary state secretaries or the minister of state in the chancellery. Nor could the governing parliamentary parties afford to have only a small B-team even be present in the plenary session.

The same is true of debates on matters of topical interest (*aktuelle Stunde*), which is not even meant to serve as an instrument of parliamentary scrutiny but, according to the rules of procedure, to allow for 'debates on clearly defined topics of general current interest' in the Bundestag. Yet it can easily be used for purposes of scrutiny, provided that the opportunity is seized. A case in point is the Bundestag's plenary session of 27 June 2018. A topical debate on maritime rescue operations in the Mediterranean called by the Left Party was at first not attended by any member of the government. Thereupon the Greens' parliamentary secretary, Steffi Lemke, tabled a procedural motion invoking Article 43(1) GG to summon the interior minister. This was, she argued, a matter of life and death, for which parliamentary secretaries of state were not adequate representatives of the federal government. The Greens had clearly been prepared for this move and were largely in attendance, and the votes of Left and AfD gave the motion the constitutionally required majority. In less than twenty minutes, Horst Seehofer was facing the house and could, once summoned, no longer remain silent, as he had done in the topical debate on his 'masterplan' two weeks previously. His responses to the criticisms were brief, flat and generally unprepared. This shows that topical debates, too, are what the opposition chooses to make of them. By turning up in sufficient numbers and with good leadership, it can at least compel the government to make a similar showing in order to fight off any applications to require the presence of the responsible minister according to Article 43(1) GG – both in topical debates and during question time. This, however, is likely to become increasingly unnecessary, since a minister, once in the firing line, will find it politically unwise to stay away from high-profile debates in the house.

III. In the Engine Room of Responsibility: The Committees

A. The Masterstroke of the 1969 Parliamentary Reform

Yet the Bundestag's true achievement in terms of parliamentary scrutiny is to be found elsewhere. Time in the plenary is scarce, and the house can at most question one or two ministers on one or two matters in an average week of its session. The effect of this kind of scrutiny thus lies above all in its symbolic enactment of parliamentary responsibility. What the plenary is not able to achieve is exercising detailed control over government business, a task that must be left to specialised committees. At their best, committees effectively multiply the plenary time available and, by doing so, significantly shorten proceedings. Far from being a matter of course, this is a historic achievement of the Bundestag.

As such, it goes back to a parliamentary reform of Germany's first grand coalition in the late 1960s. Its core was the seemingly banal rule of procedure,[15] according to which committees may deal not only with matters referred to them for discussion by the whole house, but also 'take up' other questions falling within their responsibility. Previously, the question of what a committee was allowed to discuss had indeed depended on being called upon by the house to do so. While proposed legislation usually reaches the committees after its first reading, this rule succeeded in silently and effectively preventing committees from exercising scrutiny of the government. Although the plenary would also have been able to refer a topical issue to a specialist committee, the procedure was too elaborate and the plenary time too short for this to be an effective means of responding to developments. Only since they have been entitled to take charge of an issue themselves (*Selbstbefassungsrecht*) can the committees take advantage of the instruments of parliamentary scrutiny and deploy them to influence the agenda as they see fit, for the opposition is also entitled to demand that a matter be discussed in a committee. The same rule also gave a fundamentally new and autonomous

[15] § 62 Geschäftsordnung des Deutschen Bundestages.

meaning to the committee's right to require presence according to Article 43(1) GG.[16] The committees are now able to respond to the issues of the day in any sphere of policy, and are entitled to request the presence of the minister responsible in doing so.

It is true that the committees only in the rarest of cases make formal use of their constitutional right to summon a minister, for to do so requires a majority decision. In most cases, however, they do not even need to make use of their powers, for ministers anyhow have ample reason to appear before committees. Avoiding committees carries a political cost of its own, as many have discovered. From the representatives of their own party, ministers can mostly expect support. Coalition partners, too, tend to stick together in the committees, at least outwardly. The view from the inside is often different, with committees providing coalition partners – only one of which can be in charge of a particular department – to keep an eye on each other.[17] This was previously done at the government level by the so-called 'cross-stitch method', in which a federal minister would always have a parliamentary secretary of state representing the other coalition partner to keep an eye on him. Since the parliamentary reform of 1969, the committees have increasingly brought this task under parliamentary control – a task that has only grown in importance as coalitions grow ever more heterogeneous and the need for mutual oversight between coalition partners has increased.[18]

B. Politics and Bureaucracy in the Committees

One of the key reasons for the efficiency of parliamentary scrutiny by the select committees is likely to be found within the government itself. The government is interested not only in seeing parliamentary deliberations reach an advanced stage at the politically unobtrusive committee level in order not to jeopardise its legislative agenda. It is also less eager to avoid the non-public scrutiny of committees, which helps it to avoid the public scrutiny of minsters in the plenary. Above all, however, it is only at the committee stage that the political leadership is able at any time to call upon the support of the bureaucracy, which 'shall have the right to be heard at any time' according to Article 43(2)(2) GG. Although this rule technically also applies to the whole house, it is no longer applied there, and with good reason. Article 43 GG is as important as it is ambivalent, allowing the government's political leadership to be represented in the committees by officials with no parliamentary responsibility of their own. When, in September 2018, Horst Seehofer, in his capacity as minister of the interior, came under pressure for the conduct of Hans-Georg Maaßen, the head of the domestic secret service later fired for his public denunciation of Merkel's migration policies, it was above all Maaßen himself who was left to do the talking during the five hours of questioning by parliamentarians. According to press reports, Seehofer, though present, took a back seat.

[16] See J von Oertzen, *Das Expertenparlament: Abgeordnetenrollen in den Fachstrukturen bundesdeutscher Parlamente* (Baden-Baden, Nomos, 2006) 236–38.

[17] MF Thies, 'Keeping Tabs on Partners', (2001) 45 *American Journal of Political Science* 580.

[18] On this, see R Carroll and GW Cox, 'Shadowing Ministers' (2012) 45 *Comparative Political Studies* 220; L W Martin and G Vanberg, 'Policing the Bargain: Coalition Government and Parliamentary Scrutiny' (2014) 48 *American Journal of Political Science* 13.

The parliamentary opposition parties, too, have an interest in maintaining the present form of nearly invisible government scrutiny by committee – at least they have long given up demanding far-reaching change. Why should this be so? Perhaps it is because this forum, in which they enter into direct contact with ministry officials, indeed improves their chances of influencing government action and legislation in their favour. This, in turn, is no doubt due to a peculiarity of federalism that has already been remarked upon and which explains so much: in the German political system, opposition parties are almost never fully in opposition; they are always involved in government somewhere, they are always involved somehow, and they hold the balance of votes in the Bundesrat. The parties supporting the governing coalition on the federal level today are in coalitions with every other party in the Bundestag, with the exception of the far-right AfD, somewhere in the *Länder*. As the *Länder* caucuses in the parliamentary party usually are loyal to their local party leadership, they will have to be considerate and compromise if national legislation pushed for by the federal government is heavily opposed by a coalition partner in a *Land*. In effect, a government can never simply push its legislation through with no regard for the opposition, whose deputies, for their part, do not simply dig in their heels. Within the committee's culture of cooperation and collaboration, this is entirely rational behaviour and gives the opposition a chance to see at least some of its agenda reflected in legislation. Moreover, specialist committees in a working parliament, many of whose deputies themselves have strong areas of specialisation, are conducive to bringing these members into contact with the civil service, where implicit understanding and loyalties among experts are remarkably effective even across party lines.

From these considerations, it can only be concluded that to hold committee sessions under the public eye, as is time and again demanded in the name of 'transparency', would have no benefits in the short term or even – as an isolated measure – in the long term. The contrary is far more likely to occur: public sessions have certainly not brought new audiences to the European Parliament or to *Länder* legislatures. Some Bundestag committees already conduct public hearings, though they usually involve only experts and representatives of interest groups rather than exercising scrutiny of the government or making decisions. And the most powerful committees – on budget, armed forces, domestic affairs or finance – already make the least use of existing provisions for holding meetings in public.[19] The government's willingness to subject itself to the scrutiny of committees would only diminish and the technical aspect of specialist control would suffer. In any case, it is impossible for the detailed work of legislation to take place under public observation.

IV. The Multi-Level System, Information Overkill and New Administrative Models – Aspects of Unbounded Control Tasks

The legal and institutional foundations of effective parliamentary scrutiny are thus essentially in place – scrutiny both in the plenary chamber and, in its less visible form, in the

[19] Deutscher Bundestag, *Datenhandbuch zur Geschichte des Deutschen Bundestages*, online edition (www.bundestag.de) ch 8.1.

committees. Where, then, is the problem? What has changed is the outward circumstances of parliamentary scrutiny. The Bundestag now finds itself confronted with a number of developments that, taken together, betoken the government's increasing institutional autonomy and make parliamentary scrutiny hard to enforce.

A. How to Control 'Europe'?

One such development concerns the involvement of Bundestag committees in the parliamentary scrutiny of European policy, which is expressed in an amendment to the aforementioned § 62 of the rules of procedure. This states that the committees '*shall deal promptly* with affairs of the European Union of relevance to their area of competence, independently of whether such matters have been referred to them' (my emphasis). This expansion of their involvement in European policy is the direct consequence of the constitutional court's jurisdiction of the 1990s. In a headnote to its decision on the constitutionality of the Maastricht Treaty, the court stated that in the European Union, 'democratic legitimation' was provided by 'the actions of European organs being receiving feedback from parliaments of the member states'.[20] Which is to say: European policy is domestic policy, hence the Bundestag is entitled to control it. The consequences were felt by the committees in particular. The plenary would certainly not be in any position to give such feedback, having as it was enough to do with current business, and European policy anyhow always being exceedingly technical.

At first sight, this all seems quite right. The parliament of the largest Member State has no reason to look only inwards and all the more cause to involve itself in its government's European policy. In terms of constitutional law, however, the phrasing not only went wide of the mark, but introduced an error. By transferring a notion of 'control' and the idea of an institutionalised *feedback* between government and parliament to the interaction between the EU level and national parliaments, the constitutional court made a hairline crack in the parliamentary system that would grow into a massive rupture. It was the German Bundestag's great achievement to have gained the sanction of constitutional law for feedback between parliament and government in a struggle that lasted for decades. Yet it is basic systems theory to know that one side of a feedback structure cannot be placed in feedback with a third element without unbalancing the original setup. For a government responsible to parliament to subsist in a feedback structure with that parliament has a precise meaning in constitutional law. With regard to the organs of the European Union, however, it is merely a metaphor.

The individual components of its jurisdiction on European integration, the consequences of which for parliamentary government the court seems never to have fully thought through, are mutually dependent. These include the extensively framed reservation of statutory powers and the needlessly extensive implementing legislation it demands; the institutionalised suspicion, on the part of the constitutional court, of the European Parliament; and the parliamentary committees being uncoupled from a responsible object and coupled to an irresponsible one. Make no mistake: parliamentary control of the actions of the European institutions and the link, in constitutional law, between European

[20] *Maastricht Treaty*, 89 *BVerfGE* 155, 185 (1993).

decision-making processes and opinion formation at the Member State level are constitutional questions of the highest order – questions, moreover, that are far from being satisfactorily resolved.[21] More than a few observers even argue that the court, in 1993, should have said: as long as these questions remain unresolved, Germany will not deepen its involvement. Most of them also strongly applauded the Federal Constitutional Court when it demanded stricter control of the central bank by the German Bundestag in the ECB ruling in May 2020.

Yet the terms in which the court justifies its conditional approval in constitutional terms has left the Bundestag with a role that fundamentally calls into question the role of parliament in a parliamentary democracy. Looked at closely, the imbalance between the two provisions of § 62(1)(3) of the rules of procedure is almost grotesque: committees '*shall* deal promptly with affairs of' an irresponsible supranational institution and, if they have any time to spare, they '*may* … take up other questions falling within their terms of reference', that is, those questions concerning parliamentary scrutiny of the federal government. As a result not least of the constitutional court's jurisdiction, the criterion of a constitutional responsibility as an aspect of the right of parliamentary scrutiny is structurally effaced. No doubt it was a shrewd semantic move on the part of the court to underpin this whole construction with the *Bundestag*'s supposed 'responsibility for integration' (*Integrationsverantwortung*),[22] for who could not be in favour of more responsibility at all levels? But what the court actually demonstrates here – and without the slightest indication of being troubled by the consequences – is the extent to which it recasts the Bundestag, from a ruling body with a responsible government to a controlling institution with the task of monitoring all manner of government tasks.

Under a grand coalition, in which the dialectic of majority rule and scrutiny is anyhow partially in abeyance, this sort of thing can go unnoticed for a while. Nonetheless, the fact remains that to keep constant tabs on the European Union's law-making is something entirely different from parliamentary scrutiny of the German federal government. According to the very detailed rules of procedure on European scrutiny, EU documents of all kinds and notifications of the federal government are to be referred to the appropriate committees for deliberation. The committees are also charged with ensuring adherence to the 'Principles of Subsidiarity and Proportionality'. At their behest, the Bundestag may issue rebukes for infractions and, if necessary, bring the case before the Court of Justice of the European Union, though the Bundestag is not entitled to impose political sanctions.

That scrutiny of European policy as currently practised does little to strengthen the Bundestag's influence vis-a-vis the government is evident not only from the frequent expressions of discontent heard from all members of parliament during the eurozone crisis. It is also palpable in the Europe committee, which is endowed by Article 45(2) and (3) GG with exceptional powers to act on behalf of the Bundestag while being something of a failure politically, being populated exclusively by backbenchers. Why is that the case? By no means only because until recently there was a large consensus on Europe in the Bundestag. The point is rather that a parliament can gain influence and prestige only by controlling

[21] O Tans, C Zoethout and J Peters (eds), *National Parliaments and European Democracy. A Bottom-up Approach to European Constitutionalism* (Groningen, Europa Law Publishing, 2007).

[22] Settled case law since *Lisbon Treaty*, 123 *BVerfGE* 267 (2009), ECLI:DE:BVerfG:2009:es20090630.2bve000208 (en).

a responsible government. And there is indeed a potential lever for parliamentary scrutiny: the minister sitting on the Council of the EU. To exercise control over this minister undoubtedly is very difficult indeed, and to a large extent impossible, a problem familiar from parliamentary scrutiny of foreign policy and parliamentary ratification of international treaties. In such cases, too, the government can simply respond to parliamentary objections by claiming that negotiations had been tough and no better result obtainable. Yet it would be a mistake to think that one could have it both ways, both influence in the council and the government being tied to the position adopted by the Bundestag in advance. To hold, on the other hand, each minister responsible for the positions *they* adopt is no doubt a more onerous task, though it may prove more rewarding in the longer term.

B. Scrutiny or Executive Self-Control? A Passive Parliament

A second development, which is crucial to the problem of parliamentary scrutiny as it presents itself today, concerns changed communication on the part of the government. In the first instance, parliamentary scrutiny means demanding accountability: one side asks a question and the other answers. One day, however, it must have occurred to someone that it would be more expedient for the government to account for its activities without being asked beforehand. Such obligations to accountability may be imposed for a variety of reasons. For instance, as part of the compromise on measures allowing greater surveillance of communications (the aforementioned *großer Lauschangriff*), Article 13 of the Basic Law was amended to oblige the federal government annually to inform the Bundestag of its surveillance measures – for a parliament can only scrutinise what it knows about. In the constitutional law on Europe, too, the constitutional court has interpreted the principle of democracy to impose wide-ranging obligations on the government to keep the Bundestag informed. Such obligations have since become a common pattern, and today parliamentary committees are virtually inundated with reports and information from the government.

Most of this has little to do with parliamentary scrutiny properly so-called; what parliament has effectively done here, in most cases, is to have imposed by law an obligation of self-control or evaluation on the executive body. For instance, § 66 of the Transportation of Persons Act (Personenbeförderungsgesetz) demands that the government give account of whether the law had proved effective in meeting the purposes pursued by the legislature. Of course, such reports need not always be made to parliament, but they are as a matter of course distributed as official documents to the Bundestag, for instance in the form of the 'Federal Government Report on Tourism Policy'. This may sound inconsequential, but far from it: whereas rights to information counterbalance the government's dominance of the legislative agenda, the flood of information requirements shifts the power of setting the topics of debate back towards the executive body. The federal government is able to issue reports as it sees fit within the general terms of its communication policy. They are then distributed at the discretion of the parliamentary authorities and directly referred to the committees for deliberation, regardless of whether parliament ever asked a relevant question or even signalled an interest in the matter.

By maintaining a constant flow of information in uncontroversial policy areas, the government can use its power over information as a tool against parliament. Bureaucracy will always be ahead of parliamentary opposition in the quantity, detail and quality of its knowledge. Who controls the flow of information controls the way issues are perceived and the agenda is set. The principle of parliamentary control as forming a counterweight to the government's agenda-setting power is thus structurally subverted. This paradigm shift, too, from parliamentary scrutiny to self-control on the part of the government bureaucracy, is an aspect of the progressive uncoupling of parliament and government. The assumption of controlling functions by the government bureaucracy threatens to reduce parliament to a mere government echo chamber. Information requirements imposed on the executive thus essentially and inevitably differ from what parliamentary scrutiny can and should achieve in a parliamentary system of government. Government is not an external instance for controlling the executive, but is itself the foundation of executive power.

C. The Rise of Agencies and the Limits of Inquiry Rights

There is, of course, a critical flaw to the constitutional principle binding together cabinet and parliament by means of parliamentary scrutiny: the Bundestag controls *only* the government, that is to say, the conduct of the chancellor and the ministers. Yet it has no direct control over the administration, independent state authorities or other positions of political relevance. Once again, this demonstrates the connection between parliamentary rights of scrutiny and ministerial responsibility. If parliament wishes to exert direct control over offices below the level of the federal government or beyond its remit, it can do so only by setting up a parliamentary committee of inquiry as set down in Article 44 GG. The parliamentary system of government demands this: only if federal ministers can be held responsible *for* all that happens within their sphere of responsibility, but political scrutiny does not extend to the organs of state themselves, can political responsibility be safeguarded. The cabinet acts, as it were, as the bottleneck of parliamentary scrutiny of the administration: the point at which all streams converge. The US Congress is altogether different. Its scrutiny, which is not the scrutiny of a government responsible to parliament, extends to everything in which its members might choose to take an interest. As such, it is not limited to the presidency or even the executive branch. Congress is entitled not only to summon the heads of subordinate government authorities, but also any public individual from whom it wants to hear. It was this power that led Mark Zuckerberg to explain Facebook's role in the data-sharing scandal before Congress twice in April 2018, though the Senate commerce and judiciary committees embarrassed themselves in the process.

Yet the Bundestag, too, seems increasingly to wish to apply parliamentary scrutiny at the sub-ministerial level. And indeed, if parliamentary scrutiny, following the pattern of government set down in constitutional law, was limited to the ministerial level, it would by now face tremendous difficulties. This is in large part due to organisational changes in the administrative machinery. There now exist government agencies that function in a manner altogether different from the ministerial authorities of old, in which a federal minister was at the top of a hierarchical organization for which he bore the responsibility. The Federal Network Agency (Bundesnetzagentur), for instance, in setting the prices for telecommunication services and transmission fees for the national electricity grid, does so largely independently of ministerial instructions. The Federal Financial Supervisory Authority (Bundesanstalt für Finanzdienstleistungsaufsicht, BAFin), performs its tasks de facto, if not de jure, independently. Formerly the state railway, Deutsche Bahn AG is now organised as a private company, though all its shares are held by the federal government. Every year, its management has €2.5 billion of taxpayer money to spend on the rail network. How can parliamentary scrutiny be brought to bear on such organisations?

Parliamentary investigations can barely scratch the surface of the problem. Although they may try to exercise scrutiny over all manner of things – the railways, the Federal Office of Administration (Bundesverwaltungsamt) or the German embassy in Athens – these institutions are unwieldy. The effort of bringing them under some measure of parliamentary control is, in political terms, repaid only if there are scandals to be uncovered. More than three parliamentary committees of inquiry per legislative term would be unmanageable. Indeed, the number of politically spectacular committees of inquiry obeying the confrontational logic of government and opposition in parliament has diminished: there has been none to speak of since the fifteenth Bundestag, which had to deal with far-fetched charges of electoral fraud by the Schröder government and an affair involving the issuing of visas by German consulates in Eastern Europe. More recent inquiries have had less clearly assigned roles, with parliamentarians in general casting themselves as exposing various ills in business and society, at home and abroad: surveillance by the NSA or the Volkswagen scandal of manipulated diesel emissions.

A remarkable development in its own right is the emergence of special constitutional provisions for certain areas outside ministerial control. One such provision concerns the parliamentary oversight panel (Article 45d GG), which is charged with keeping tabs on the activities of the intelligence services. Officially, such bodies are created because organisations prone to scandal require particularly close scrutiny. But such organisations, by being scandal-prone, are always a risk to the minister responsible – doubly so when, as with the Federal Intelligence Service (BND), political authority lies with the chancellery. The creation of a special parliamentary body to look directly at the services short-circuits parliamentary responsibility to the ministers' advantage. If something goes wrong, it is enough to change the head of the service concerned. In September 2018, the then head of the domestic intelligence service (Verfassungsschutz), Hans-Georg Maaßen, was compelled to explain himself in person to the oversight panel and the interior committee for comments he had made to the tabloid newspaper *Bild*. The minster of the interior, who is in charge of the Verfassungsschutz, was able to take a back seat, performing a moderating role. This arrangement serves to protect the ministers responsible.

D. Government Scrutiny by Corporate Governance: An Unconstitutional Fallacy

Even more worrying is the fact that many parliamentarians today serve on the federal government's various supervisory and advisory bodies. Members of the Bundestag are thus, under corporate law, directly involved in the corporate governance of quasi-state-run businesses and quasi-autonomous administrative bodies. For example: does it make sense that the parliamentary SPD's spokeswomen on transport policy is on the supervisory board of Deutsche Bahn AG? One may argue that it offers an insight into the problems of a major organisation that could scarcely be obtained only by reading its annual reports. However, members of parliaments may find their activities held against them by others. In this case, the minister for transport, as the minister responsible, may well counter any complaints about the state of the network by arguing that deputies should take the matter straight to management. The administrative board of the federal agency charged with oversight of the financial market and banking (Bundesanstalt für Finanzdienstleistungsaufsicht), too, consists not only of representatives of government, commerce and academia, but also of five members of the Bundestag. Should his own department have failed in its supervisory duties, the presence of these deputies on the board offers a handy excuse to the minster concerned. As for the regulatory agency concerned with network industries (Bundesnetzagentur), half of its supervisory body consists of parliamentary representatives – sixteen each from the Bundestag and the Bundesrat. Corporate law here leads to a form of parliamentary pseudo-responsibility, since the supervisory body can nominate the president, but only the government can dismiss him.

Why are such models even practised? Privatising state enterprises and outsourcing tasks of the state into autonomous administrative bodies or quangos was all the rage in the 1980s and 1990s. Often cited as an example was the American idea of 'independent agencies' which, though part of the executive, are subject only to limited control by the president: hence their 'independence'. Instead, they are to varying degrees directly controlled by Congress. This direct control by Congress in the absence of presidential responsibility is a political aspect that cannot easily be transferred to a parliamentary system of government. Nonetheless, members of parliament have an obvious interest in exercising direct control of this kind. By sitting on a supervisory board, they expect – and most probably with good reason – their prestige to be enhanced and generally to have an opportunity to exert greater influence than they could in everyday parliamentary business. After all, two members of the Bundestag find the time to involve themselves in the design of postage stamps as members of the finance minister's artistic advisory panel.

Ought this model to be generalised in constitutional law and parliamentary rights of scrutiny be extended beyond the federal government? There certainly is no shortage of possible applications. Should the president of the Federal Networks Agency be made to explain a rise in postage to parliament, or the head of the railways the latest fare increase? Should not the president of the Bundesbank be held answerable to the Bundestag for the policies of the ECB? All manner of scenarios might be imagined, and they might all serve to raise public awareness of parliament's work. But none of this would contribute to holding a parliamentary government to its responsibility. Public interest could no doubt be generated by questioning the manager of the German football team in the parliamentary sports committee after an inglorious first-round exit. Yet such a departure from its focus on the parliamentary responsibility of government would lead the Bundestag in a direction more strongly resembling the legislature in a presidential system. Whether such a perspective may be plausible or desirable is another matter. But as long as the Federal Republic has parliamentary government, uncoupling parliamentary scrutiny from the federal government's responsibility constitutes a weakening of ministerial responsibility.

7

The Future of Parliamentarianism and the German Constitution

Reunification marks a historic boundary, dividing the constitutional history of the Federal Republic into two contradictory parts. The parliamentary system of government evolved alongside the tasks of integration faced by the old Federal Republic – a process of integration that addressed mainly issues of interior and social policy. The constitutional institutions of the Basic Law succeeded in integrating all social groups into the West German state. That this was possible is due not least to substantial, and indeed historic, legislation passed in the decades after World War II. Much to the irritation of subsequent generations, Nazi elites were integrated by a famous civil service law of 1951 (the so-called G 131). Workers were integrated by the 1952 Works Constitution Act, the Capital Accumulation Act and dynamic pensions; refugees from the former German territories in the East by the Equalisation of Burdens Act; students by public education loans and university co-determination; and women by the Equal Rights Act of 1958, no-fault divorce, maternity protections and reformed abortion law. By such means, many social groups came to appreciate that party politics and parliamentary majorities offered them a good chance at seeing their interests reflected, and indeed advanced, in legislation.

Yet at the time the Federal Republic was not in possession of full sovereignty and had rather less responsibility in foreign affairs and defence to bear than it does today. Writing in 1960, Ernst Forsthoff, a pupil of Carl Schmitt and an outstanding conservative intellectual of the postwar period, went so far as to describe West Germany's institutional structure and democratic normalisation as a

> form of abiding, within the framework of the free world, at a moment … in which the historical role of the German people could not be but essentially passive. What changes it will undergo once this historical phase has ended is impossible to foresee.[1]

We now know that this phase ended with the country's reunification. Since then, no comparable feats of integration have been achieved. To the West Germans, a positive attitude to the constitution seemed so self-evident that they saw little need to win over their new compatriots. While reconstruction took place in the East by means of civil service cooperation and financial programmes, no comparable effort was made to renew what was now the country's common constitutional framework. The supposed pinnacle of efforts begun at reunification, the 1994 constitutional reform, resulted only in small-scale revisions that might as well have been made in 1980 or 1985. By 1990, the Bundesrat had become subject to party-political

[1] E Forsthoff, 'Die Bundesrepublik Deutschland – Umrisse einer Realanalyse' (1960) 14 *Merkur* 821.

interests to such a degree that the five new federal states were unable to bring their votes – around a quarter of the total – to bear in a coordinated fashion as a single interest. Moreover, the East Germans were faced with the choice of joining the western parties or forming a regional party of their own, a role that fell to the successor of the former East German state party SED, which had rebranded itself as the Party of Democratic Socialism (PDS), an ancestor of today's Left Party (Die Linke). Yet a regional party was destined to remain a foreign body in the constitutional framework of parliamentary government, just like the Scottish National Party is a foreign body in the Westminster system. Although Die Linke had participated, since 2002, in a succession of state governments, it had no comparable prospects or ambitions at the federal level, making its oppositional role somewhat ambiguous. The situation has changed since considerable parts of the eastern German electorate have chosen to make the AfD their political voice.

1990 marked a turning point – above all in foreign policy. After a brief euphoric interlude of juridification – when many observers and participants thought that the old political form of the European state would in due course give way to a supra-national federation and, ultimately, global governance – there followed a long stretch of disillusionment. In the crisis of the European Union, which has continued virtually uninterrupted since 2008, the dominant institution proved not to be the ones on which constitutional hopes had been pinned – not, that is, the parliamentary and democratic forces of the European Commission and Parliament. Instead, the renaissance of intergovernmental rule in crisis alongside an unchained central bank helped Germany to become, in the words of Christoph Schönberger, 'the reluctant hegemon'. This perpetual summit diplomacy has led to all decision-making processes being concentrated at the heart of government. Under the impression of the simultaneous failure of the UN, NATO, the WTO and the G8, international politics has entered a phase of 'de-institutionalization', to use a euphemism put about by the German foreign ministry. The reverse side of this trend is the foreign ministry losing power and foreign affairs coming under 'presidential' control. (The history of the State Department in the Trump administration is but the most extreme form of this development.) Meanwhile, discussion of the social and political consequences of mass migration is poisoned and deadlocked.

Anyone asking, in such circumstances, about the future of parliamentary democracy must explain what they mean by the term. Of course, the state will continue to need an institution like the Bundestag to produce binding decisions. But this is not to say that the parliamentary system of government as it is now practised in the Federal Republic has a future or what its future development is likely to be.

What developments are possible that could fundamentally change the current situation? It may be that a new political movement emerges that sweeps aside the established party system. Yet it seems unlikely that the success of Emmanuel Macron's La République en Marche should be imitated in Germany any time soon. German law largely excludes loosely organised movements from the polls by compelling them to organise themselves in the static form of parties.[2] Whether such legal demands constitute a secret cartel of the establishment parties or whether they are stipulated by the constitution itself is now the

[2] S Schönberger, 'Rechtliche Hürden für neue Parteien' in M Morlok, T Poguntke and G Zons (eds), *Etablierungschancen neuer Parteien* (Baden-Baden, Nomos, 2016) 71.

subject of intense discussion, not least under the impression of En Marche's success.[3] In any case, Article 21 GG requires parties to organise themselves in accordance with democratic principles, that is to say, they must have a membership able to make policy decisions by majority votes in a way that mere movements do not, and party offices must be subject to periodic elections. Nonetheless, it is at least conceivable that even within the existing party system, a movement of a kind may form, if only for the purpose of changing the law on political parties.

I. What Chances for Minority Governments?

If things remain as they stand, developments seem to point inexorably to minority governments or, at least, minority governments receiving the tacit support or 'toleration' of another party – although as recently as 2017, Angela Merkel affirmed that she was 'highly sceptical' of such ideas. There are two constitutionally plausible ways by which a minority government might come about. One would involve a party – or only one or a few members of parliaments – withdrawing from a coalition, thereby depriving it of its majority. This was briefly the case when the FDP pulled out of its coalitions with the CDU in 1966 and the SPD in 1982, and also when Willy Brandt's government lost its parliamentary majority in 1972. These minority governments, however, were short lived: new coalitions were soon formed in 1966 and 1982, and Willy Brandt regained a comfortable majority in the election of November 1972.

The other constitutional possibility is for a minority government to be formed.[4] According to Article 63(1) GG, the federal president must first propose a candidate for election as chancellor by the Bundestag. For this candidate to be elected, Article 63(2)(1) GG requires the votes of a majority of the Bundestag's members. Only if no such overall majority can be reached – and not for any other candidate either (a stipulation of Article 63(3) GG) – another vote would take place after fourteen days had elapsed (Article 63(4)(1) GG). In this, the absolutely last vote, in which any number of candidates may stand, the rules are changed: now, any relative majority, including that of the largest parliamentary party, is enough. The decision on whether the successful candidate goes on to form a government then passes into the hands of the federal president, who either proclaims the candidate elected by relative majority chancellor or proceeds to dissolve the Bundestag. Assuming the minority to evince a clear will to govern and given the manner in which all previous incumbents have performed their office, the latter scenario is highly unlikely. Whenever the Bundestag has been dissolved, it has been by close agreement between the president and the government.

An intermediary form is the 'tolerated minority government' of a chancellor elected with the votes of a party which, while not entering into a coalition, would abstain from pursuing an open policy of opposition. The possibilities for such toleration range from a

[3] See most recently C Gusy, 'Parteienrecht en marche?', *Verfassungsblog*, 6 September 2019, https://verfassungsblog.de/parteienrechtenmarche/.

[4] See the comparative survey in G Strohmeier, 'Minderheitsregierungen in Deutschland auf Bundesebene – Krise oder Chance?' (2009) 56 *Zeitschrift für Politik* 268.

covert majority government, in which one party is bound by formal agreement, but receives no ministries, to ad hoc agreements to cooperate in certain essential policy fields.

Once formed, a minority government can expect to be in a reasonably secure constitutional position, for there is no legal way to remove it other than Article 67 GG. This applies all the more when, as in the current German Bundestag, the opposition is split, with strong fringes on the left and right that are unlikely to form a majority government between themselves. Unlikely, that is, but not impossible, as the Italian (Lega and Cinque Stelle) and Greek (Syriza and ANEL) examples show: *les extrèmes se touchent*.

But would such a government not be likely to fall apart no later than the next budget deliberations? By no means, because even without a federal budget passed by parliament, the government, for historical reasons, has considerable fiscal discretion (Article 111 GG).[5] What little is denied the government in the absence of a budget is unlikely to be of much political consequence as long as the minority government is formed by a centrist party and can at least count one left-wing party to form a legislative majority in the Bundestag. Given the implications of such behaviour on redistributive policies, it is highly unlikely that the Social Democrats, the Greens or the Left Party would use the Bundestag's budgetary powers as a weapon against the government, thereby plunging the country into a budget-less state. Is there not, then, a good argument to be made from constitutional law in favour of trying out minority governments within the German system?

II. A New Chance for a Bargaining Democracy?

What makes minority governments an interesting scenario in the German political system is its dual constitution. Minority governments would have to reckon with the Bundesrat and bureaucratic coordination between the *Länder* and the federal level. The German constitution, it has been argued, offers 'ideal conditions for a successful minority government': cooperative federalism, good relations between specialists across party boundaries, the ability to forge informal coalitions in certain policy areas, and the overall German culture of 'negotiation-based democracy':

> Regardless of what coalition of parties is in power in Berlin, the representation of state governments in the Bundesrat means that all relevant parties are involved in federal legislation and thus in governing at the federal level. Since the founding of the Federal Republic, the opposition has always had a share of the power, at least by influencing legislation.

The key question here is whether this is an argument for or against a minority government? According to this logic, the reinvigoration of parliament would consist in relieving it of the political burden of decision-making – a task that would be left entirely to the much-vaunted institutions of federal policy coordination. Germany's supposed suitability for minority governments would accordingly be based on the government's ability partly to escape its dependence on parliamentary opinion formation by instead making itself dependent on non-parliamentary constitutional factors. The political consequence would be coordination

[5] W Heun, *Staatshaushalt und Staatsleitung: Das Haushaltsrecht im parlamentarischen Regierungssystem des Grundgesetzes* (Baden-Baden, Nomos, 1989) 309–20.

at the federal level and corporatism: in short, bureaucratic rather than parliamentary government. The argument is plausible because it assumes that the dualistic structure of the German constitutional order enables an alternation between a parliamentary and a federative, bureaucratic form of politics. Yet this would in fact be an altogether different form of government in disguise, one in which the Bundesrat played a far stronger role as a reserve of legality. In 1948, a majority in the constitutional convention at Herrenchiemsee had opted for this model, and that it was not adopted in the Federal Republic is thanks to the parliamentary council in the following year. The original idea had been to have the right to form a government pass to the federal second chamber if the Bundestag was unable to form a majority.[6] There is nothing to be said in favour of returning to that model, thereby undoing the peculiarly German separation of powers between politics and bureaucracy in the latter's favour.

III. A Renaissance of Parliamentarianism?

During the lengthy process of forming a government in 2017–18, the advocates of minority government seemed to expect from it nothing less than a renaissance of parliamentarianism. 'In questions of domestic politics', wrote the distinguished historian Heinrich August Winkler in the *Süddeutsche Zeitung*,

> such a minority government would rely on changing majorities, that is to say, on the support of the SPD one day and of the Greens or the FDP the next. The Bundestag and its committees would take on new significance; the CDU/CSU could sharpen its profile, as could its respective partners.[7]

In this notion, a minority government entails a parliament that is no longer faced with *faits accomplis* by the chancellery and the governing coalition and is used only as an echo chamber for political communication. A government that would humbly put its proposed legislation before the house as a whole and would solicit support for it in view of the shifting nature of parliamentary majorities. That would thereby take all key debates out of committees and coalition meetings back into the plenary. That would perhaps even not so much govern as let parliament itself decide. Really?

Winkler no doubt is correct in assuming that a minority government today would be nothing like a minority government in the Weimar Republic – and moreover at a fundamental political level the parties represented in the Bundestag today are still united by a 'broad constitutional consensus' and

> a high degree of agreement on foreign policy, with the exception of the Left Party and the AfD. A minority government of the largest parliamentary party … would not cause to fear being without a parliamentary majority in key questions of foreign and security policy.[8]

Yet the fact that most parties feel bound by reasons of state in matters of foreign and European policy is not simply a matter of the application of practical reason, but is quite crucially a

[6] Art 88 Abs 1 HChE, in Bundesarchiv (ed), *Der Parlamentarische Rat: Akten und Protokolle*, vol 2 (Boldt, Boppard, 1981) 597.

[7] HA Winkler, 'Nur keine vierte Groko!' *Süddeutsche Zeitung*, 23 November 2017.

[8] Ibid.

strategic element of their will to form a majority and participate in government – as the path taken by the Greens from their roots in communist splinter groups to the pro-NATO policies of Joschka Fischer. Moreover, the shifting dynamics of stances on European and foreign policy taken in the context of debates on migration policy since 2017 demonstrates that a broad constitutional consensus on foreign policy should not be taken for granted.

The idea that a higher degree of political dissociation between parliamentary opinion formation and government policy would strengthen parliament derives once more from the idea that parliament's task was above all to deliberate on projected legislation. Yet in parliamentary system of government, parliament's strength is founded on the close personal and institutional links between parliamentary and executive action. To normalise minority government as anything more than a stop-gap would not strengthen this link – much the contrary.

IV. Constitutional Implications

Constitutions are of course anything but axiomatic structures, from which claims regarding the behaviour of future actors in the system of government might be deduced. By the same token, to take a sceptical view of the constitutional consequences of minority governments is not a forecast, but an extrapolation from certain realities of German constitutional law as they stand today. The consequences of an end to majority parliamentary government need not resemble those that unfolded after May 1930. In any case, the weight of that historical parallel is too much for any deduction to bear.

The fact that the constitution, in Article 63(4) GG, allows for and indicates the path to a minority government does not in itself say anything about its consequences for parliamentary democracy. As we have seen, even the parliamentary system of government in which a majority government would have to prove itself is a creation of the constitution only in certain of its rudiments, but is above all the product of seventy years of constitutional development in the Federal Republic. The emergence of government and parliamentary majority as a unit of joint political action has taken on a specific sub-constitutional form over the many years of its operation within the German system of government. Although this constitutional development is of course reversible, nobody should be deceived as to the consequences of doing so: each of the three mediating institutions discussed in this book would find its accustomed workings fundamentally questioned and would each face barely foreseeable challenges.

This of course applies first of all to the popular parties in their shrunken state. The ability of governing parties to impose commitment and strike compromises depends on governing coalitions committing themselves, not ad hoc to certain policy areas, but rather to an entire programme for a fixed term of government.[9] It is possible to accustom a party to taking a joint line in many policy areas for a certain period of time and with a particular coalition partner. What cannot be done, however, is to commit a popular party to brokering compromise with changing parties on changing issues for anything more than a transitional

[9] K Strøm, WC Müller and T Bergman, *Cabinet Governance: The Democractic Life Cycle in Western Europe* (Oxford, Oxford University Press, 2007).

period without imposing compromises on those parties in turn. The tool for achieving such compromise is to force them to take on government responsibility themselves. For this reason, the model of toleration, though it has proved viable at the state level, cannot successfully be transposed to the federal level. Compared to the Bundestag, state parliaments have barely any controversial legislation to pass. The Bundestag does not have the option of muddling through a legislative term without major legislation. In the end, there is also little empirical evidence that minority governments pursue a more inclusive strategy of legislation.[10]

If parties cannot agree on package deals, it takes a great deal of time and effort to negotiate each policy project from scratch. Moreover, ad hoc majorities are highly volatile. What would a governing party do if, having put together a narrow parliamentary majority for a piece of legislation, it found itself faced with an altered mood in parliament when it came to that legislation being implemented? And, assuming that ministers would find it less easy to cooperate with parliamentary parties that could not be expected to give consistent support to the government – how could an ad hoc majority in parliament exercise effective control over the government? It is likewise irrelevant to invoke, as German advocates of minority government as a response to political polarisation often do, the Scandinavian example. For one thing, the Scandinavian system is even more oriented towards consensus than the German. What is more, Scandinavian legislatures are de facto unicameral, which means that they need not confront the problem of qualified legislative majorities being imposed by the second chamber. A lower degree of ideological coherence in political parties, which makes ad hoc coalitions easier to form,[11] is moreover considered a typical feature of presidential democracies.

A transition to minority governments would also have consequences for the institutional role of the chancellor and the chancellery. The chancellor's standing is enhanced not least by the pressure to form coalitions, in which the chancellor can act as mediator between the coalition parties. Meanwhile, the need for compromise with another party also enforces coherence within the party. It was remarked upon at the time how little elation Angela Merkel (unlike the rest of CDU leadership) displayed on election night in 2013, when it seemed for a while that the CDU/CSU had gained an overall majority. Indeed, she seemed visibly relieved when early polls were proved wrong. She will, in any case, have felt gratitude for the constitutional court, which in July 2012 had declared the electoral law, as it then stood, unconstitutional on account of the many overhang seats it produced. Had it not done so, the CDU/CSU would have gained an overall majority in the Bundestag with 41.5 per cent of the vote. Merkel had reason to fear the centrifugal forces working within a party ruling with an overall majority of its own – forces that are likely to be all the greater in a minority government, whose members would constantly be seeking to form majorities for their own particular policy priorities.

The chancellery owes its institutional role not least to its functioning as a mediating instance between the government and the Bundestag. The fact that the largest part of the legislative agenda can be planned and enacted through the (largely informal) cooperation of

[10] S Ganghof, S Eppner, C Stecker, K Heeß and S Schukraft, 'Do Minority Cabinets Govern More Flexibly and Inclusively? Evidence from Germany' (2019) 28 *German Politics* 541.

[11] JA Cheibub, A Przeworski and SM Saiegh, 'Government Coalitions and Legislative Success under Presidentialism and Parliamentarism' (2004) 34 *British Journal of Political Science* 565.

chancellery, ministries and the council of elders is due to the existence of a reliable majority of the coalition parties in the parliamentary steering committees. Although the constitution equips a minority chancellor with the tool of the 'legislative emergency' (Article 81 GG) – never yet used – this instrument, as its name suggests, relies not on a minority government finding support from ad hoc coalitions, but rather on the chancellor, the president and the Bundesrat bypassing the parliamentary majority. A legislative emergency can be declared when, on losing a vote of confidence, the chancellor, rather than requesting the president dissolve the Bundestag, continues as the head of a minority government. By contrast, a chancellor who comes into office as the head of a minority government (according to Article 63(4) GG) is not entitled to the tool of legislative emergency as a matter of course. In this situation, the president may set into motion a special procedure for urgent legislation whereby the Bundesrat, once the Bundestag has rejected a bill twice, can pass it into law by a vote of its own. In this procedure, the Bundesrat acts as a 'reserve of legality', as it was called in the 1948 constitutional convention at Herrenchiemsee.[12] In other words, the legislative emergency, too, presupposes a dualist constitution. Even in extremis, the Basic Law does not privilege government business *within* the parliamentary process, but rather by bypassing the parliamentary process altogether.

In reality, however, the instrument of legislative emergency is unlikely to be of much use to a minority chancellor – even if he has a president at his side who is willing to go along with it. The very eventuality of a government having a majority in the Bundesrat but not in the Bundestag is highly unlikely. Since the Bavarian CSU lost its absolute majority in the election of 2018, no party currently holds an overall majority in any of the sixteen state legislatures of Germany. There are no more votes in the Bundesrat that could be freely cast by any party without having to confer with its coalition partner in that respective state, which means that a single-party minority government could not absolutely rely on any support in the second chamber. Moreover, the legislative emergency is limited to a maximum of six months during a single term (Article 81(3)(2) GG), making not a regular pattern of government, but at best a recourse in a situation of crisis.

Finally, how would the constitutional court respond to a minority government? The answer is anything but clear if one considers the extent to which the court's rulings have contributed to the development of the parliamentary system of government. Although the court justifies its commitment to the statutory provision – that is, to there being a firm legal basis to any state action that might infringe upon basis rights – mainly with reference to basic rights and the rule of law, its political durability depends in large part on the federal government being able to satisfy its will to legislate, that is to say, actually realise its legislative agenda. Should the model of a federal government lacking a firm parliamentary majority establish itself for longer than a transitional period, the court may find itself under pressure to be more generous. Much the same goes for the procedure, chiefly developed in the jurisdiction of the constitutional court, of the Bundestag's and the Bundesrat's communication of European policy according to Article 23(2) and (3) GG. The Act on Cooperation between the Federal Government and the German Bundestag in Matters concerning the European Union (Gesetz über die Zusammenarbeit von Bundesregierung und Deutschem

[12] Bundesarchiv (ed), *Der Parlamentarische Rat: Akten und Protokolle*, vol 2 (Boppard, 1981) 282 and *passim*.

Bundestag in Angelegenheiten der Europäischen Union, EUZBBG), which governs the implementation of this constitutional provision, is clearly designed with a majority government in mind.

Of course, none of the consequences discussed here would preclude a minority government. But every change that the act of forming a government without the majority backing of a parliamentary coalition would bring its wake would eat away at the parliamentary principle of the system of government that developed, over time, at the sub-constitutional level. The idea that a minority government, emerging from the current situation, would be able to make up for the dissolution of established procedures in some way – even to the extent of reinvigorating parliamentarianism – is at best overly hopeful, at worst naïve, and in any case without foundation in constitutional law. The likeliest prospect for minority governments with variable majorities in the parliamentary system of the Federal Republic is this: strong personalities at the head of the government would be encouraged to pursue a plebiscitary style of politics by which they would put pressure on the opposition to agree to legislation. Rather than reinvigorating parliamentary government, a successful minority chancellor would thus be more likely to enhance the plebiscitary element of government at the expense of the parliamentary.

V. Institutional Alternatives

Other scenarios for the further development of the parliamentary system of government could be realised only by means of formal amendments to the constitution.

There certainly is scope for pushing back the influence of state governments on national politics and hence the federalist counterweight to the parliamentary system. Article 79(3) GG safeguards only the principle of the several states' involvement in federal legislation against any constitutional amendment. It does not require the Bundesrat in its present form. Of course, recent history teaches us humility where the chances of institutional reform at the federal level are concerned. Since the Bundesrat itself must approve any change to the constitution by a two-thirds majority, its position seems unassailable. The covid crisis has been a period of growing political influence of the *Länder* governments as the struggle for the succession of Angela Merkel in the chancellery demonstrates. The two frontrunners in the race are the two most important German minister presidents (of Bavaria and North Rhine-Westphalia), but no major politician from the federal level.

Reforming the Bundesrat system is a tough task: since all parties involved in government at the *Länder* level have an interest in upholding the status quo, any impetus to change would have to come from the outside. Already, the accomplishments of the federalism reform of 2006, which tried to reduce the instances of legislation requiring approval by the second chamber, are being undone and fields of cooperative federalism have been established in constitutional law. All those involved seem blithely to accept the need for further instances of coordination – a sure sign that they see no alternative to grand coalitions for the time being. But must the Bundesrat really continue in its present form for all eternity? Arguments for its replacement by a senate of delegates elected directly or indirectly by the states can still be heard. Such a senate would, after all, no longer consist of deputies beholden to the state executives, but rather of genuine federal politicians. But what would be gained by such a change? The present involvement of *Länder* bureaucracies in framing legislation is, after all, the complement to their responsibility for implementing federal laws. A senate would break this connection, regardless of how it might be composed or elected.

It is, moreover, only to be expected, in the last years of a long chancellorship, to hear arguments raised in favour of limiting the chancellor's term of office. While opposition politicians are driven by despair, constitutional lawyers consider it a matter of principle. Are the rules for office of the Basic Law, they sometimes claim, not founded on a 'peculiar, asymmetrical conception in constitutional law of limiting the powers of the highest state functionaries', a 'normatively unequal treatment of the president and the chancellor'?[13] Leaving aside that there is no example of political offices being subject *both* to recall by parliamentary majority at any time *and* term limits – and hence that there is no inconsistency here to speak of – the argument depends on a completely misleading parallel between the constitutional position of an elected president and a head of government responsible to parliament. The whole demand is as insubstantial as that for a limit on the term of office for the British prime minister. A president, in his second term, need no longer face the electorate, whereas a chancellor would be in danger of losing her parliamentary party's support long before her term ended. When Angela Merkel stepped down from the CDU leadership in October 2018, she drove her party into a phase of succession struggles that has lasted ever since (her handling of the covid crisis brought her some new support, however). Term limits would thus be a clear signal that the parliamentary system of government was being remade as a presidential one.

The most obvious institutional alternative, hence, is the straightforward transition to a presidential system that would only for reasons of tradition still call the centrepiece of the executive the 'chancellor'. That model, too, has its advocates. The standard arguments runs as follows: if a chancellor is elected by direct ballot, he would be independent of a fixed coalition of parties. Coalitions could be formed for each piece of legislation depending on the issue, giving the smaller parties an opportunity to get involved without jeopardising the functioning of democracy. Electoral threshold would no longer be required. In elections, citizens would again have a simple, clear choice between competing individuals rather than between a multitude of ideologically similar parties.

It is certainly true that a presidential system and pure proportional representation are not fundamentally incompatible, though the examples of France and the United States might suggest otherwise. The Argentine constitution is only one example of such a combination of principles. The problems of such an admission that we have been living in a presidential system for a long time, at least in practice, become apparent at second glance. Even a presidential chancellor could scarcely govern with pure ad hoc coalitions. Legislation needs legislative majorities. If it's not parliament, then it's the Bundesrat who would compel a chancellor to commit to a stable coalition. Here the same problem occurs as with minority governments: the parties' capacity for compromise to a large extent derives from the pressure to form a government. And anyway, who would seriously consider the transition to a presidential democracy to be a desirable constitutional development? Across the world, the great monocratic offices are struggling. On the one hand, the institutional boundaries to their power seem no longer to apply; on the other, they find themselves hemmed in by

[13] M Kloepfer, 'Herrschaft auf Zeit – das Amt des Bundeskanzlers', *Frankfurter Allgemeine Zeitung*, 18 February 2016; most recently J Kersten, 'Parlamentarismus und Populismus' [2018] *Juristische Schulung* 936.

institutional and structural constraints. Donald Trump may already have done irreparable damage to the US presidency, and the president of the French Fifth Republic seems unlikely to regain his former political stature. Even the papacy, since the plebiscitary pontificate of Karol Wojtyła, seems to be staggering from crisis to crisis. Is this really the situation in which it would be wise to exchange the collegial structure of parliamentary government for an authoritarian model?

All the more interesting is an idea that has been proposed by the political scientist Steffen Ganghof.[14] Its basic normative assumption is that in present constitutions, the binary opposition of parliamentary and presidential government has lost its former relevance, which leaves room for a more creative institutional fabric of the conditions of political stability, inclusive legislation, oversight and control. His idea is that the key functions of parliaments – making and unmaking of governments, legislation, parliamentary scrutiny, debate – can be institutionalised fairly independently of each other rather than being bundled as they have been until today. The particular appeal of Ganghof's reform idea for the German political system lies not least in his refusal to be carried away by such unlikely prospects as the abolition of the Bundesrat. His suggested reform is based on a modified system of proportional representation quite unlike that currently used in elections to the *Bundestag*. In his model, parliament would be elected along purely proportional lines, with national party lists and no minimum threshold. Yet this vote would also produce – without, that is, a further vote in parliament – what he calls a 'confidence chamber', in which only the strongest parties with a share above a certain threshold would be represented, still according to their relative strength. Voters favouring smaller parties may nonetheless influence the confidence chamber's composition by stating their order of preference. With a first vote for party A, a second and third order vote for parties B and C could be cast, the latter counting only if party A fails to reach the 'confidence threshold'. The core of the model is the exclusive function of that confidence chamber: legislation would still be a matter for the proportional plenary chamber, while the making and unmaking of government would be solely for the confidence chamber to decide. Compared to the present system, this would lower the hurdles for the formation of new parties without endangering the stability of government. Parliament's legislative decision-making function would be uncoupled from its support of the government.

Such an arrangement, which Ganghof himself calls 'semi-parliamentarianism', would be quite unlike the parliaments familiar from the constitutional history of Europe. It would produce, within parliament, a group of privileged members of the confidence chamber. The key question then is how to prevent the abuse of that privilege. Would the members of the confidence chamber hesitate to use their influence on forming the government also to further their influence in the legislative process? Within the legislative chambers we know, all members enjoy by law the same legal status. Such inequalities and privileges as obtain within the corporation are the result of free self-organisation and procedural choice. Democratic representation is representation by *equal* representatives. This equality is not just a legal technique for calculating majorities and as such tied to parliament's authorised decision-making powers, but is also an aspect of the symbolic representation of parliamentary government.

[14] S Ganghof, 'Combining Proportional and Majoritarian Democracy: An Institutional Design Proposal' [2016] July–September *Research and Politics* 1; S Ganghof, 'A New Political System Model: Semi-Parliamentary Government' (2018) 57 *European Journal of Political Research* 261; S Ganghof, *Beyond Presidentialism and Parliamentarism. Democratic Design and the Separation of Powers* (Oxford, Oxford University Press, forthcoming, 2021.

Equality between deputies represents the legal equality within civic society and the nation. This is one of the reasons why Marx and Lenin condemned parliamentarianism as the institutional form of class rule. Does the model of semi-parliamentarism imply abandoning the principle of egalitarian representation in order to stabilise the government? Ganghof counters objections of that kind by stating the categoric difference between equal rights of citizens and fair electoral rules. Equality does not necessarily need to be 'symbolised' by equal representation. The exclusion of minor parties from the process of government formation, in his conception, is of no other sort than other disproportional aspects of electoral law such as the 5 per cent threshold.[15] Votes could even be compensated for a higher confidence threshold with a lower or indeed no representation threshold at all. And still, the model of semi-parliamentarism appears to have a certain presumption in favour of a constitutional model based on the separation of powers. In parliamentary systems, the legislative function and the governmental function of parliament probably cannot be separated so easily. It is, as this book has shown with the example of the German political system, precisely the point of this form of government that the government must also present its legislative agenda to the majority which supports it in parliament. This is the only way that the government's dominant position in the legislative process is well justified in normative terms.

The parliamentary and, above all, federal implications of such a model of semi-parliamentarism cannot be discussed in any adequate depth here. It shows, however, that there are reform proposals that lead out of the idiosyncrasies of German debates on constitutional reform, which have remained unchanged for decades. Three decades after reunification, the constitutional concepts and patterns shaped in the old Federal Republic are on the one hand indispensable: there is no other language and tradition of democratic constitutional law in Germany. On the other hand, the institutions from which these patterns emerged and which these concepts once described are changing as rapidly as the expectations placed on the constitutional system. In fields such as gender representation in electoral law, this is already evident today, while in others it is more subtle. Constitutional jurisprudence today also sees itself confronted with entirely new conflicts of social justice, ecological rights and the control of private power. To what extent can a constitutional court play an active role in such problems? The fact that they are brought before the Federal Constitutional Court shows that at least those who do so no longer suspect that they will be solved within the system of parliamentary politics. In particular, the call for more effective action against global warming will not be limited to hitherto isolated decisions such as that of the Dutch Hoge Raad,[16] but will also confront the Federal Constitutional Court with the issue of ecological justice. Are the current institutions of parliamentary government still capable of articulating and mediating the political conflicts? The dilemma of the German understanding of the constitution has always been a diffuse longing for the juridification of politics. This longing sees the purpose of public law above all in protection against political decisions, and regards politics as a spectacle as long as administrative functions and the protection of fundamental rights do not fall below an acceptable level. But it would be fatal if the largest Member State were to adopt this attitude in the forthcoming constitutional reform of the European Union after Brexit.

[15] Ganghof, *Beyond Presidentialism and Parliamentarism* (n 13).

[16] Hoge Raad, 19/00135, ECLI:NL:GHDHA:2018:2591.

INDEX

Lightning Source UK Ltd.
Milton Keynes UK
UKHW050828130721
387081UK00004B/209

9 781509 943395